Benson Saler
Understanding Religion

Religion and Reason

Founded by Jacques Waardenburg

Edited by
Gustavo Benavides and Michael Stausberg

Volume 48

Walter de Gruyter · Berlin · New York

Benson Saler

Understanding Religion

Selected Essays

Walter de Gruyter · Berlin · New York

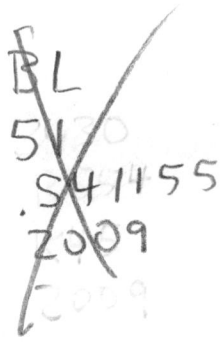

♾ Printed on acid-free paper which falls within
the guidelines of the ANSI to ensure permanence and durability.

ISSN 0080-0848
ISBN 978-3-11-021865-7

Library of Congress Cataloging-in-Publication Data

A CIP catalogue record for this book is available from the Library of Congress.

Bibliographic information published by the Deutsche Nationalbibliothek

The Deutsche Nationalbibliothek lists this publication in the Deutsche Nationalbibliografie; detailed bibliographic data are available in the Internet at http://dnb.d-nb.de.

© Copyright 2009 by Walter de Gruyter GmbH & Co. KG, 10785 Berlin

All rights reserved, including those of translation into foreign languages. No part of this book may be reproduced or transmitted in any form or by any means, electronic or mechanical, including photocopy, recording or any information storage and retrieval system, without permission in writing from the publisher.

Printed in Germany
Cover design: Christopher Schneider, Laufen
Printing: Hubert & Co. GmbH, Göttingen

To Michael, Judith, and Bethel

Preface

Twelve of the essays selected for this collection were published between 1997 and 2007. One essay, "Culture in Phylogenetic Perspective: An Appreciation of the Contributions of A. I. Hallowell," was not actually published; it was read at a conference at Aarhus University in 2006.

Most of the published essays were originally conference papers. While they were reworked for publication, they retain, I think, vestiges of an oral flavor. In first preparing them for a live audience that could not go back and read troublesome passages, I strove for auditory clarity. At the same time, however, I wanted to convey a fair amount of information, and to do it within the time periods assigned to me. Those two goals do not always support one another. For that and other reasons, I welcomed opportunities to publish my efforts, in the hope that interested readers would better understand the various points I try to make. And now, with even more enthusiasm, I welcome the opportunity to re-publish, to arrange the selections in thematic order so that they support one another, and to provide further comments by means of an introductory essay. I am very pleased, moreover, to acknowledge my gratitude to the editors, Gustavo Benavides and Michael Stausberg, and to the publisher, Walter de Gruyter, for making this collection possible.

Concord, Mass.   Benson Saler

Contents

Part I Orientations

Introduction 3
The Ethnographer as Pontifex 31

Part II Homage to Three Pioneers

E. B. Tylor and the Anthropology of Religion 51
Culture in Phylogenetic Perspective: An Appreciation of the
Contributions of A. I. Hallowell 82

Part III Beliefs

On What We May Believe About Beliefs 95
Finding Wayú Religion 116
On Credulity 132
Secondary Beliefs and the Alien Abduction Phenomenon 147

Part IV Studying Religion: Some Conceptual Issues

Family Resemblance and the Definition of Religion 159
Conceptualizing Religion: The Matter of Boundaries 172
Comparison: Some Suggestions for Improving the Inevitable ... 181
Biology and Religion: On Establishing a Problematic 188
Toward a Realistic and Relevant „Science of Religion" 196

References Cited 224

Index 237

Part I Orientations

Introduction

As the reader will discover, the essays that follow cover a range of topics associated with secular, academic efforts to understand religion. They do not, however, systematically map the great diversity of subject matters in what Edward Burnett Tylor terms "Religion in all its bearings" (Tylor 1958 II: 445, 1871). That is not because I deem it unnecessary to examine religion as broadly (as well as deeply) as possible. Rather, it is because religion is so complex that no one student is likely to be able to describe and discuss it "in all its bearings." If, however, we are to expand our understandings as best we may, we ought to keep it in mind that religion is more than beliefs of a certain kind and rituals of a certain kind.

Religion amounts to, among other things, a variable congeries of social phenomena within and sometimes between human societies. Indeed, as the anthropologist Robin Horton (1960: 24) states in his definitional efforts, religion constitutes "an extension of the field of people's social relationships beyond the confines of purely human society." And, to be sure, it variably expresses and otherwise relates to a complexity of values that define important psychological and cultural dimensions in human life. Lest we forget, moreover, it is worth affirming that the intensity of commitment to religious ideas may vary from person to person, in small-scale societies as well as in our own, just as punctiliousness in the exercise of rites may vary not only from individual to individual but perhaps over individual lifetimes as well. In short, there is not only a fair amount of heterogeneity in what we identify as religions, but also among religion-bearers.

The essays in this collection touch on some of the heterogeneity. But they also point to some recurring features of religion and religion-bearers throughout the world. Simultaneous posits of differences and natural resemblances suggest some of the analytical and theoretical tensions of "modernism." That is, they suggest recognition of seemingly opposable or perhaps even "contradictory" intellectual biases: a preference for the general and an acknowledgement of the particular, a celebration of the different and the hope of discovering what is common, and a longing for the enduring while accommodating to the transient.

Although I identify myself as a modernist (the essays gathered here testify in support of that self-identification), I also find much of worth in certain postmodernist perspectives. Most especially, I am impressed by postmodernist caveats concerning the implications that a respect for differences may have for the desire to develop stabile classifications. If we truly value differences, some postmodernists ask, does that not negatively impact the notion that we can systematically attend to the world through the mediation of stabile categories? Awareness of this issue affects my efforts to deal with the problem of conceptualizing religion as well as some other matters in the study of religions.

Each of the essays is preceded by a brief abstract that indicates part of what is covered in the selection that follows. The reader should be warned that I tend to wander in my writings, so that the abstracts do not disclose the full contents of the essays.

I have sorted the essays into four broad topical divisions or "Parts." The topic headings relate to sets of interests addressed by the essays. I turn now to a discussion of each of the divisions and their contents.

Part I Orientations

This section contains two essays: the present "Introduction," written specifically for the collection, and "The Ethnographer as Pontifex." While it would be redundant to introduce the Introduction that you are now reading, some remarks about the orienting functions of the "Pontifex" essay are in order here.

Ethnographic monographs continue to be the traditional professional publications of socio-cultural anthropologists. In most anthropology departments throughout the world, graduate students are usually expected to engage in ethnographic research as part of their training. Indeed, ethnographic fieldwork of some duration and substance – and the writing up of what one learned in the field – often amount to something of a *rite de passage* that marks the transition from being a matriculated student to being a professional anthropologist.

I expand on discussions of ethnography in the anthropological literature by suggesting a sacerdotal analog. Just as some religious communities may suppose that their priests or shamans connect the realms of the divine and the human, so, too, do anthropologists hope that ethnographers will connect us to the culturally other. Ideally at least, ethnographic monographs are ethnographic bridges. We traverse them in hope of new understandings, new understandings of human cultural diversity – including, perhaps, new understandings of ourselves as we may relate to, while simultaneously differing from, the culturally other. In that idealized sense, then, the ethnographer is a "*pontifex*," a Latin term that literally means "bridge-builder." Understanding, to be sure, is never complete nor, if we think about it critically, completely secure. But even partial and provisional understandings can be gratifying.

I chose this essay for purposes of general orientation because it touches on some of the difficulties – and some of the rewards – of trying to understand and convey the religious concepts of others.

Part II Homage to Three Pioneers

Of the various pioneers whose works prefigure contemporary efforts to understand religion, I discuss three in this division: Edward Burnett Tylor, Lucien Lévy-Bruhl, and A. Irving Hallowell. I will comment on each. Before doing so, however, there is a general point that I would like to make.

It seems to me that some of my contemporaries are impatient when they encounter references to various nineteenth and early twentieth century students of religion. To be sure, significant changes have occurred over the years in philosophy, in the philosophy of science, and in the impacts made on our thinking by advances in linguistics (which many now think of as a cognitive science), cognitive, developmental, and evolutionary psychologies, evolutionary biology, the neural sciences, and, indeed, the social contexts or ambiences in which scholarship has come to be situated. We can now do better in explaining religion than scholars of yesteryear, some of our contemporaries say, so why should we spend time and energy in harkening to voices from the past? There is, I think, a credible, general answer to that question: that understanding where we come from and how we got here provides a sobering historical dimension to our appreciation of our current worldview and our awareness of the provisional nature of all claims to knowledge.

The best of yesteryears' scholars were serious and intelligent persons who cultivated imaginative (if not ultimately sustainable) ideas. Their work was the best available in their time periods, relative to the intellectual ambiences in which they operated and from which they derived their sense of problems. They not only lacked the rich data that more recent archeology, more recent historical studies, and more recent ethnography make available to us, but they also lacked recourse to the understandings – and, indeed, stimulations – afforded us by recent advances in the contemporary cognitive, neural, and evolutionary sciences. In rejecting or setting aside various of the constructs and theories of our predecessors, we ought not to disdain their authors. Those authors often displayed personal courage and integrity in the face of prejudices and antagonisms current in their societies, and they deserve our admiration for doing so. Further, they sometimes evinced a shrewd sense of problem, and they addressed questions that we more or less continue to address. Despite our overall criticisms of their work, moreover, we can still find in their writings insightful observations, pleasing and revealing turns of phrases, and visions of new directions that are exciting and worth cherishing. Finally, we ought to note that some of our predecessors developed critical and self-critical sensitivities, sensitivities that we would be fortunate to emulate.

E. B. Tylor. Tylor's most famous publication, the two volume *Primitive Culture* (1871), was of major importance in establishing cultural anthropology as a discipline in modern secular universities and in rendering the word "culture" the key vocabulary term of that discipline. Concepts of culture eventually diffused out well beyond anthropology, and they are still widely employed for conceptually organizing and discussing many aspects of human life. Many persons, anthropologists and non-anthropologists alike, moreover, deem religion a sort of department or constituent of culture, thanks in no small measure to the influence, whether recognized or not, of Edward Burnett Tylor.

In his 1871 work, Tylor outlines for us what he regards as the evolution of religion. And, as some commentators note, in describing the evolution of religion, Tylor in effect describes what he takes to be the evolution of mind. His evolutionary efforts, however, are not without their critics. Much of what he wrote is highly speculative, the product of imaginative armchair theorizing, his data base being a jumble of descriptions of the beliefs and practices of different peoples compiled from a diversity of sources. A Just-So story, Evans-Pritchard and some other critics opine. Further, Tylor's style of evolutionary conjectures are vulnerable to the same analytical criticisms that are leveled at the similar evolutionary conjectures of other nineteenth century cultural and social theorists.

Various late nineteenth century theorists suppose that cultural and social evolution is unilineal. That is, it proceeds progressively, from lower stages to higher stages, in much the same lineal fashion, wherever it takes place. (Major posited stages, in some schemas, are "lower, middle, and upper savagery," "lower, middle, and upper barbarism," and "civilization.") Facile assumptions are made to the effect that similar consequences (similar evolutionary stages found in different loci) are the products of similar causes (universal laws of the mind operating in distinct historical contexts). Not every society, it is allowed, actually passes through each stage. Some social orders, it is claimed, become arrested at one stage or another and do not progress further. The peoples of such arrested social orders are viewed, in effect, as our "contemporary ancestors." They are held to represent, in our own time, what our ancestors were once like, before our ancestral lines evolved further. Ethnographic studies of such peoples, it is suggested, are therefore all the more valuable because they can reveal to us our own past. By comparing the different societies and cultures of the world, it is maintained, we can trace the evolutionary history of humankind (and better appreciate the civilization that we enjoy). This, basically, is what the nineteenth century "Comparative Method" was all about.

Critics soon pointed out that diffusion – the spread of culture traits or complexes from their places of origin or invention to other places, where they are often adopted by local peoples – is likely to short-circuit the identification and alleged integrity of unilineal evolutionary "stages." A more thoroughgoing attack on the evolutionist's position, however, was penned by the anthropologist Franz Boas. In an 1896 paper ("The Limitations of the Comparative Method in Anthropology"), Boas played an important role in turning many anthropologists away from the kinds of evolutionary studies favored by Tylor, Lewis Henry Morgan, and their ilk. And, perhaps through the operation of a psychological mechanism known to us as "stimulus generalization," Boas turned numbers away from other sorts of imaginable inquiries respecting cultural evolution as well.

Boas maintained that the work of his evolutionist contemporaries rested on logical and methodological flaws. Thus, for instance, Boas argued against the evolutionists' supposition

> that if an ethnological phenomenon has developed independently in a number of places its development has been the same everywhere; or, expressed in a different form, that the same ethnological phenomena are always due to the same causes. This leads to the still wider generalization

that the sameness of ethnological phenomena found in diverse regions is proof that the human mind obeys the same laws everywhere. It is obvious that if different historical developments could lead to the same results, that then this generalization would not be tenable. Their existence would present to us an entirely different problem, namely, how it is that the developments of culture so often lead to the same results. It must, therefore, be clearly understood that anthropological research which compares similar cultural phenomena from various parts of the world, in order to discover the uniform history of their development, makes the assumption that the same ethnological phenomenon has everywhere developed in the same manner. Here lies the flaw in the argument of the [19th century evolutionist] method, for no such proof can be given. Even the most cursory review shows that the same phenomena may develop in a multitude of ways. (Boas 1940 [1896]: 273)

After giving several ethnological examples of how different causes can sometimes eventuate in similar effects, Boas goes on to write that

> We have another method, which in many respects is much safer [than the comparative method of the evolutionists]. A detailed study of customs in their relation to the total culture of the tribe practicing them, in connection with an investigation of their geographical distribution among neighboring tribes, affords us almost always a means of determining with considerable accuracy the historical causes that led to the formation of the customs in question and to the psychological processes that were at work in their development. The results of inquiries conducted by this method may be three-fold. They may reveal the environmental conditions which have created or modified cultural elements; they may clear up psychological factors which are at work in shaping the culture; or they may bring before our eyes the effects that historical connections have had upon the growth of the culture.
>
> We have in this method a means of reconstructing the history of the growth of ideas with much greater accuracy than the generalizations of the comparative method will permit. (Boas 1940 [1896]: 276)

So great was the influence of Boas's critique that many anthropologists eschewed evolutionary studies during most of the twentieth century. Not all did, of course. Thus, for instance, Julian Steward conceived of multi-evolutionary lines, and Leslie White suggested that we can study socio-cultural evolution in terms of an increasing harnessing and control of energy. Numbers of anthropologists, nevertheless, frowned on studies of social and cultural evolution.

Many twentieth century anthropologists not only rejected the evolutionary conjectures of nineteenth century authors, but they roundly distanced themselves from much else that those authors advocated. In Tylor's case, this amounted to an example of throwing out the baby with the bath-water. Tylor not only suggested an evolution of religion and mind, but he accompanied his suggestion with a radical proposal for the reform of our civilization. Ironically enough, some anthropologists ignored the radicalism of his reformist agenda (the baby) because they did not want to sully their hands in the evolutionary context of his proposal (the bath water).

Tylor holds that when cultures evolve, some elements from older forms of culture may survive into the new. These "survivals," as he terms them, had usually played significant – and in that sense appropriate – roles in the stages of culture in which they originated. But as survivals into new (newly evolved) cultural orders, they may be out of harmony with the new. Indeed, Tylor suggested, they are likely to prove to be stultifying relics, inhibiting further cultural progress. It is the task of the anthropologist, Tylor proclaims, to identify such elements, and by so identifying them help to eradicate them.

The last chapter of the first volume of *Primitive Culture*, and the entire second volume, are dedicated to Tylor's theory of religion. Not to "Religion in all its bearings," but mainly to the "intellectual" aspects of religion. Religion, indeed, is portrayed by Tylor as the first great theory in human history, a theory that seeks to answer questions about dreams, death, visions and the like by drawing on human sensory experiences. The "great doctrine of Animism," as Tylor conceives it, has lingered on, from the dawn of human history to the religions of today, Christianity included. A close reading of Tylor suggests that while he has a certain appreciation of Animism, which he regards as the product of rational but mistaken thought, he nevertheless deems its expression in the religions of our "civilization" to be another survival (or collection of survivals), ready to be exposed as such by the anthropologist, as a beneficial service to humankind (at least in Euro-American societies).

In recent years, we have witnessed a proliferation of atheistic advocacies contained in several well publicized books. Some of these are more than tinged by polemical pigments. That is especially the case, I think, for Richard Dawkins's *The God Delusion* (2006). Dawkins, indeed, seems to justify the sobriquet awarded him by *Discover* magazine, that of being "Darwin's Rottweiler." But, as the cognitive science of religion shows us, theism is better explained by avoiding pejoratives and insults. And Darwin, in my opinion, is not in need of Rottweilers.

One of the notable things about the recent spate of atheistic publications is that they are published, easily purchased, and widely reviewed despite the severity of some of their assertions. Their authors, insofar as I am aware, are not publicly shunned or barred from appearing on television, at least in Euro-American societies. I think that that is all to the good. Tylor, however, operated in a less accepting social order. That, in all probability, had something to do with the way he argued. Without necessarily endorsing Tylor's theory, his conclusions, or his reformer's zeal, we can nevertheless admire his courage in advancing them. And we can respect the subtlety of their packaging.

Overall, I think that Tylor is mistaken on a number of issues. He is mistaken not only for the reasons given by Boas in 1896, but for others as well. Most importantly, I think, he not only misunderstands evolution as it may apply to culture, but his views of religion and mind are narrow, and they are constructed on an unsubstantial foundation, at least when compared to the understandings now afforded us by the contemporary cognitive science of religion. We now have good reasons to suppose that theism is "natural" in humankind, and that it is atheism that is somewhat anomalous and very much in need of explanation (Atran 2002; Barrett 2004; Boyer 1994; Saler and Ziegler 2006). Tylor, nevertheless, is an important pioneer, one who blazed new paths. Ironically, some contemporary anthropologists, who declare themselves to be dedicated to the improvement of humankind, fail to appreciate the pioneering efforts in that regard of their nineteenth century predecessor and benefactor, Edward Burnett Tylor.

Lucien Lévy-Bruhl. It is common, among both anthropologists and scholars in departments of religious studies, to assert that all human societies "have" religion. Or, to invoke the more qualified formulation given by Durkheim, one might say that religion is found in all societies now known, thus leaving open the possibility that some human societies of yesteryear lacked religion – but, if so, they did not survive as challenges to universalist claims about the distribution of religion. Insofar as I am aware, the only major "classical" scholar to enter a counter-claim is the French philosopher, Lucien Lévy-Bruhl. In the concluding chapter of his first book on "primitive mentality," a work published in 1910, he suggests that among such living peoples as the Arunta and Bororo we do not really find what we typically take to be religion. Religion, he muses, is a differentiated product, emerging from a prior form of thought, a form of thought evinced by the Arunta and Bororo.

Lévy-Bruhl championed the idea of "mentalities." This, broadly characterized, is the notion that distinctive forms or modes of thought, different mentalities, are evinced by the members of different human social collectivities. That was hardly a new idea in Lévy-Bruhl's time, nor is it one that has now been finally discredited. In crude form it is found in sweeping stereotypes of national characters and ethnic groups. But as developed by Lévy-Bruhl, and by members of the French school of *mentalité* historians who came after him, the basic idea was refined and rendered more sophisticated (if still unpalatable to some critics).

By tracing some of the complexities and subtleties of Lévy-Bruhl's developing thoughts on the matter of "mentalities," we afford ourselves a window on the development of an interesting modernist construct. While the essay included here attempts to do that, it also calls attention to the importance of some related matters. Thus, for instance, it deals to some extent with the issue of affectivity in thought. As Lévy-Bruhl notes, his European contemporaries tend to separate out cognition from affect and motor action. But such categorical compartmentalizing, he suggests, can mislead us when we deal with "primitive thought," which allows so great a penetration of the affective into the cognitive that many of the thoughts of so-called primitive peoples are more "felt" than "thought."

When anthropological fieldworkers criticized Lévy-Bruhl for what they regarded as an unbalanced view of how the peoples that they studied think, he responded to their criticisms generously. He allowed that his early writings distorted both "primitive" thought and our thought. That is, "primitives" are more commonsensical than he had previously maintained, and our thought includes more of the "mystical" and the affective than was provided for in his earlier comparisons. Further, and quite importantly, from his fourth book on, through the sixth and last book and the posthumously published *Notebooks*, Lévy-Bruhl reproblematized the comparison of mentalities. He held that the difference is not really based on a difference *in logic*, as he had previously supposed, but as pivoting on substantive differences in relative degree, where the "primitives" are considerably more accepting of physical incompatibilities than we, and where they are more given to a working marriage of the cognitive and the affective than we.

These issues, and some end note information on the views of certain others pertaining to the "modes of thought" question, are discussed in the essay. Over and above those discussions, however, is the matter of reflexivity, the matter of self-criticism. From 1910 to his death in 1939, Lévy-Bruhl continually subjected his own thoughts on the "primitive mentality" question to his own critical review. He is, indeed, a paragon of self-criticism. Like Tylor, Lévy-Bruhl depended on the published reports of ethnographers, missionaries, explorers, colonial officials, and others for his data on "primitive" peoples. (While Tylor spent some time in Mexico, he was not really a fieldworker, and Lévy-Bruhl was even less of one.) When, however, such accomplished field ethnographers as Bronislaw Malinowski and E. E. Evans-Pritchard criticized him, Lévy-Bruhl was quick to take their strictures seriously and to modify his views when he found their criticisms convincing. In his openness to external criticism, as well as in his disciplined and internally generated self-criticism, he constitutes a predecessor worthy of our admiration and emulation, regardless of any skepticism that we may harbor regarding the particulars of his theories.

A. Irving Hallowell. Unlike both Tylor and Lévy-Bruhl, Hallowell was a fieldworker. His ethnographic writings on the Northern Ojibwa are landmarks, both in their clarity and because they go beyond ethnographic reportage by stimulating our wider analytical and theoretical interests. One of the hallmarks of Hallowell's work is his carefully worked-out effort to convey in English his understandings of Ojibwa categories with minimal distortion of Ojibwa cultural subjectivities.

An example of Hallowell's scrupulousness in that regard can be found in what he says about our word "supernatural." That term is widely encountered in religious studies. But Hallowell avoided it in his ethnographic writings, and he explicitly calls out attention to that avoidance. Thus, for instance, he remarks that to apply the expression "supernatural persons" to characters in Northern Ojibwa myths "is completely misleading, if for no other reason than the fact that the concept of 'supernatural' presupposes a concept of the 'natural'. The latter is not present in Ojibwa thought" (Hallowell 1960: 28).

Accepting a notion of the "natural" that more or less resembles Durkheim's (1965 [1912]: 41–43) emphasis on *impersonal* natural laws and "the immutability and the inflexibility of the order of things," Hallowell finds no real analog of that understanding in Ojibwa thought. Rather, for the Ojibwa, as Hallowell describes them, the events of the world are subject to the operation of will, purpose, and intelligence. The Ojibwa universe is populated by a large diversity of sentient objects. (By "object," here and elsewhere in this volume, I mean two things: in logic, any member of a class, and in psychology, anything of which we take cognizance.) These different objects – human beings, thunderbirds, anthropomorphic healers without noses who live in rocks, a giant turtle, etc. – are all named. As far as I can tell from my reading of Hallowell, the Ojibwa do not lump the many non-human objects that they conceptualize into a named macro-class. But Hallowell does. He calls them "other-than-human persons." Why he terms them "persons" is touched on in the essay on Hallowell. Here, however, I focus attention on the "other-than-human" designation.

Hallowell deems "other-than-human" more neutral, and thus less distorting, than the term "supernatural." He regards the latter as "a reflection of *our* cultural subjectivity" (Hallowell 1960: 21, emphasis in original). And he gives it as his opinion that "It is unfortunate that the natural-supernatural dichotomy has been so persistently invoked by many anthropologists in describing the outlook of peoples in cultures other than our own" (Hallowell 1960: 28).

Some anthropologists have been convinced by either Durkheim's or Hallowell's argument, and they avoid using the term supernatural in ethnographies where the people described appear to lack a natural-supernatural distinction (e.g., Godfrey Lienhardt 1961: 28). Others, however, opine that the term can be extended analogously to objects in non-Western worldviews that would be termed supernatural by us, and that doing so is convenient (e.g., Marvin Harris 1975: 514). Hardly anyone in either camp, however, describes in more than a sentence or two (if that) what "supernatural" may mean as a Western category. The Swedish anthropologist Åke Hultkrantz (1983) is a notable exception, and his discussion of the term is well worth reading.

In 1974 I was invited to present a paper at one of two memorial sessions in honor of Hallowell to be given by some of his former students at the 1975 annual meeting of the American Anthropological Association. I accepted the invitation, and I announced that I would focus on Hallowell's remarks about the supernatural as they may relate to the Western intellectual history of that term. I assumed that there was a substantial, published intellectual history to access. I soon learned, however, that my assumption was mistaken. Much of what I could find by way of intellectual history was written by Roman Catholic theologians whose theological concerns led them to address issues that, at that time, I had difficulty in understanding. While the publications of Henri de Lubac (1934, 1946) and certain others were valuable as, in part, intellectual histories, a number of other works were of lesser relevance to my project. In any case, I presented a paper as scheduled, and a revised version, "Supernatural as a Western Category," was published (Saler 1977), its flaws notwithstanding. I have remained interested in the topic, however, and I have worked on it over the years as a "back burner" project.

In my 1977 paper, I more or less endorsed Hallowell's views. I did so, however, while recognizing that many persons find use of the term "supernatural" to be convenient in lectures and publications. To justify repudiating it, as Durkheim, Hallowell, and others realized, requires an outlay of words. As it happens, I eventually bowed to the convenience argument, and for many years used the term myself (though sometimes putting it in quotation marks, in deference to my own unease).

Recently, however, I have thought of a possible way out of my difficulty. A similar idea independently occurred to the Finnish scholar, Ilkka Pyysiäinen (2001). We both think that Pascal Boyer's (1994) distinctions between "intuitive" and "counter-intuitive" ideas may go a long way toward resolving debate over the applicability of the natural-supernatural distinction. While it is probable that not all peoples consciously make a distinction between the intuitive and the counter-intuitive, I agree with Boyer that such a distinction is, in effect, universally operative in human thought. In light of that understanding, a reasonable argument could be made for replacing "natural" with "intuitive" and for replacing "supernatural" (as well as "unnatural") with "counter-intuitive" in scholarly accounts of non-Western worldviews. While this may at first seem inelegant, it would prove to be somewhat analogous to Hallowell's use of the expression "other-than-human persons" in preference to "supernatural persons." That is, it would be less distorting of the cultural subjectivities of some of the peoples about whom we write.

Part III Beliefs

I suspect that discussions of "beliefs" constitute the largest subject matter in publications authored by academic students of religion. Such discussions, moreover, are quite varied in what they cover. There are, for instance, numerous expositions and historical treatments of the creedal or doctrinal orthodoxies and heterodoxies of religions and religion-bearers (the beliefs of the latter may differ in interesting ways from beliefs associated with the former, even to the point of being undoctrinal or credally unstable); beliefs as they may relate to rituals and organizational structures; studies of the substitution of beliefs (or the acquisition of new beliefs) in cases of religious conversion; beliefs of a "secular" or "scientific" sort as they may resemble or differ from religious beliefs; and on and on. It is my impression, however, that fundamental considerations of what we may be talking about when we talk about beliefs are not as frequently encountered, or as frequently referenced, in anthropological and religious studies literatures. What, indeed, does it mean – or may it mean – to say that anybody believes anything? And, if we can agree on some answer to that question, how do we know that somebody believes something? While some scholars have dealt with these questions, numbers of others appear not to have read what they wrote.

The first essay in this section, "On What We May Believe about Beliefs," considers some fundamental questions. Inasmuch as the topic posed by such questions is of great complexity, the discussion provided is inevitably partial and incomplete. Other essays in Part III enlarge the coverage of belief (without, of course, exhausting what might be profitably explored). Thus, for instance, "Finding Wayú Religion" asks if beliefs always constitute systems. Many anthropologists proceed as if they do, even to the extent of envisioning overarching systematicity in religious beliefs and worldviews.

Now, as I suggest in "Finding Wayú Religion," it seems reasonable to expect to encounter subsystems of beliefs. Domain specific beliefs often amount to what the philosopher Stephen Stich (1996) calls "doxastic neighborhoods." Such "neighborhoods" are clusters of beliefs that relate to one another syntactically. Tuned to specific areas of interest, they tend both to support and to constrain each other. But what about much larger "systems"?

It is one of the aims of theologians in Western societies to construct large, inclusive, and internally coherent doctrinal systems. They may begin, for instance, by subjecting fragments of scripture to analysis, and, through the exercise of reason, sometimes stimulated by what other theologians have written, to arrive at fresh understandings. Interestingly enough, in their studies of "belief systems" numbers of anthropologists and other academics who study religions make parallel (if more circumscribed) efforts.

Underlying secular academic efforts to describe (and perhaps to some extent to construct) belief systems are various suppositions – themselves beliefs – that may not be consciously considered or, at any rate, explicitly expressed. Thus, for instance, many academics believe that the world is orderly, and that the sciences and social sciences must seek to reveal (and perhaps explain) that order. Since beliefs are part of the world, they, too, will demonstrate order if one looks closely and reasons well. Some academics, moreover, give a specific twist to that idea. Impressed by the achievements of linguists, some attempt to import linguistic models and analytical procedures into the study of various cultural domains (e.g., the much misunderstood "emic"/"etic" distinction introduced by the linguist Kenneth Pike).

I cannot attempt a responsible review here of that subject. It must suffice for me to register my own belief: that when it comes to the study of religious beliefs, linguistic models and methods are best employed in mapping and analyzing "doxastic neighborhoods." Beliefs with a mutuality in focus are likely to be more reliably accessed by certain eliciting procedures than a disparate range of beliefs. Further, the models that we may eventually develop of their syntactic and semantic relationships are likely to be better supported than claims about entire "belief systems." Indeed, I think it doubtful that most people actually entertain coherent "belief systems" of any appreciable scale. Most people are concerned with the press of daily life, and their beliefs are likely to be pointed primarily to specific problems and concerns, and only secondarily (if at all) to the achievement of some overarching coherence among the many doxastic neighborhoods that they visit and re-visit in the course of their lives.

The above discussion relates primarily to the essay "Finding Wayú Religion," though it touches on some of the concerns of other selections in this section. I offer some comments on those other essays below.

"On What We May Believe About Beliefs." If I were to expand this essay, I would add a section on distinctions drawn in the cognitive science of religion between "intuitive beliefs" and "reflective beliefs" (Sperber 1997) or, in an alternative phrasing, between "non-reflective beliefs" and "reflective beliefs" (Barrett 2004). Similar distinctions have been made by others, employing somewhat different vocabularies (see Pyysiäinen 2004 for a listing and discussion of some of them).

Intuitive or non-reflective beliefs are conceptualized as unconscious beliefs. Beliefs, that is, that are normally outside of the believer's conscious awareness and that are not subject to review and reflection. They may, however, come into awareness as intuitions or when challenged, or when reflective beliefs that depend on them are challenged. Most of our daily actions accord with these beliefs, even though we are not usually conscious of them. Thus, for instance, we behave in ways that indicate that we take it for granted that rocks will fall to earth if we throw them up in the air, that we cannot walk through solid material barriers of substantial thickness or tensile strength, that we are likely to harm ourselves if we fall from an appreciable height on to a hard surface, and so on. The "intuitive knowledge" and "intuitive expectations" of which some cognitive scientists speak rest on intuitive beliefs.

Reflective beliefs, in contrast, are conscious beliefs. We may not be consistently aware of them, but in situations of appropriate stimulation we summon them into awareness and perhaps subject them to reflection and review. The creedal statements of theologians are examples of reflective beliefs. But reflective beliefs themselves depend significantly on intuitive or non-reflective beliefs. The latter serve as default options for the former and they enhance the plausibility of reflective beliefs that harmonize with them. Indeed, the longevity or successful transmission of reflective beliefs depends in part on their harmonic interactions with our intuitions, and our intuitions represent a nascent coming into awareness of non-reflective beliefs. Further, inasmuch as people typically draw on memory in formulating novel – and therefore not entirely novel – reflective beliefs, intuitive beliefs once again suggest their importance by sculpting or coloring memory.

In light not only of the plausibility of the above distinction, but also in light of experimental evidence in favor of it, some proponents of the cognitive science of religion maintain that people often do not actually believe what they say that they believe. Indeed, much of what people "really" believe is "theologically incorrect" (Barrett 1996; Boyer 2001; Slone 2004). That is, a person's intuitive beliefs may be at odds with certain of the theological or cultural dogmas that that person articulates by way of conscious endorsement. Evidence in support of this claim is for the most part based on experiments and the close analysis of narratives. Thus, for instance, a well schooled Christian may declare that his god is both outside of time and omnipresent. But when that same believer is asked to tell stories about god, the deity in his narratives is likely to go from place to place, one place at a time, in accordance with our intuitive beliefs about persons and our expectations about their behavior as it expresses what amounts to an intuitive physics.

The odd – and really interesting thing – about all this is that while intuitive beliefs may (as in the above example) seem to contradict or be out of joint with reflective beliefs, they also support them. Thus a god who is everywhere at once is clearly a departure from our normal expectations about the behavior of persons. Yet, at the same time, we can feel comfortable or familiar respecting god because the deity conforms in other respects to our general ideas and expectations about persons. Thus, for instance, god has intelligence, will, and purpose, and on occasion is both recipient and source of messages.

Reflective beliefs, it should be noted, do not displace or erase intuitive beliefs. Both sorts co-exist. Intuitive beliefs are, as it were, available 7/24, and they are typically invoked – indeed, automatically invoked – when there is need for rapid ("online") thinking and action. Reflective beliefs, in comparison, may be invoked in more leisurely settings where reflective thought ("offline thinking") can be advantageous socially and in other ways.

Creedal or doctrinal religions such as mainstream Christianities supply our major examples of religions that celebrate reflective beliefs. Such religions, Pascal Boyer (2004: 224) points out, supplement (rather than displace) non-doctrinal religions. Like non-doctrinal religions, they are founded on intuitive beliefs, but they represent an "additional growth." They are, as Boyer puts it, "a secondary, derivative development of a much more general human tendency to imagine important supernatural agents" (2004: 28). Most religion, Boyer writes, "has no doctrine, no set catalogue of beliefs that most members should adhere to, no overall and integrated statements about supernatural agents. Most religion is piecemeal, mostly implicit, often less than perfectly consistent and, most importantly, *focused on concrete circumstances*" (2004: 28, emphasis in original). And that, I believe, is something that we can and should believe!

"Finding Wayú Religion." I have already commented on part of this essay elsewhere in the Introduction. But I will supplement my remarks with an observation. Wayú religion is a good example of a religion that is "piecemeal, mostly implicit, often less than perfectly consistent," and "*focused on concrete circumstances.*" Concrete circumstances include the dead. The motives of the dead are thought to be transparent and limited, actually quite sensible in their own way, and it is equally sensible for the living to seek protection against the baleful attentions of the dead. Religion for the Wayú is largely a practical way of handling certain kinds of threats to wellbeing. And it provides a ritualized way of transcending (but probably not resolving) ambivalence, for at the same time that the Wayú fear their dead, they also mourn them.

"On Credulity" One sometimes hears it said that "People will believe anything." That is too broad a statement. There are good arguments, and some evidence, for not accepting it across the board (e.g., Boyer 1994, 2001). Thus, for instance, to borrow an example from Boyer

(2001: 52), it is extremely doubtful that any normally cognizing adult would proclaim it as an article of faith that "There is only one God! He is omnipotent. But He exists only on Wednesdays." This set of statements is likely to be adjudged false, and probably foolish. For those with a logical bent and an understanding of the meaning of "omnipotent," there may well seem to be an incompatibility between being omnipotent and not existing most of the time. We normally take existence to be a precondition for having powers. And being omnipotent would presumably include the power to exist. More generally, moreover, it is counter-intuitive to suppose that any person – our god in this example is a "He" – comes into existence and goes out of existence and comes back into existence again on a regular basis. Persons, even as spirits and ghosts, are usually credited with a continuous existence or "lifetime," whether it be short or long. Spirits or ghosts may hide themselves from us most of the time, but that does not make them non-existent. If they were truly non-existent, they could neither hide nor show themselves. Without further laboring the point, it deserves to be said that there are some imaginable beliefs (as in Boyer's example) that most people are unlikely to accept or try to spread. Not everything goes! Our inference systems balk at some prospects.

Having said that, it must also be said that there are a huge number of beliefs that different people do appear to accept. While many such beliefs may be similar to others when it comes to themes and the intuitions that support them, there is still quite a lot of variety in apparent content.

Recognition of that fact inclines some people to label much of humankind as credulous, as being willing to accept beliefs too readily. People who talk that way usually mean beliefs of the sort that Dan Sperber and others call "reflective" or "non-intuitive." But while people often do accept such belief with little in the way of what critics would deem "objective evidence," they may nevertheless be acting in a socially responsive – and perhaps responsible – manner. Some of our beliefs derive from hearing our fellows voice them; we begin to speak as they do, without necessarily being aware of it. Others are imparted to us quite consciously and often deliberately, and we accept them on authority. Still others become established in our cognitive archives through still more complex process that relate to our mimicry of speech and our acceptance of authority. And some are acknowledged (if not truly accepted) in order to be companionable, or so as not to give the appearance of rejecting persons by rejecting their beliefs.

In addition to concerning ourselves with the semantics and syntactics of beliefs, we can also learn much from investigating their pragmatics. That in itself is a broad field of inquiry. In my essay "On What We May Believe about Beliefs," I note that people do not just "have" beliefs. They usually deploy them in social transactions of diverse kinds. People use their beliefs for relating to others as well as in monitoring and directing the self. In my essay "On Credulity" I explore some of the social functions of beliefs. But it is only a modest effort at exploration, for the topic is as complex as it is important.

"Secondary Beliefs and the Alien Abduction Phenomenon." Most of us who have written about Alien Abductions focus on people who claim to believe that they have been abducted. Those making such claims – some call them "experiencers" – often furnish dramatic tales, and they usually appear to be convinced of the truth of what they relate. I indicate this in my essay, but perhaps too pallidly. Numbers of experiencers tell their stories with such evident sincerity that I sometimes feel almost churlish in not believing them. A sociologist who studied the alien abduction phenomenon, and who generously supplied me with information and advice when I began my studies, was even more impressed than I by the shows of emotion and other narrative displays of his informants. He interviewed a woman who claimed to have been abducted, and he was, he told me, dazed by her story and how she presented it to him. He emerged from an interview of many hours a convert: he came to believe that people actually have been abducted by aliens. While he tries to appear "even-handed" (his words) in his scholarly publications, he personally believes that at least some abduction stories are true.

My interest in "secondary believers" – my term for people who do not claim to have been abducted, but who affirm belief in the reality of alien abductions – has perhaps spared me greater emersion in the affectively-charged worlds of "primary believers" (the abductees or experiencers). Secondary believers articulate their beliefs, but usually without emotional displays approaching the intensity demonstrated by primary believers. Secondary believers believe, but sometimes in hedged or tentative fashion, and often with overt recognition of the probable skepticism of their academic interviewer.

Now, my essay in this collection deals with persons who profess belief. There are, however, numbers of people with an interest in UFOs and abductions who are not believers so much as they are persons who suspend disbelief at certain times and in certain places. I do not deal with them in my essay. I will, however, say a little about them here, for considering them helps us to expand our understandings of what it may mean to believe – and to not believe.

Some people who take more than a casual interest in UFOs and abductions tell their interviewers that they don't fully believe in the reality of either, but that they think that they are possible. Further, some add that it would make for a more interesting world (or universe) if there were extraterrestrials who take a genuine interest in human beings. And so, because they think that it is possible that alien spacecraft are monitoring us, and because the prospect is exciting or entertaining, they do what they can to learn more. Learning more may consist of reading about the subject and perhaps discussing it with others. Some persons, however, attend lectures, participate in organizations such as MUFON (Mutual UFO Network), interview people who claim to have seen unusual things in the sky and/or to have been abducted, compile records, and the like. Some are weekend researchers, and they often act as if they do believe, while still claiming to have "an open mind." In the course of their research they may be indistinguishable from hardcore believers, but that is because they suspend disbelief, at least for a time.

That point was driven home to me at a MUFON meeting that I attended in Connecticut some years ago. The meeting was much the same in structure as an academic conference. There were volunteered and invited papers, session chairmen who varied in how severely they enforced the time limits for papers, registration fees, badges, a printed program, and questions from the audience following paper presentations. One presenter gave a paper on "Bigfoot," one of several names applied to what is usually described as a mysterious giant primate glimpsed in northern latitudes. The presenter, who held a Master's Degree in Anthropology from a respected university, justified the inclusion of Bigfoot at a UFO meeting by claiming that those giants originated as extraterrestrials. They came to earth, he said, sixty-five million years ago, established a number of colonies, and for the last sixty-five million years have been regularly visited by spacecraft from their home planet. He then proceeded to give us some ethnographic information about Bigfoot, and he illustrated some of his points with anecdotes that I enjoyed. He told us, moreover, that his information came from interviews that he had conducted with more than one hundred Bigfoots (or, if you prefer, Bigfeet). These interviews, he added, were all conducted by mental-telepathy. After his paper, a few people in the audience asked polite questions calling for clarification of some details, and then we went on to the next paper in the session.

Now, although I didn't conduct a survey, I suspect that most of the people in the room did not believe what they were told about Bigfoot. At least some (myself included) deemed the presentation entertaining, and entertainment sufficed. A rather different reception was accorded a plenary lecture given by a U.S. astronaut later that same day. Many in the astronaut's audience appeared to hang on to his every word as he recounted remarkable things that he had observed in space, and as he gave reasons for concluding that the U.S. federal government was engaged in a long-standing cover-up designed to restrict the knowledge that we humans are not the only intelligent species in the universe.

What I have just described is actually quite common in our society and probably in other societies as well. In watching, say, a vampire film on television, one can usually enjoy the story more if one suspends one's disbelief. To proclaim stoutly that there are no such things as vampires is unlikely to enhance the entertainment value of the film. Without further elaborating the point, suffice it to say that people often simulate belief – or, to approach it from a different angle, people often suspend disbelief – because doing so is fun. There is sometimes a playfulness in pretending to believe or in not strenuously disbelieving. And playfulness of that sort may be more widespread in human life than is commonly allowed for in scholarly tomes on "belief."

Part IV Studying Religion: Some Conceptual Issues

This last section of the collection touches on a number of issues of varying concern to contemporary academic students of religion. But its center of gravity, so to speak, is the problem of conceptualizing and defining religion.

While I think of definitions as tools, as means to ends rather than as ends in themselves, I do not want to suggest that they are unimportant. Constructing or critically considering definitions can be valuable exercises for crystallizing our thoughts and for conveying them to others. Definitions, moreover, can serve as heuristics, as devices for pointing us in certain directions. And, of course, they are useful for explicitly and publicly marking out some area of inquiry, some field for exploration. This last point is strongly affirmed by Melford E. Spiro in a classic paper dealing with the definition and explanation of religion. Spiro (1966: 90) maintains that while "a definition cannot take the place of inquiry, in the absence of definitions there can be no inquiry – for it is the definition, either ostensive or nominal, which designates the phenomenon to be investigated." On the same page, moreover, he writes that when the term religion "is given no explicit ostensive definition, the observer, perforce, employs an implicit one."

Religion is a matter that has come in for a lot of definition making, definition minimizing or avoidance, and (to a lesser extent) definition rejection.

I deal with definition rejection very briefly here. The rejecter may claim that what is usually meant by common uses of the term religion can be better described, explicated, and perhaps explained by using other terms. Thus by way of a widely known example, Wilfred Cantwell Smith (1962) recommends that we substitute the expressions "faith" and "cumulative traditions" for "religion." While Smith is still in the approximate area of what we conventionally call religion, although disinclined to employ the actual term religion, more extreme rejecters move further away. Timothy Fitzgerald, for instance, claims that religion "cannot reasonably be taken to be a valid analytical category since it does not pick out any distinctive cross-cultural aspect of human life" (Fitzgerald 2000: 4). We ought to desist from trying to use religion as an analytical category, Fitzgerald suggests, and go on to study power relations and values in human life. While Smith, Fitzgerald, and other rejecters provide some arguments in favor of their positions, the great majority of people associated with the academic study of religion continue to use the term religion, as do people in the larger societies that support their research. At the very least, an argument for retaining religion as a category term can pivot on the convenience of the term, in analogy to a similar argument made in favor of the term "supernatural" (see my discussion of that latter term earlier in this Introduction). I think, however, that stronger arguments can be made for retaining religion, especially if we conceptualize it and define it in an improved way – which is what I attempt to do in several of the essays in this section of the collection.

Some authors provide only minimal definitions of religion. These usually declare that religion centers on beliefs and practices that relate to posited "supernatural," "superhuman," or "spiritual" beings or agents. Edward Burnett Tylor (1871), for example, offers "the belief in Spiritual Beings" as his "minimum definition." Still other authors avoid stating a definition, apparently depending on their readers to have some understanding of what "religion" means. The strategy of either minimizing or avoiding definitions is useful to some extent. Rather than get bogged down in definitional issues, issues sometimes dismissed as pertaining more to the purview of lexicographers than that of scholars of religion (e. g., Boyer 2004: 27), authors are free to move on to matters that they may deem of greater substance or weight. I, however, prefer to confront definitional issues.

As I see it, problems of conceptualizing and defining religion are central to the academic study of religion. In my opinion, they should be faced explicitly and, if need be, addressed at some length. I opine, however, that efforts to define religion in essentialist fashion – to specify, that is, necessary features or conditions that must be met if phenomena are to be labeled properly as "religion" or "religions" – are very likely to be inadequate and, worse, misleading. Religion, in my view, cannot be clearly demarcated from all else. It is an analog phenomenon in a world that is mostly analog, and it has no clear boundaries. Assigning it sharp boundaries is likely to cut out phenomena that might otherwise be productively considered and included. Indeed, it tends to focus our attention on a small number of variables, to the detriment of a more expansive appreciation of religion. Some people attempt on occasion to transcend those limitations to some extent. Thus, for example, they may talk of "quasi-religions," "semi-religions," or "secular-religions," by which they usually mean clusters of phenomena that strike them as resembling religions in interesting ways, but not sufficiently enough to be simply and accurately pronounced "religions." Hyphenated "religions" are not usually taken to be real or "full" religions. Lexically treating them as if they have something "religion-like" about them, however, can serve as an effective rhetorical device for calling attention to something deemed worthy of emphasis in phenomena so labeled.

I think of religion and religions differently. My conceptual preferences are succinctly summarized in the last paragraph of the essay "Towards a Realistic and Relevant 'Science of Religion'." The approach that I favor, I write, "emphasizes central tendencies rather than essences, fuzzy peripheries rather than sharp boundaries, resemblances rather than identities, and typical features rather than distinctive ones." I discuss these preferences in the essays referred to in this section, and it would be redundant of me to go over them here. I do, however, want to enlarge slightly on my preference for "typical features" over "distinctive features."

The expression "distinctive features" is well known in linguistics, where it is employed in classical discussions of phonemes and certain other matters. When employed in definition making in the social sciences, a so-called distinctive feature is usually deemed to mark off the phenomenon credited with expressing it from all else. Ideally, at least, a distinctive feature indicates something unique or special about the phenomenon that "has" it. Thus, for instance, in his classic 1966 essay, Spiro maintains that "culturally postulated superhuman beings," and their supposed powers to help or harm human beings, constitute "the core variable" necessary for any acceptable definition of religion. And religious institutions are distinguished from all other institutions, Spiro claims, only because of their references to culturally posited superhuman beings.

Rather than think of religion in terms of "distinctive features," I prefer to think of it in terms of *typical features*. These are features that, in our conceptualizations, are deemed typical of what we mean by religion. They are typical, and therefore usually to be expected. But they are not on that count necessary, nor are they always to be encountered.

Swans are typically white. But there are some black swans. And tigers are typically striped. But there are some albino tigers that lack stripes. We have no difficulty in accepting black swans as swans and albino tigers as tigers. We accept them as, respectively, swans and tigers on other grounds. That, in my opinion, is how we may best approach religion. I flesh-out that idea in several essays in this section, but especially in "Conceptualizing Religion: The Matter of Boundaries." I will not replicate that discussion here other than to say that it includes a consideration of the possibility that "gods" are contingent rather than necessary elements in religion. In the essay alluded to, argument centers on Theravada Buddhism. In considering the different views of Melford Spiro and the anthropologist Martin Southwald regarding the matter of theism and Theravada Buddhism, I opt for the position espoused by the philosopher W. D. Hudson. Hudson argues that while theism is among the family resemblance predicates of Buddhism, it is not found in all forms of Buddhism.

The most pointed discussions of the metaphor of family resemblances in this collection are found in two essays, "Family Resemblance and the Definition of Religion" and "Towards a Realistic and Relevant

'Science of Religion'." A more detailed treatment is given in my book, *Conceptualizing Religion* (Saler 2000a [1993]).

The expression "family resemblances" was not invented by the philosopher Ludwig Wittgenstein. It, and similar expressions such as "family faces," have long been in colloquial use in various European languages to assert or to suggest resemblances in physical characteristics among persons related by consanguinity. Wittgenstein, however, made the expression into a major philosophical conceptual tool. In his famous discussion of the term game, he asks what the many types of games have in common. He cautions us not to say that they must have something in common, for otherwise they would not all be called games. Rather, he instructs us to look and see if there is anything common to all. And when we look and see, we do not find commonalities, we find "similarities, relationships, and a whole series of them at that" (*Philosophical Investigations* I.66). I apply this understanding to the category religion, and I recommend that we conceive of instantiations of that category as being linked by family resemblances, not by mutual expression of one or more distinctive features. This, as I try to make clear in the "Family Resemblance" essay, does not free us of problems. Analytical categories are likely to confront us with difficulties regardless of how they are organized. And family resemblance categories, I maintain, have their own special difficulties. But such difficulties are not fatal. Conceptualizing the category religion as a family resemblance category is, in my opinion, a first step well worth the effort. But I do not think that it suffices. I argue that we can best serve our definitional interests by also taking into account certain insights derived from prototype theory.

Arguments in support of an emphasis on resemblances are found in the essay "Comparison: Some Suggestions for Improving the Inevitable." That work points to the inevitability of comparisons in monitoring the world. Making comparisons is part and parcel of many of our cognitive activities. Thus, for instance, our understandings of newly encountered events, and our predictive confidence respecting those events, often depends on the resemblances that we apperceive between such events and our established representations. We may not always be consciously aware of the making of comparisons. But when we are, and when we reflect on them, it is the relative strength (or weakness) of resemblances, not the "digital" yes or no of identities, that is usually of functional significance. In light of that understanding, a philosophical overview on resemblances may further strengthen our commitment to the idea of resemblances. In the "Comparison" essay, I supply such an overview by drawing on the philosopher H. H. Price. Price argues in favor of what he calls "The Philosophy of Resemblances," as opposed to "The Philosophy of Universals." His argument, I think, lends additional support to the argument that I make for how we may best conceptualize religion.

Finally, there is the matter of religion and the evolutionary sciences. As my earlier discussions of Tylor, Hallowell, and evolution in this Introduction indicate, evolution has long been a topic of interest – and of controversy – among numbers of anthropologists and various other students of religion. Controversies today, however, are for the most part different in various ways than the controversies of yesteryear, owing in great measure to the emergence of a far more sophisticated and empirically referenced understanding of evolution. Indeed, new disciplines and sub-disciplines such as genetics and molecular biology have arisen over the last century, stimulated in part by technological breakthroughs such as the electron microscope and the electronic computer. New disciplines and sub-disciplines, along with progress in longer established fields of evolutionary research, have resulted in impressive advances in our knowledge. And, as one may expect, today's evolutionary scientists are not in full agreement among themselves about certain important details. I will not try to expand on this observation here. Suffice it for me to point to a specific difference in opinion respecting one such matter among some contemporary students of religion.

Some contemporary scholars who view religion in evolutionary perspective deem religion to be an evolutionary adaptation. They hypothesize that affect-laden ideas, constructs, and practices of the sort that we typically associate with religion conferred advantages on the members of small groups of Pleistocene hunters and gatherers who entertained them and transmitted them to their offspring. In the view of these students of religion – we can call them "adaptationists" –, shared commitments of a supernaturalistic cast promoted social solidarity within small bands. This organizational benefit, it is supposed, constituted a competitive advantage over other small groups of Pleistocenne hunters and gatherers who were less ideationally and affectively integrated, and it was therefore adaptive. A leading exponent of the adaptationist point of view is the biologist David Sloan Wilson, the author of *Darwin's Cathedral: Evolution, Religion, and the Nature of Society* (2002).

Other contemporary students of religion who view religion in evolutionary perspective do not opine that religion originated as an adaptation. These scholars – we can call them "derivationists" or "spandrelists"

– think it likely that various of the affect-laden ideas, constructs, and practices that are central to religion developed as byproducts of the evolution of adaptive capacities and dispositions that we humans would presumably enjoy even if there were no religions. In this view, what we call religion is a "spandrel" or aggregate of "spandrels" (Scott Atran 2002 holds that there was no "it" to have evolved, for the elements that we deem central to religion did not all evolve together). The term spandrel was borrowed from architecture and first utilized in evolutionary studies by the biological scientists Stephen Jay Gould and Richard C. Lewontin. They use it to mean a non-adaptive evolutionary development, that is, an architectural byproduct of other evolutionary changes. While spandrels may sometimes take on functional utility, Gould and Lewontin caution against inferring an adaptive origin from a current utility. This accords with the point of view espoused by most "derivationists" or "spandrelists" who study religion Thus, for instance, Pascal Boyer (2001, 2004) affirms that religion derives from, and is "parasitic" on, evolved propensities that are important in human life regardless of whether or not we have religion.

I count myself a proponent of the derivationist or spandrelist view. Not only does it nurture powerful theories that purport to explain much, but the adaptationist alternative strikes me as unconvincing. The kinds of religion available to our Pleistocene ancestors were probably only modestly "adaptive" (fitness enhancing), if even that. I see no compelling reason to imagine that those religions joined band members together in consequence of commonly endorsed creeds, or by virtue of taking directions from religious guilds, or through participation in socially inclusive rituals that served as distinctive badges of group membership. In short, I am skeptical that Pleistocene religions conferred crucial organizational or solidarity advantages on some small human groups in competition with others. I think it likely that Pleistocene religiosity was starkly anthropomorphic and animistic, to a large extent fear-triggered, intellectually shallow, and interpersonally variable as to both beliefs and rites.

My essay, "Towards a Realistic and Relevant 'Science of Religion'," affirms my enthusiasm for invoking the evolutionary sciences in our efforts to account for religion. In doing so, it describes and admires some of the work of the archeologist Steven Mithen. My remarks about evolution, moreover, are incorporated into a larger set of advocacies respecting an idealized science of religion. Such a science, in my opinion, would realistically takes human beings (rather than religions and cultures) as its phenomenal subjects. Further, its theorizing would be relevant to the theorizing of other sciences, particularly the biological sciences.

The essay, "Biology and Religion: On Establishing a Problematic," makes the point that some scholars focus on religion as something to be explained or understood, whereas others discuss religion mainly in order to illustrate or illumine something else. Obviously, gravitating toward one or the other choice will have consequences. The major thrust of my essay is to evaluate critically someone else's discussion of religion, and by so doing to support a conclusion about how we may best attempt to connect cultural phenomena to their possible biological substrates. I focus on Walter Burkert's book, *Creation of the Sacred: Tracks of Biology in Early Religion* (1996), which is largely devoted to making religion the thing to be understood against a posited biological landscape.

Walter Burkert is one of the world's leading classicists. His *Creation of the Sacred* is in many respects in keeping with his renown as a scholar of ancient Greek religion and other forms of religion in the ancient Mediterranean basin. It is erudite, lucid, thoughtful, and insightful. For all that, however, I find it disappointing. I agree with an observation voiced by the philosopher Daniel Dennett: Burkert, Dennett (1998: 122) writes, "has whetted my appetite beyond what he can satisfy with his feast of good suggestions." While Dennett credits Burkert with being an "alert and imaginative guide" to available sources on religion developed by anthropologists and historians, Dennett holds that he is more a guide than a theorist (Dennett 1998: 127). I agree.

Burkert attempts to sketch for us some of the biological "landscape" that underlies religion. I judge the word "landscape" to be a felicitous choice. And I think the same of the expression "tracks of biology." Unfortunately, however, I opine that Burkert is not a very convincing tracker, nor does he substantively deliver on landscape. He strikes me as being vague respecting certain important points in his perspective, as neglecting or rejecting culture in cases where there are reasons to take it seriously, as hinting at homologies where he can only demonstrate analogies, and in other respects as seeming to dismiss the canons of science that I extol elsewhere (e.g., Burkert 1996: 22). But above all, I think that he fails to propose mechanisms that intervene between expressions of religiosity and posited biological substrates.

That is, Burkert suggests that various human religious behaviors relate to genes giving "recommendations" or to "more original processes in the evolution of life" (Burkert 1996: 22), without supplying a persuasive account of how religious behavior is linked to these presumably more fundamental factors. How do we go from one to the other? What are the likely explanatory mechanisms? Burkert does not tell us. That failure, as I indicate in my essay, is a failure to note, meet, and transcend a cautionary consideration advanced by Leda Cosmides, John Tooby, and Jerome Barkow (1992: 3): "[T]o understand the relationship between biology and culture, one must first understand the architecture of our evolved psychology ... Past attempts to leapfrog the psychological – to apply evolutionary biology directly to human social life – have for this reason not always been successful."

Having already endorsed the above statement by Cosmides, Tooby, and Barkow in the Biology and Religion essay, I conclude this Introduction by endorsing it again. The need that it suggests for a consideration of intervening variables in the construction of explanatory mechanisms is crucial for the emergence of a realistic and relevant science of religion. And so, too, is a consideration of other fundamental epistemological issues as they relate to the study and understanding of religion. It is this latter consideration that connects my essays in this collection. I very much enjoyed writing them, and I hope that the reader will find them useful.

The Ethnographer as Pontifex[1]

Abstract: Using the Doctrine of the Trinity as an example, this essay considers some issues attendant on understanding and translating religious concepts. It argues that the task of the ethnographer is explication rather than translation in the narrow sense of finding correspondences (glosses) across languages. It suggests that there is an analogy between the work of the ethnographer and what some religious communities expect of their priests. Ideally, the ethnographer is a bridge-builder (pontifex), facilitating a crossing into the sensibilities and sensitivities of others.

Incident at Cajamarca

Some of the difficulties attendant on understanding and then translating religious concepts are illustrated by an incident that occurred during the Spanish conquest of the Inka Empire. The first verbal exchanges between the Spaniards and the Inka ruler ("*The* Inka") Atahuallpa were mediated by an interpreter named Felipe. According to the chronicler, Garcilaso de la Vega, nicknamed "El Inka," Felipe was

> a native of the island of Puna, a man of very plebeian origin, young – for he was scarcely twenty-two – and as little versed in the general language of the Incas as in Spanish. He had in fact learned the language of the Incas, not in Cuzco, but in Túmbez, from Indians who speak barbarously and corruptly as foreigners; we have already explained that to all the Indians but the natives of Cuzco this is a foreign language. He had also learnt Spanish without a teacher, but merely by hearing the Spaniards speak, and the words he heard most often were those used by the ordinary soldiers ... Though baptized, he had received no instruction in the Christian religion and knew nothing about Christ our Lord, and was totally ignorant of the Apostles' creed. (Vega 1966: 682)

As may be expected, Felipe translated poorly from one language to the other. Thus when Fray Vicente de Valverde addressed a long and uncompromising speech to Atahuallpa in which he outlined the Christian

---

[1] "The Ethnographer as Pontifex." In Paula G. Rubel and Abraham Rosman (eds.), T*ranslating Culture: Perspectives on Translation and Anthropology*, 197–212, Oxford and New York: Berg, 2003.

faith and demanded The Inka's submission to the Pope and to the Emperor, Felipe mangled the translation. He did so not out of malice, the chronicler tells us, "but because he did not understand what he was interpreting, and spoke it like a parrot" (Vega 1966: 682). Among other things, "Instead of God three in one, he said God three and one make four, adding the numbers in order to make himself understood. This is shown by the tradition of the *quipus*, or annual records in knots, kept at Cajamarca, where the event occurred" (Vega 1966: 682).[2]

Garcilaso, while clearly no admirer of Felipe, does not blame him entirely for mistranslating Fray Vicente's speech. Felipe, he claims,

> could not express it [the doctrine of the Trinity] in any other way; for there are no words or phrases in the Peruvian language for many of the concepts of the Christian religion, such as Trinity, Holy Spirit, faith, grace, Church, sacraments, and similar words. These are totally unknown to the gentiles, and the words have never existed, and still do not exist [twenty-nine years later], in their language. For this reason, when the Spanish interpreters of these times wish to express these ideas adequately, they have to seek new words or phrases, or use with great care suitably dignified expressions in the old language or else lay hands on the many words the cultured and scholarly Indians have taken from Spanish and introduced into their own languages, adapting them to their own ways of speech. The Indians of today do this with great elegance, thus helping the Spaniards to find the words that are lacking, so that they can say what they want and the Indians can understand the sermons that are preached to them. (1966: 682)

I return eventually to Garcilaso's remarks about how the doctrines of Christianity may be "adequately" conveyed to Peruvian Indians. Here, however, I want to consider one particular doctrine, that of the Trinity.

Felipe added three Gods and one God and came up with four, at least partly, it seems, out of profound ignorance. But even well schooled and greatly respected Christian theologians have confessed to difficulties in understanding the doctrine of the Trinity. They nevertheless proclaim it to be central to their faith and of crucial significance for their salvation. The doctrine of the Trinity, moreover, has proven difficult

---

2   The quipu was a mnemonic device consisting of knots of different kinds tied in various positions on strings. The types of knots, their locations, and their syntactic relations to other knots were assigned semantic values that stimulated and constrained the memories of specially trained personnel. A collection of quipus, as at Cajamarca, was in effect a sort of archive. By referring to these records, Garcilaso de la Vega does what good historians normally do: he supports his narrative by citing sources for it.

to translate from one language to another, beginning with efforts to render Greek formulations of it into Latin.

Difficulties in understanding and conveying the doctrine of the Trinity are traceable in part to a major factor affecting the comprehension and translation of many religious ideas: the matter of their partial counter-intuitivity. I explore that point by first describing certain problems posed by theologians respecting the doctrine of the Trinity. I go on from there to consider some recent theoretical claims about the counter-intuitive aspects of religious ideas, and certain of the implications of such claims for translation.

The Doctrine of the Trinity

Despite a fair amount of heterogeneity in opinion among Christian theologians, they commonly recognize certain constraints on their theologies. Two are especially relevant here.

The first we may term anthropocentric pragmatism. That is, thoughtful theologians generally evaluate their theological options in light of this consideration: what may be the likely consequences – indeed, the potential harm – of any doctrine for the possibilities of human salvation? (Placher 1983: 69)

The second, adapting and amending a theoretical construct advanced by Brian K. Smith (1987), can be called the principle of "canonical reflexivity." Smith maintains that a religion is to be identified by the repeated references or returns, if only formulaic, that its adherents make to some canon, whether written or oral. The canon is invested with authority, and the positive references that people make to it are definitive of their faith or perspective, even if they do not explicitly discuss its substance. (Many Hindus, for example, are ignorant of what is contained in the Vedas, but their regard for the chanting of those works in Sanskrit is important to their identity as Hindus.) By resting religion on this one criterion, Smith is forced to identify "Marxism" and "Freudianism" as religions. I criticize him elsewhere for doing so (Saler 2000a [1993]). And while I do not hold that canonical reflexivity is either necessary or sufficient for identifying religion, I acknowledge that it is often important in religions.

These two principles relate to the development of the doctrine of the Trinity. The New Testament depicts Jesus Christ as more than a man. At the same time, however, he is canonically distinguished from the Heavenly Father (e.g., "the Father is greater than I" [*John* 14: 28]). What, then, is Jesus? And how is he related to the Father? And if human salvation comes through Jesus Christ, what other considerations might that implicate? Thus, for instance, if Jesus were a creature, as Arius claimed, he would have come into existence at some time, and doing so betokens change. If he had changed once, from nothing to something, might he not change again? And dare we entrust human salvation to a creature capable of change (Placher 1983)?

These and other considerations entered into the development of the doctrine of the Triune God. Much of the early argument in the developing Church focused on the relationship of the Second Person of the Trinity (the Son) to the First (God the Father). While the Third Person (The Holy Spirit) was discussed, it received less polemical attention in the first few centuries – albeit argument over whether the Spirit "proceeds" *both* from the Father "and from the Son" ("*filioque*"), as Augustine of Hippo and the Western Church proclaimed, or only from the Father, as the Eastern Church maintained, proved to be of major divisive significance within Christendom.

The Council of Nicaea (325 A.D.) was called by the Emperor Constantine largely to settle the issue of whether the Son is co-eternal with the Father or whether, like a creature, he had come into existence at some time. The Council concluded that the Son is co-eternal with the Father and that he is "begotten not made," his begetting, by eventual consensus, being an eternal begetting, for unlike creatures he was not begotten at some point in time. Further, the Council, in proclaiming the Son to be "true God from true God," also declared him to be "of the same substance (*homoousios*) as the Father."

This matter of being *homoousios* proved to be theologically problematic. While the translation of this Greek term – *homo*, 'same' + *ousios*, 'substance' – by Latin-speaking churchmen was generally in harmony with the literal meaning assigned to it by their Greek-speaking colleagues, there were divisions among both Greek and Latin speakers as to the theological interpretation of the term. Some churchmen at the Council apparently understood "the same substance" to mean of the same divine stuff, which would be somewhat like saying that two pieces of oak furniture are of the same substance because they are both made of oak wood. But Athanasius, a leading fourth century theologian, insisted that the term means the very same substance, which would be analogous to saying that our two pieces of oak furniture are cut from the very same oak tree (adapted from Placher 1983). Some of the theologians who supported the idea of the same divine stuff (oak in general) rather than the very same stuff (the same oak tree) eventually endorsed the claim that the Son is *homoiousios* with the Father, of a "similar substance" rather than of the same substance.

Arius held that "There was a time when the Son was not." The debate at Nicea between those who inclined to his opinion and Athanasius and his supporters was influenced significantly by Greek philosophy. Indeed, Alan Kolp (1975: 101) suggests that "Without noting it the Arian controversy is a struggle over the correct use of Platonic philosophical categories." The Athanasian *homoousios* theology was eventually strengthened by the Cappadocian Fathers, Basil the Great, Gregory of Nyssa, and Gregory of Nazianzus, who creatively reformulated certain Greek metaphysical categories. They maintained that the Father, Son, and Holy Spirit are all of one *ousia*, one 'substance', but they are three *hypostaseis* ('individuals', 'persons').

This terminology immediately raised problems in Greek, where the terms *ousia* and *hypostasis* were sometimes employed as synonyms for 'substance', as in some of the writings of Athanasius (Placher 1983: 78). And it raised problems for translation into Latin, for, as Placher (1983: 78–79) points out,

> Since the time of Tertullian, Latin-speaking Christians had made a parallel distinction between three *personae* ... and one *substantia*. Unfortunately, *substantia* is the literal Latin translation of *hypostasis* (both words mean "that which stands under"), so horrified Latin-speaking Christians read Greek references to "three *hypostaseis*" as meaning "three *substantiae*."

Eventually, however, things were more or less sorted out by those who took the trouble to acquaint themselves with the peculiarities of usage in Cappadocian theological Greek and the problems encountered in translating from that discourse to Latin. The Cappadocian Fathers assisted in clarifying understandings by extended explications. They declared, for instance, that while the Three Persons are each distinct, they always act in perfect harmony and concert, unlike any other three persons. Further, the Three Persons of the same divine *ousia* are the only form that *ousia* has ever taken or could ever take (Placher 1983: 78). And, of course, and in case anyone was not aware of it, they called attention to the fact that they were using the terms *ousia* and *hypostasis* in special, non-synonymous senses.

Difficulties in Comprehending the Doctrine of the Trinity

Despite the attempts at clarification described above, and others as well, many theologians (to say nothing of ordinary Christians) deem the doctrine of the Trinity exceedingly difficult to understand. Some, indeed, declare it to be beyond the powers of human comprehension, at least in this life. Thomas Aquinas takes that position.

In the first of his two *summas*, the *Summa contra gentiles* (Bk. IV, Chapt. 1), Thomas writes that there are three ways for humans to obtain a knowledge of things divine. The first is by the unaided exercise of human reason and the third is by the post-mortem attainment of the Beatific Vision, wherein the human mind will be elevated to more powerful understandings. The second, which is the one that most directly concerns us here, is by revelation from God. Thomas declares, however, that revealed truths – he supplies two examples, the Incarnation and the Trinity – are given to us "not, however, as something made clear to be seen, but as something spoken in words to be believed" (SCG IV, I: 5). The truths of the Incarnation and Trinity, the "angelic doctor" teaches, are not merely difficult to understand; they are, in a profound sense, impossible to understand, at least in this life. Yet they are fundamental facts of reality and of crucial importance for the possibility of human salvation. In short, one of the greatest theologians in Christendom maintains that his religion turns on certain truths that the faithful must accept but cannot fully fathom.

A more contemporary consideration of the difficulty of understanding the doctrine of the Trinity (and thus, by implication, the difficulty of translating it) is given by John Henry Newman in his *An Essay in Aid of a Grammar of Assent* (1985 [1889, 1870]). Newman's Grammar is a major nineteenth century work dealing with the epistemology of belief.

Newman is concerned with what is involved in apprehending, inferring, and assenting to propositions. He characterizes apprehension as the mind's imposition of sense on the predicate of a proposition. Inference is the relating of a proposition to others as a conclusion. And assent is the mind's acceptance of the truth of a proposition.

While John Locke (1959 [1689]) holds that assent is conditional, that it can be proportional to evidence, Newman denies it. He allows that inference may be conditional, but not assent. Assent, he says, does not admit of degrees (1985: 32).

"The terms of a proposition," Newman writes,

do or do not stand for things. If they do, then they are singular terms, for all things that are, are units. But if they do not stand for things they must stand for notions, and are common terms. Singular nouns come from experience, common from abstraction. The apprehension of the former I call real, and of the latter notional. (1985: 22)

In the case of real propositions, that is, "the terms stand for things external to us" (1985: 13) insofar as there are impressions of those things in the imagination. In the case of notional propositions, in contrast, the mind is directed to its own creations rather than to "things." The apprehension of a proposition, moreover, varies in strength because, according to Newman, "what is concrete exerts a force and makes an impression on the mind which nothing abstract can rival. That is, ... because the object is more powerful, therefore so is the apprehension of it" (1985: 31).

Newman's distinction between "real" and "notional" beliefs resembles to some extent distinctions that certain contemporary philosophers draw between "*de re*" and "*de dicto*" beliefs (see, for example, Woodfield 1982: v-xi). Rather than digress to sketch the similarities (and differences), however, I focus instead on the applications that Newman makes of his own distinction to what his Church teaches about the Trinity.

The dogma of the Trinity, Newman says, consists of nine propositions. Each of the nine, taken separately, can be the object of real assent, for the devout can image each by a lively act of the imagination. But if the nine propositions are taken together as a "systematized whole," that combination "is the object of notional assent" (1985: 91). The nine propositions, in Newman's words, are these:

> 1. There are Three who give testimony in heaven, the Father, The Word or Son, and the Holy Spirit. 2. From the Father is, and ever has been, the Son. 3. From the Father and Son is, and ever has been, the Spirit. 4. The Father is the One Eternal Personal God. 5. The Son is the One Eternal Personal God. 6. The Spirit is the One Eternal Personal God. 7. The Father is not the Son. 8. The Son is not the Holy Ghost. 9. The Holy Ghost is not the Father. (1985: 91)

Combining the nine into a whole, says Newman, produces a theological mystery — that is, an affirmation that is beyond our full comprehension and that is to be accepted on faith. Newman remarks that the Holy Trinity in Unity "is never spoken of as a Mystery in the sacred book, which is addressed far more to the imagination and affection than to the intellect" (1985: 90). Nor is it termed a mystery in the Apostles', Nicean, and Athanasian Creeds, "which have a place in the Ritual" and are "devotional acts ... of the nature of prayers, addressed to God; and in such addresses, to speak of intellectual difficulties would be out of place" (1985: 90). Further, it is not called a mystery in "Confession after confession, canon after canon," though Popes and Councils "have found it their duty to insist afresh upon the dogma" (1985: 91). But the "custom is otherwise," Newman informs us, "as regards catechisms and theological treatises. These belong to particular ages and places, and are addressed to the intellect." And in them, he relates, "the mysteriousness of the doctrine is almost uniformly insisted on" (1985: 91).

The Counter-intuitive

While numbers of Christians maintain that the Trinity is a divine mystery revealed to finite human minds by God, and that the theologians whose doctrines about it became mainstream were guided by the Holy Spirit, a secular intellectual history of the doctrine takes a different tack. A major impetus to that development, as suggested earlier, was a certain tension or paradox in the canonical texts, which presented Jesus as more than a man yet as distinct from God the Father. The unfolding doctrine of the Trinity, in secular perspective, was in large measure the unfolding of efforts to resolve that tension or paradox. Numbers of theologians, moreover, attempted to do so in ways that would not challenge scriptural authority or jeopardize the possibility of human salvation, given the fan of understandings and hopes that motivated and constrained those efforts.

A major problem is reconciling the Three with the One and the One with the Three. Conventional Christian theological applications of those numbers to the Godhead contravene present day, ordinary uses of numbers in the West and associated intuitions about numeration in our society. Newman, cognizant of that circumstance, opines that in speculating about "the Supreme Being, ... it may be unmeaning, not only to number with other beings, but to subject to number in regard to His own intrinsic characteristics. That is, to apply arithmetical notions to Him may be as unphilosophical as it is profane" (1985: 39).

Closely related to that problem is the problem of reconciling the individuation of the Three Persons of the Trinity with their eternal and perfect unity in thought and action. The explications that Christian theologians furnish respecting the individuation of the three Persons, for example, do not fully jibe with the understandings that many contemporary Westerners entertain about the nature of individualism. Nor, I think, are they entirely harmonious with the somewhat different understandings of Westerners of yesteryear. In both cases, experience and folk belief-desire psychology testify that individuals often disagree in significant ways and pursue different ends. Thus even when the believer accepts it on authority that three individual divine Persons always act in complete agreement and concert, how might s/he explain it meaningfully to others – to Atahuallpa, say, who had difficulties with his brother, or, for that matter, to those of us non-believers who have logged many hours in attendance at department meetings?

In addition to the above problems, there are others, such as the problem of understanding (let alone translating) the concept of "eternal begetting." In short, the doctrine of the Trinity – the doctrine that the one true living God who created all else consists of three eternal Persons of the same substance who always act in perfect concert – is difficult to comprehend because it violates several of our work-a-day intuitions and expectations about numbers, identity, personhood, and procreation – and, more broadly, it violates our intuitions about living things.

The Persons of the Trinity, the "living God" of mainstream Christianity, are not merely different sorts of "persons." They violate a constellation of ontological assumptions – a constellation of assumptions in Western societies and, according to Pascal Boyer (1994), a constellation of assumptions likely to be found, more or less, among people in other societies – about persons and, more broadly, about living things, that structures expectations. Persons, as exemplars of living things, are physical objects and therefore visible. Their identity, sentience, and intentionality are individuated. Predicates that might well apply to individual persons (e.g., "is lustful," "is contentious," "is malleable") are doctrinally declared to be inapplicable to the Persons of the Trinity. And some of the predicate terms that are applied to the Persons of the Trinity (e.g., "perfect in knowledge," "unchangeable," "one in understanding and purpose") are not usually applied to human persons, either individually or collectively. Further, and especially among those who champion "negative theology," it is sometimes claimed that predicate terms applied to divinity do not mean the same things that they mean when applied to human persons: that, for instance, God is not "wise" in the same way that Alan Greenspan is "wise," but in a special way applicable only to God.

Now, the counter-intuitive plays important roles in human life. It is, for example, associated with modern science, especially insofar as modern science transcends and subverts naïve realism. And it is often invoked to good effect in science fiction (Disch 1998). But it may well be so salient and consistent in the configuration and transmission of religious ideas as to mark them off from other ideas. Such, at any rate, is one of the arguments of Pascal Boyer in his complex book, *The Naturalness of Religious Ideas: A Cognitive Theory of Religion* (1994).

Boyer (1994: 35) observes that

> Religious representations typically comprise claims or statements that violate people's ideas of what commonly takes place in their environment. For instance, some entities are described as invisible, yet located in space, intangible yet capable of mechanical action on physical objects; things fly in the air instead of falling to the ground, aging and death do not affect certain beings, and so on.

Indeed, not only do religious representations violate intuitive expectations, but, according to Boyer, "Religious notions would not be interesting, would not be attention demanding, if they complied with intuitions about ordinary events and states" (1994: 48). This, however, does not mean that there is nothing intuitive or ordinary about religious ideas.

As Boyer sees it, the sorts of religious ideas that will be transmitted from one generation to the next – the religious ideas that will prove successful in the competition, so to speak, among ideas for places in human memory – are those that strike an optimal cognitive balance between the intuitive and the counter-intuitive (1994: 121). Their intuitiveness, their harmony with expectations supported by ordinary ontological assumptions and commitments, invests them with plausibility and renders them learnable. But their violation of such expectations, their seeming intuitive unnaturalness "to the subjects who hold them" (1994: 3), makes them interesting and "attention demanding." If the mix is right, they are more likely to be remembered and more likely to be transmitted to the next generation than ideas that are either unexceptional or entirely counter-intuitive.

In addition to attempting to account for the transmission of religious ideas, Boyer also attempts to account for "important recurrent features in the religious representations that can be found in very different cultural environments" (1994: vii-viii). He takes pains to point out, however, that he is not postulating substantive universals in religious ideas (1994: 5). Rather, beyond our minimal recognition that in many human groups there are ideas "concerning non-observable, extra-natural agencies and processes[,] ... the similarities between religious ideas are a matter of family resemblance rather than universal features" (1994: 5). I fully agree with that position, and I would add that since we deal cross-culturally with *resemblances* rather than *identities* (Saler 2000a [1993]), the problem of translating is all the more difficult. While ideas, say, about witches in two societies may show appreciable conceptual overlap, there are also likely to be significant differences, and a scrupulous translator will have to take pains to avoid obscuring important differences in relevant contexts.

Boyer links his consideration of transmission processes with his appreciation of family resemblances among religious representations in different cultural settings. He aspires to explain both by working toward a complex theory of the cognitive foundations of religious ideas. Suffice it for present purposes to foreground only certain features of his theorizing.

Boyer argues that there are universal features (following Needham 1972, I prefer to say natural resemblances) in human cognition. People throughout the world, for instance, tend to distinguish between living things and artifacts and they develop similar general understandings of what is normal for each. These and other widely distributed cognitive resemblances both motivate and constrain the transmission of religious ideas. Among other things, we humans develop rich, domain-specific ontologies, both explicit and tacit, in our attentions to the world, and those ontologies provide us with a host of expectations and intuitions in all walks of life, including the religious. The "intuitive assumptions that are used in all religious representations," Boyer (1994: 121) writes, "provide the main substance of all inferences and conjectures." But they also constrain the acceptability of counter-intuitive claims. Further, Boyer argues, while religious ideas are subject to selective pressures in the transmission process, their contents are likely to be underdetermined by that process.

The processes that we call socialization and enculturation do not account for the richness of many religious ideas. Individuals enhance their religious claims by making inferences from their established ontological assumptions and expectations. The richness of religious ideas, Boyer argues, therefore need not depend on exhaustive cultural transmissions. On the basis, moreover, of cross-cultural ethnographic data, experimental studies of concept development in children, and certain arguments advanced by evolutionary biologists and evolutionary psychologists, Boyer suggests that on the level of such macro-categories as person, plant, animal, and artifact, people throughout the world have similar ontological assumptions and expectations, and so can be expected to make similar inferences, and to respond in similarly orderly ways to the inferences of their fellows. This would account for the recurrence of certain religious ideas in diverse cultural settings. And, I would add, it enhances the prospects for warrantable explications of religious ideas across populations.

Boyer claims, in general argument and with the support of some ethnographic examples, that religious believers themselves often sense something "unnatural" or counter-intuitive in their beliefs – that, in fact, an apprehension of the unnatural or counter-intuitive, however inchoate, sparks the imagination and in that wise renders the beliefs attractive. Believers may not render their sense of the "unnatural" immediately explicit, but it can be fathomed, in my experience, on asking them to explicate and extend their assertions.

I agree with Boyer' general argument about the counter-intuitive, and I recommend that we attempt to capture and convey some appreciation of our informants' sense of it – and of the intuitive structures that render it both possible and significant – in our ethnographies.

Some anthropologists (e.g., Leach 1967), however, perhaps because of their commitments in the "rationality" debate that has occupied the attentions of many of us, describe and analyze beliefs in ways that mask, minimize, or explain away violations of the intuitive, thus seeming to render those beliefs less troublesome for their readers to apprehend and in some sense accept. That, of course, in a crude, uninformed, but not apparently ideological fashion, is what Felipe of Puna did in mistranslating Fray Vicente's profession of the doctrine of the Trinity: he added the numbers, Garcilaso tells us, "*in order to make himself understood*" (1966: 682, emphasis added). But intelligibility purchased at the cost of fidelity is not worth much.

My suggestion that our ethnographies of religious ideas include explicit considerations of the counter-intuitive – and its dependence on the intuitive – is a facet of a more inclusive suggestion: that we strive for fidelity in a "global" sense. I have in mind "translation" – good translation – very broadly conceived. Perhaps I can make my widened understanding of translation clearer by briefly comparing it to translation in a narrower, more conventional sense.

Garcilaso's Solution and Explication

The chronicler Garcilaso de la Vega, it may be recalled, was concerned with how Christian ideas might be "adequately" expressed to Peruvian Indians. Garcilaso had an interest in good translation. Translation is always motivated. In Garcilaso's case, there was not only the hope of benefiting the souls of the Indians, but also concern for minimizing stresses stemming from the incorporation of the conquered into a new order. Garcilaso himself traced roots to both the Indians and the Spaniards. His father was a *conquistador*, and his mother was an Inka noble, a second cousin to Atahuallpa.

When Spanish interpreters of "these times," Garcilaso wrote, wish to express Christian ideas adequately, "they have to seek new words or phrases, or use with great care suitably dignified expressions in the old language or else lay hands on the many words the cultured and scholarly Indians have taken from Spanish and introduced into their own languages, adapting them to their own ways of speech" (1988: 682).

Garcilaso's solution is to coin new terms and expressions, to use with great care possible correspondences (glosses) across languages, and to adapt loan words. These are conventional instruments of translation in a narrow sense, and they can be productive where the translator is sensitive and skilled.

Although the solution endorsed by Garcilaso may serve for purposes of religious conversion (or, at any rate, the appearance of religious conversion), it is inadequate for anthropological purposes. If by "translation" we mean translation in the narrow sense sketched above, then the anthropologist, I think, should subsume translation in explication. Indeed, in my opinion the task of the ethnographer is *explication* rather than "translation" in the narrow sense of glossing expressions in one language with terms from another or with freshly minted neologisms. Such explication involves the examination of contexts in which targeted expressions occur and the analysis of any encountered polysemy. Our intellectual grasp and appreciation of key terms will be enhanced by an understanding of the domains with which they are associated in native usages.

A well known example of explication is found in Evans-Pritchard's (1956) discussion of the Nuer term *kwoth* ('spirit'). I am aware that some anthropologists suggest that Evans-Pritchard's explication of that term is biased by his personal religious proclivities. I do not know enough about the case, however, to evaluate that claim. Regardless of possible inaccuracies or other deficiencies in the contents of what he writes, however, the form of his explication deserves admiration on two counts. First, Evans-Pritchard examines how the term is used in different contexts, and even though his examination may not be exhaustive, he demonstrates the polysemy of *kwoth*, and he makes efforts to deal with it in ways that we, his readers, may comprehend. Second, his explication is alive to the significance of tropes; and although his fame in that regard largely rests on his analysis of the "twins are birds" metaphor, he alerts us generally to how a sensitivity to tropes might expand our understandings of religious terms and expressions, and so enlarge and potentially improve the translation task.

Efforts to achieve "global" fidelity in the ethnography of religious ideas are efforts at explication that include discussion of the environments and likely polysemy of important religious terms, the determination and exploration of relevant and revealing tropes, and systematic efforts to make explicit what is significantly implicit, both with respect to the intuitive structures and understandings that support the plausibility of religious ideas and the counter-intuitive features of those ideas that render them memorable. Yet more, I think, is required. Serious efforts should also be made to learn who professes or endorses the reported ideas, for not everyone in a given population may do so. Attempts, moreover, should be made to assess the relative strength of professions of belief, which may well vary from hedged or weak affirmations to those that seem vigorous and confident. These efforts will collectively support and make more convincing the anthropologist's theorizing about the functions of religious ideas in discrete populations and in human history.

Efforts at global fidelity are not solely focused on the human population under study. They are also inevitably motivated, weighted, and constrained by considerations relating to the eventual target audience of the ethnographic monograph.

The ethnographer has the difficult task of conveying, as accurately and as cogently as possible, what s/he has come to understand about religious ideas studied in the field to an audience (often largely of other anthropologists though sometimes a wider audience) that lacks comparable knowledge and experience of the field situation. Explication of categories and ideas encountered in the field, moreover, is attempted in the language of the eventual target audience, the readership of the ethnographic monograph. In addition to using that audience's "ordinary language," explication is also likely to involve the so-called professional analytical categories of anthropologists. And these, in the overwhelming majority of cases, are specially refined and often contested versions of Western folk categories (see Saler 2000a [1993] for "religion"). In short, conveyance depends on the artful and problem-plagued application and adjustment of categories from different sources, sources that themselves answer to different interests. Such conveyance, in any case, constitutes "translation" in that term's fundamental etymological senses: 'transfer' and 'transformation'. It amounts to a task of mediation or bridge-building between disparate but not entirely incompatible clusters of understandings. It is, indeed, something of a secular analog to what some religious communities expect of their priests.

The Ethnographer as Pontifex

Dictionaries and other sources in English generally state that the "literal" meaning of *pontifex* is "bridge-builder," from the Latin *pons*, bridge + *facio*, to do or to make.

Emile Benveniste (1971 [1966]: 255–256) relates the Latin *pons* and the Greek *pontos*, 'sea', to the Sanskrit *pánthah*, one of several terms in Vedic texts for 'road'. That particular Sanskrit term for 'road', he writes, "implies difficulty, uncertainty, and danger, it has unforeseen detours, it can vary depending on who is traversing it … It is indeed … a 'crossing' attempted over an unknown and often hostile region …" Its sense of crossing rather than road, Benveniste opines, "explains the diversity of the documented variants."

Although we may start with the sense of 'road' as crossing associated with the Sanskrit term *pánthah*, Benveniste writes, "this sense is no more 'primordial' than the others; it is only one of the realizations of the general signification defined here." Thus in a Latin approximation to the realization of such a general signification, "*pons* will designate the 'crossing' of a stream of water or a dip in the ground, hence a 'bridge'." A bridge crosses something, and it may facilitate our crossing.

In ancient Rome the term *pontifex* (pl., *pontifices*) was applied to the members of a college of priests, the leader of which was called *pontifex maximus*. There were probably three members in the days of the monarchy, and they advised the king on religious matters. By the time of the late Republic they numbered sixteen, and they administered the *ius divinum*, the laws governing the state cult, which included the regulation of the official calendar. They were termed "bridge-builders," some classicists speculate, because they may have had charge of the Pons Sublicius, a bridge over the Tiber River that was invested with a sacred significance (Bailey 1932: 162).

In the early Christian church a bishop was termed pontifex, but that term was eventually reserved for the Bishop of Rome, the Pope. In contemporary Roman Catholic sources the symbolism of bridge-building, of bridging two domains, the divine and the human, is often made explicit, and I use the term pontifex analogously here.

The ethnographer is, metaphorically, a 'bridge-builder', one charged with the task of facilitating a 'crossing' into the sensibilities and sensitivities of others. The major purpose of ethnographic bridges, of ethnographic monographs, is to allow the reading public to cross-over to new understandings, new understandings of others and perhaps of themselves. And among the building materials utilized to construct such bridges, creatively figured analogies and glosses are salient.

An analogy is a way of establishing resemblances between things that otherwise differ. Ethnographers not only depend on analogies in their descriptions, but they are beholden to them in recognizing problems and interests. Numbers of populations, for example, have no term or category for what we call "religion," but the ethnographer recognizes "religion" in their societies by observing local assertions and other behaviors reminiscent of what s/he deems to be religious behaviors elsewhere. Religion, that is, is established by analogy. And that, of course, suggests an important question: analogy to what?

Ironically enough, I think that some students of religion have done a better job of exploring the religious categories of other peoples than those of the populations for which they write, with the consequence that their analogies might not be as detailed nor as cogent as they could be. As I put it elsewhere,

> If we suppose that there is warrant to construct bridges of some sort to span the semantic chasms that separate us from others, we would do well to remember that bridges normally have two anchoring foundations, one on either side of what they span. Much mischief, I think, has accrued from our failures to prepare the ground profoundly enough on *our* side of the divide. (Saler 1993: 124–125).

Glosses can be viewed as lexical analogies, and they can be problematic in ways that are similar to those of other forms of analogy. Take a case put to me by the editors: Malinowski's use (in *Argonauts of the Western Pacific*, 1922) of the gloss 'flying witches' for the Kiriwinian term *muluk-*

wausi. Has Malinowski, I am asked, "actually captured the meaning" of the Trobriand concept to which his gloss refers? I think that he has, but not because of the gloss itself, although it is plausible both analytically and holistically.

The gloss is plausible in these ways: First, when broken down into its components, those resonate with our understandings. We identify flying as a mode of locomotion. And we identify witches as malevolent beings who utilize magical means to harm others (although I suspect that the term was somewhat less ambiguous in Malinowski's day, since in our time Wicca, *The Wizard of Oz*, and certain television serials and cartoons support the understanding that not all witches are bad). Second, the expression is holistically meaningful, for the idea of flying witches is well established among us, and it is an idea that occurs in many other societies. That is, there are family resemblances among the flying witch representations in numbers of cultural settings (our witches, for example, typically fly on broomsticks, whereas those of the Fang of Cameroon typically fly on banana leaves [Boyer 1994]).

Still and all, Malinowski's gloss 'flying witches' is inadequate by itself, despite its overlap with our ideas. Fortunately, however, Malinowski supplies more than a gloss. He provides us with an explication of certain relevant Trobriand ideas, and by so doing justifies his gloss.

Again, "translating" ("glossing") in a narrow sense is unlikely to suffice for anthropological purposes. More is required if we are to cross-over to warrantable understandings. The "global fidelity" of which I have spoken is, of course, a desideratum and an ambition, unlikely ever to be achieved in full. But there are degrees of approximation, and we should aim for the maximum possible.

Some persons claim that adequate translation is impossible. They aver, indeed, that attempts at bridge-building or crossing-over are inevitably and fatally subverted by cultural barriers encoded in language. That, however, strikes me as too pessimistic a point of view. There are, of courses, difficulties in crossing-over the barriers of language and culture. For the most part, however, those difficulties are extensions of the difficulties that we encounter in understanding others in our own society. As extensions, to be sure, they are rendered complex by the necessity of dealing with newly encountered lexicons and grammars. Yet, as Boyer's work suggests, there is reasonable hope that such barriers can be overcome, if not completely then sufficiently enough to satisfy most of our needs.

We would do well to remind ourselves that even where we suppose that we control the language and are familiar with the culture, we encounter difficulties in understanding. Indeed, we cannot honestly claim full comprehension of our spouses, children, parents, and colleagues, let alone the Three Persons of the Trinity, but we go on trying, sometimes with apparent if only limited – but nevertheless gratifying – success. And, lest we forget, we also experience genuine difficulty in understanding ourselves. Indeed, of all the commandments that humanity has saddled itself with, perhaps the most difficult to obey is the Delphic Imperative, "Know Thyself!" Such difficulties in understanding may help explain why even persons accounted to be non-religious sometimes avail themselves of priests.

Part II Homage to Three Pioneers

E. B. Tylor and the Anthropology of Religion[1]

Abstract: An understanding of Tylor, it is suggested, can be enhanced by a knowledge of what he was against as well as what he advocated. In presenting his theory of the origin and evolution of religion, Tylor, as J. Samuel Prues and others claim, is advancing a theory of the evolution of mind. And while Tylor, unlike the literary critic Harold Bloom, does not explicitly describe his approach to religion as „religious criticism," it amounts to that. But unlike Bloom (or, mutatis mutandis, Mircea Eliade), Tylor does not hold that religion rests on „an irreducibly spiritual dimension" in human life.

1

In light of the retrospective theme of this Annual Meeting,[2] it is fitting that we pay homage to Edward Burnett Tylor (1832–1917). His appointment as Reader in Anthropology at Oxford in 1884 was the first academic appointment of an anthropologist *qua* anthropologist in the English-speaking world. And in his two volume classic, *Primitive Culture* (1871), Tylor, as Kroeber and Kluckhohn (1952: 150–151) observe, „was deliberately establishing a science by defining its subject matter."

Yet although Tylor is not far removed from us in time, and while he writes in a language very similar to our own, we might nevertheless take note of Lesley Hartley's lines, „The past is a foreign country; they do things differently there" (*Prologue, The Go-Between,* 1953). Despite Tylor's pleasing and seemingly lucid prose, his concerns, sensitivities, and insensitivities do not fully match ours. If we are to improve our scholarly understanding and appreciation of his efforts, we must try to learn as best we can what Tylor was against as well as what he advocated, and what he hoped to achieve within the context of the intellectual ambiance in which he operated.

---

1   „E.B. Tylor and the Anthropology of Religion." *Marburg Journal of Religion* 2 (1): 1–3, 1997.
2   This paper was read at The Annual Meeting of the American Anthropological Association in San Francisco, November 21, 1996. The retrospective theme of the meeting focused on the history and accomplishments of anthropology.

Thus, for example, Tylor's theorizing was motivated in significant measure by his disagreements with degenerationist theories of the religions of so-called „savages." He hoped to replace such views with an evolutionary, progressivist perspective on the development of human religiosity. Yet while we can recognize the importance to Victorians of arguments about whether or not some contemporary religions were degenerations from so called „higher" forms of religiosity, we cannot, I think, cathect such arguments to the same extent, or in the same ways, that Tylor did.

Tylor's evolutionary account, as is well known, largely deals with the development of what he calls „the intellectual ... side of religion" (1958 [1873, 1871], II: 444–445), to the explicitly confessed near-neglect of other important aspects of religion. He justifies this by declaring that

> Scientific progress is at times most furthered by working along a distinct intellectual line, without being tempted to diverge from the main object to what lies beyond, in however intimate connexion.... My task has been here not to discuss Religion in all its bearings, but to portray in outline the great doctrine of Animism, as found in what I conceive to be its earliest stages among the lower races of mankind, and to show its transmission along the lines of religious thought. (Tylor 1958, II: 445).

But in attempting to portray „the great doctrine of Animism" and „to show its transmission," Tylor does far more than outline a theory of the evolution of religion. As his work unfolds, J. Samuel Preus observes,

> we see that Tylor is writing the history of the mind. Repeatedly, he refers to his project as describing „the course of mental history," the „laws of intellectual movement," the history of laws of mind," the „history of opinion," „intellectual history," and so on. (Preus 1987: 133).

Marvin Harris (1968: 202) opines that „the basic point of *Primitive Culture* seems to be that the human mind has the ability to perfect itself by thinking more clearly." And George Stocking (1987: 192) waggishly remarks that in Tylor's presentation, „It was as though primitive man, in an attempt to create science, had accidentally created religion instead, and mankind had spent the rest of evolutionary time trying to rectify the error."

But beyond treating the evolution of religion as window on the development of mind and culture, Tylor suggests an even more ambitious agenda. Research into the history and pre-history of humankind and „the doctrine of the world-long evolution of civilization," he writes, have their „practical side, as *a source of power destined to influence the course of modern ideas and actions"* (1958 II: 529, emphasis added). It is „the practical office of ethnography," Tylor declares,

> to make known to all whom it may concern the tenure of opinions in the public mind, to show what is received on its own direct evidence, what is ruder ancient doctrine reshaped to answer modern ends, and what is but time-honoured superstition in the garb of modern knowledge" (1958 II: 531).

Apposite to Tylor's sense of „the practical office of ethnography" is his concept of „survivals." He conceptualizes these as cultural elements or complexes („adhesions") that once made a certain sense within the contexts in which they were developed, but that have lingered on beyond their time and are out of intellectual harmony with later cultural settings. These stultifying elements, Tylor declares, need to be identified so that they might be eliminated. He concludes his great work with this ringing – and radical – declaration:

> It is a harsher, and at times even painful office of ethnography to expose the remains of crude old cultures which have passed into harmful superstition, and to mark these out for destruction. Yet this work, if less genial, is not less *urgently needful for the good of mankind*. Thus, active at once in aiding progress and in removing hindrance, *the science of culture is essentially a reformer's science*. (1958 II: 539, emphasis added).

2

In Tylor's view, as A. I. Hallowell was fond of pointing out in lectures, our ancient forebears were moved by curiosity. Puzzled by their experiences of dreams and of visions, and desirous of achieving a satisfying account of death, they derived and melded from their experiences notions about animating principles and ghost-souls. Then, by a process that we call stimulus generalization, they extended the idea of individual souls out from humanity to the non-human world. By a further extension they developed ideas about independently existing spirits of various sorts. They thus propounded the two complementary parts of „the great doctrine of Animism," belief in souls and belief in other spiritual beings.

Tylor supposes that the theory of animism is the first great theory in human history. Not only that, but it is so powerful and appealing that it has continued on in a variety of elaborated and modified forms, and may be discerned in the Christianity of his own time.

„The beliefs and practices of savage religion," Tylor affirms in the first volume of *Primitive Culture,* are far from being „a rubbish heap of miscellaneous folly." Rather, they are „consistent and logical in so high a degree as to begin, as soon as even roughly classified, to display the principles of their formation and development" (1958 I: 23). Yet while „these principles prove to be essentially rational," they work among „savages" „in a mental condition of intense and inveterate ignorance" (1958 I: 23). Indeed, the great doctrine of animism is founded on inadequate observation and childlike inference, though the product of rational minds.

Animism, Tylor suggests, illustrates not only the rational yet error-prone nature of human thought, but also a human propensity, especially well marked among so-called „savages," to rest understandings closely on experiences. Tylor, as Robert Lowie points out (1948 [1924]: 109), derives the theory of animism „very largely not from ratiocination about observed phenomenon but from the immediate sensory testimony of dream life."

Two further observations about Tylor's perspective can be usefully entered at this juncture. One is about his views on what some anthropologists term „the psychic unity of humankind." The other has to do with the implications of his theory of human religiosity for the religions of his time — and ours.

Both in his *Researches Into the Early History of Mankind* (1865) (Stocking 1987: 160) and in *Primitive Culture,* Tylor supports the idea of the psychic unity of humankind. Though he does not employ that exact expression in his theorizing about religion, the concept is crucial for his application of the comparative method. As Preus (1987: 138) notes,

> Tylor's confidence that he can understand the savage mind because it is essentially rational is the basis for his conviction that he can understand the continuity of human religiousness from the earliest times in which it affords a glimpse of itself.

In the matter of the implications of Tylor's theory respecting religions in modern society, suffice it to summarize the conclusions reached by two major contemporary scholars. The logical thrust of *Primitive Culture,* Stocking writes (1987: 195), is „clearly to reduce Christianity to the same category of 'mythology' with which Tylor prefaced his discussion of the development of animistic belief." And Preus maintains that we may conclude from Tylor's great work that „*religion itself is a survival*" (1987: 139, emphasis added).

3

Tylor's theory of religion has come in for strong and diverse criticisms. Thus, for example, Evans-Pritchard dismisses Tylor's speculations about the origins of soul and spirit concepts as having „the quality of a just-so story" (1965: 25); Durkheim rejects the possibility that religion, an enduring phenomenon, could be founded on an illusion; and Malinowski, Radcliffe-Brown, and Margaret Hodgen enter their various criticisms of Tylor's „doctrine of survivals."

Overall, many critics note that Tylor slights the social and emotional dimensions of religion. Later anthropologists, of course, emphasized religion's social aspects and consequences, with such regularity and redundancy, indeed, that in 1966 Clifford Geertz (1966: 1–2) complained that still more cases addressed to the same functionalist points might well convince people within and without our profession „that anthropologists are, like theologians, firmly dedicated to proving the indubitable." The emotional dimension of religiosity, however, has not been developed with the same intensity and cogency, despite the efforts of some analysts. Sudies thus far undertaken, however, suggest that affectivity can play havoc with Tylor's „doctrine of survivals," for, as Spiro (1984: 338) succinctly puts it, „Many apparently arbitrary cultural propositions make sense in terms of emotions."

While many of the specifics of Tylor's theorizing are unacceptable to us today, we may nevertheless appreciate his reformer's impulses. Those, of course, were grounded in, and focused on, Victorian intellectual controversies. But if we abstract his impulses from that foreign country which is the past, we might say that Tylor's approach to religion can be broadly described as „criticism," in analogy to contemporary literary criticism. Such criticism, despite a number of fiercely competing theories about what it should be and what we might hope of it, generally attempts *to interpret*, to *situate*, and to *appropriate* for some purpose. Tylor did not talk about „religious criticism" as such. But his effective efforts in that direction, I think, are of greater interest and relevance to anthropologists than those of the literary scholar Harold Bloom.

Bloom does talk about religious criticism, which he describes as „a mode of description, analysis, and judgment that seeks to bring us closer to the workings of the religious imagination" (1992: 21). Yet while that sounds promising, Bloom soon tells us that just as the literary criticism that he learned to practice „relies finally upon an irreducibly *aesthetic* dimension," religious criticism analogously „must seek for the irreducibly *spiritual* dimension in religious matters or phenomena of any kind" (1992: 21). Talk of an irreducible spiritual dimension, however, reminds us of Mircea Eliade and others who assert unconvincingly that religion rests on something irreducibly religious, such as „the sacred" or „the transcendent," and that religion is therefore „autonomous" and „*sui generis.*"

While Tylor held that religion universally rests on animism, he was far from claiming that religion is autonomous and *sui generis*. Rather, in his view it arose from a welter of sensory and psychological factors. Although „the animism of lower tribes," Tylor holds, is „self-contained and self-supporting," for it is maintained „in close connexion with the direct evidence of the senses on which it appears to be originally based," and so seems to explain itself (1958 II: 84), it is not founded on some irreducible religious disposition. The lack of such foundation is further attested to by the development of mind and the evolution of culture. The „doctrines and rites of the higher races," Tylor writes, „show survival of the old in the midst of the new," and, indeed, „*abandonment of the old because it is no longer compatible with the new*" (1958 II: 84, emphasis added). „For our knowledge of our own history," Tylor muses,

> it is deeply interesting that there should remain rude races yet living under the philosophy which we have so far passed from, since Physics, Chemistry, Biology, have seized whole provinces from ancient Animism, setting force for life and law for will (1958 II: 269).

Finally, for those of us who may aspire to the broad sense of criticism given earlier, and who do so from a secular stance, Tylor send us a message from the past. In secularism, he declares, „the feeling and imagination which in the religious world are bound to theological belief, have to attach themselves to a positive natural philosophy, and to a positive morality" (1958 II: 536). It is here, I suspect, that our contemporary anthropology of religion is most deficient, especially as potentially significant criticism.

We have not really agreed among ourselves about the larger purposes and commitments of contemporary research, and that weakens us as a scholarly community. I have elsewhere argued that considerations of purpose ought to shape our analytical categories (Saler 1993), and that pragmatic argument can be extended, I think, to our professional identities. If that mélange of startling lights and disconcerting shadows that some call postmodernism has convinced us of anything, it ought to have convinced us that there is no such thing as the disinterested pursuit of truth. But what, then, are our interests?

Lévy-Bruhl, Participation, and Rationality[3]

Abstract: Focusing on the theories of the admirably self-critical Lucien Lévy-Bruhl, this essay touches on a diversity of issues respecting arguments about modes of thought, emotions as they may relate to cognition, and notions about rationality. From 1910 until his death in 1939, Lévy-Bruhl published six books on what he thought of as „primitive mentality." After World War II, eleven of his notebooks – preparations, it seems, for a seventh book – were recovered and published. While the notebooks affirm in final form Lévy-Bruhl's retrenchment from positing a difference in logic between so-called primitive mentality and what he supposed to be our mentality, they reaffirm and further develop certain other attributions that he had emphasized in his first book on the subject.

Our concern with rationality in the study of religion invites a number of questions about „rationality."

First, What do we – or what should we – mean by „rationality"? That question is obvious and easy to frame. But it is not easy (or perhaps even possible) to find a simple answer to it that all scholars of religion would accept. Some persons, for example, prefer to identify rationality with conformance to the fundaments of standard (two-valued) Western logic: Identity (A is A), Excluded Middle (either A or not-A), and Non-Contradiction (not both A and not-A). Others, while not necessarily abjuring the formalisms of Western logic, are inclined to stress pragmatic instrumentality, whereby rationality is to be judged in terms of the selection of appropriate means to accomplish recognized ends. And still others persons may be given to emphasizing other possibilities. These include various kinds of posited coherences among human activities or between human activities and other things, and sweeping normative or prescriptive assertions to the effect that rational beliefs are those that we ought to hold and rational acts are those that we ought to perform.

Postmodernists, however, suggest a rethinking of the question. They generally maintain that criteria of rationality are largely or entirely cultural formulations, and that transcendental standards of rationality

---

[3] „Lévy-Bruhl, Participation, and Rationality." In Jeppe Sinding Jensen and Luther H. Martin (eds.), *Rationality and the Study of Religion*, 44–64. Aarhus: Aarhus University Press, 1997.

proffered by different theorists either cannot be supported or are so abstract as to be vacuous unless they are culturally situated and colored.

A second question about rationality to be considered here is this: what tends to be associated with our understanding of rationality? That question is not as obvious as the first, and it is in greater need of explication. To reframe it: if we operate with some understanding of rationality, what other understanding might accompany that understanding?

Lévi-Straussian structuralists have sensitized us to „homologies of thought." We are prepared, in consequence, to countenance the possibility that in Western discourses each member of the paired distinction „rationality/irrationality" may be associated with discrete members of other paired distinctions.

Deconstructionists, moreover, have alerted us to the probability that in expressing paired distinctions, the first expressed member of each pair is likely to be privileged over the second. Participants in a discourse, furthermore, may not always realize that they tend to commit themselves to preferences or biases by committing themselves to conventional expressions of distinctions.

In the English-speaking community to which I belong, for example, one normally says „rationality and irrationality" rather than „irrationality and rationality." And one normally says „thought and emotion" rather than „emotion and thought," and „thought and action" rather than „action and thought." Catherine Bell (1992) calls our attention to the role played by the privileging of thought over action in theorizing about religion, and we would do well to consider the possible consequences of the other two examples just given.

In this paper I explore the two questions posed above – what might we mean by rationality?, and what tends to be associated with our talk about rationality? – by relating them to the theorizing of Lucien Lévy-Bruhl (1857–1939) repecting so-called „primitive mentality." That French scholar played an influential role in supporting and disseminating the idea that there are distinct modes of thought among the peoples of the world.

Lévy-Bruhl held that the members of some small scale, nonliterate societies can be characterized as operating with a distinct mind-set, one that differs significantly in certain respects from that found in what he broadly thought of as modern Western civilization. Among the most salient features of that mentality, he supposed, are an unconcern for, or a veritable indifference to, „contradictions" (which he eventually modified in his final writings to a tolerance for physical impossibilities rather than logical contradictions); an absorption in the „mystical," by which he meant a realized disposition to suppose that the world is filled with powers and entities that are not usually accessible in any direct way to normal human vision, hearing, or other senses (albeit „primitive" peoples may find what they take to be evidence for the existence and activities of suprasensible realities, including what may be remembered of dreams); and a certain marriage of what we call the cognitive and the affective in which the latter is much the dominant spouse, so that many of the ideas of so-called primitives are more felt than thought.

Lévy-Bruhl: Myth and Reality

When I was in graduate school, there was a popular legend – or, if you will accept the term, a popular myth – about Lévy-Bruhl that was recited around academic campfires to hordes of note-taking anthropology students.

According to that narrative, Lévy-Bruhl published six imaginative but flawed books on the mentality of so-called primitive peoples between 1910 and his death in 1939. Those works, it was alleged, challenged widely held (if somewhat variegated) anthropological opinions about the „psychic unity" of humankind. The substance of that challenge, the myth continued, was evaluated and refuted by numbers of anthropologists, including such masterful fieldworkers as Bronislaw Malinowski and Edward E. Evans-Pritchard, who knew „primitive" peoples at first hand. In consequence of their criticisms, it was claimed, Lévy-Bruhl came to see the errors of his theories, and he more or less recanted them. In eleven posthumously published notebooks, he abjured much of what he had previously affirmed, thus drawing closer to, if not actually endorsing, opinions widely held by anthropologists.

This inspiring story pleased me and many of my fellow graduate students. It helped to rescue so-called primitive peoples from seeming inferiority. It drove home the importance of ethnographic fieldwork, for which most of us were then preparing, as antidote to armchair theorizing. And it resonated strongly with an ancient and powerful parable in Western traditions, that of the Prodigal Son (see, for example, *Luke* 15).

The Lucien Lévy-Bruhl of the myth that I encountered as a graduate student was, in effect, anthropology's adopted prodigal son, worthy of a fatted calf because of his posthumously published recantation. But while it is the case that he altered his views in the *Notebooks*, the sope and significance of the changes entered were greatly exaggerated. As Robin Horton points out, what Lévy-Bruhl

> retains is more significant than what he withdraws. Thus, although his final picture of primitive thought allows a good deal of common sense in alongside the mystical, and although his final picture of modern thought allows a good deal of the mystical in alongside common sense, his characterization of the mystical remains unrepentantly the same. (Horton 1973: 257–258)

Horton (1973: 258, n.1) adds that the greater part of the *Notebooks* „is taken up, not with recantation but with clarification of the two key concepts" that Lévy-Bruhl advanced in his first book on primitive mentality in 1910: mystical orientation and participation.

In my reading of Lévy-Bruhl's works on „primitive mentality," the views that he expressed in 1910 are continually under his own critical review in the succeeding years. He elaborates on some, modifies others, and eventually withdraws still others.

Thus in the *Notebooks,* Lévy-Bruhl caps more than twenty years of retrenching from the notion of „prelogical mentality" (1975 [1949]: 39, 47) by finally abandoning it as „a badly founded hypothesis" (1975 [1949]: 47). He does so for several reasons: the term „prelogical" had confused or distracted many of his readers; it was a crude way of pointing to something that can be better explicated as the expression of a „mystical orientation;" and, as his critics had suggested, it lacked balance in characterizing the socially formulated mentations of „primitive" peoples. Indeed, in the *Notebooks* he acknowledges that such peoples „no more support a formal contradiction than we do," but that while they reject what is *logically* impossible, they do not reject what is physically impossible (1975 [1949]: 62), and they are relatively tolerant of „incompatibilities."

Lévy-Bruhl's final abandonment of the notion of a clearly marked and crucial distinction in *logic* bewteeen modes of thought is perhaps the most important retrenchment in the *Notebooks*. Lévy-Bruhl disavows a difference in mentalities – and hence in rationalities – based on formal differences in logic. It is worth quoting him on that point:

> I no longer speak of a prelogical character of the primitive mentality, even when clarifying the misunderstandings which this term has occasioned. From the strictly logical point of view no essential difference has been established between the primitive mentality and ours. In everything that

touches on ordinary, everyday experience, transactions of all sorts, political and economic life, counting, etc., they behave in a way that involves the same usage of their faculties as we make of ours. (1975 [1949]: 55)

In the *Notebooks*, moreover, while Lévy-Bruhl makes extensive use of „the affective category of the supernatural," a construct that he had made the subject of his fourth book, *Le Surnaturel et la nature dans la mentalité primitive* (1931), in one section he appears to drop it. (The *Notebooks*, we need to remind ourselves, are not a book, and inconsistencies in them might have been eliminated or otherwise resolved had they been turned into a book by their author.) In any case, Lévy-Bruhl affirms in one section (1975 [1949]: 106) that he no longer needs „the affective category of the supernatural" because his mature understanding of participation now renders it unnecessary. „The affective category of the supernatural," he writes in the *Notebooks*, „is participation" (*ibid.*). In the *Notebooks*, indeed, Lévy-Bruhl virtually exults in a more profound understanding of participation. He abandons what he once called „The Law of Participation," but he affirms strongly that „What exists is the *fact* (not the law) that 'primitive man' very often has the feeing of participation" between himself and other objects, so that at one and the same time he may be both a human being and something else. No less frequently, Lévy-Bruhl maintains, so-called primitive man „imagines similar participations" between other objects (1975 [1949]: 61).

Different commentators trace the development of Lévy-Bruhl's thought in different ways, depending on what they find especially interesting. Maurice Leenhardt, for example, sees „a great gap" between the first book and the sixth, *L'Expérience mystique et les symbols chez les primitifs* (1937), in which, Leenhardt opines, Lévy-Bruhl „qualifies endlessly" (Leenhardt 1975: xiv).

Robin Horton (1973: 256–257), however, groups together the sixth book and the *Notebooks* because they both respond positively to a major criticism voiced by anthropological fieldworkers. Lévy-Bruhl, some complained, had slighted common-sensical thought among „primitives," and had characterized such peoples as more absorbed with the mystical than is actually the case. „Mystical," as Lévy-Bruhl describes it in his first book, „implies belief in forces and influences and actions which, though imperceptible to sense, are nevertheless real to 'primitive' peoples" (1985 [1910]: 38). In the sixth book and in the *Notebooks* Lévy-Bruhl accepts the criticism of ethnographers, and he takes pains to present „primitive" thought as oscillating bewteeen the common-sensical and the mystical.

Jean Cazeneuve separates the first three books from the last three because the fourth book, *Le surnaturel et la nature* (1931), advances some important refinements and qualifications of the earlier theories. In the earlier works, Cazeneuve remarks, the matter of differences in mentality was posed „in terms of logic," and „at the very least the hypothesis of different mental habits was adduced" (1972 [1963]: 22). Lévy-Bruhl, in describing „primitive mentality" as „prelogical," had not meant that it was illogical or irrational, but, rather, alogical and non-rational. Prelogical, as he himself characterizes it in his first book, is preeminently a mentality that „does not bind itself down, as our thought does, to avoiding contradiction" (1985 [1910]: 78). But in his later works, Cazeneuve writes,

> The discovery of the affective category [of the supernatural] even modifies the way of problematizing „primitive mentality." The description of archaic mentality is no longer so much that of specific characteristics of the mind, constituent or acquired, *as that of the role of affectivity in thought* (Cazeneuve 1972 [1963]: 22, emphasis added)

Lévy-Bruhl himself, we may note, groups together the last two books because he opines that their treatment of participation marks a more sophisticated stage in the development of his theorizing than the earlier works (Lévy-Bruhl 1975 [1949]: 108–109)

In what follows, I try to clarify certain aspects of what Lévy-Bruhl came to understand by participation, and to connect those understandings to our interests in rationality and the study of religion. While Lévy-Bruhl's theories have been deservedly criticized over the years, we continue to refer to them. We do so, I think, for two major reasons. First, Lévy-Bruhl played an important role in establishing questions about modes of thought, questions that we continue to address. Second, some of Lévy-Bruhl's claims resonate with later findings. I will point to such a resonance by referring to some of the work of two contemporary anthropologists, the Norwegian Unni Wikan, and the North American Catherine Lutz. I relate their understandings to Cazenueve's important remark about Lévy-Bruhl's shift of emphasis from „specific characteristics of the mind," as exemplified by the notion of „prelogical mentality," to „the role of affectivity in thought," as exemplified by a more profound conceptualization of „participation."

Participation

„Participation" is an ancient construct in Western philosophy and theology, where it is often conceptualizied as an ontological function invoked in efforts to answer two broadly posed questions: What is the justification for grouping different individual objects together into one *genus* or class? And how do we account for the fact that the things of our experience exist and manifest the qualities that they apparently do? „Participation," Charles Bigger (1968: 7) writes, „is the name of the 'relation' which accounts for the togetherness of elements of diverse ontological type in the essential unity of a single instance." And Durkheim (1965 [1912]: 270) remarks that „today, as formerly, to explain is to show how one thing participates in one or several others."

The Plato of the Middle Dialogues held that when a multiplicity of individuals are conceived as constituting a *genus* or class by virtue of some common attribute, that attribute exists independently in perfection in a superior realm, that of the things that are (τὰ ὄντα), the realm of Being. The realm of Being consists of the transcendent Forms or Ideas. They can be comprehended only by the mind, and they are incorporeal, unchanging, and eternal. Another realm, that of the things that become (τὰ γιγνόμενα), the realm of Becoming, is the inferior realm of the sensibles, the particulars of our experience. They are apprehended by the senses, and they are finite, mutable, contingent, and dependent.

Participation relates these two realms. The relationship, however, is asymmetrical. The sensibles, the entities of the realm of Becoming, exist and have their apparent qualities because they participate, if only for a brief time, in the realm of Being, the realm of the intelligibles. And the realm of Being exists independently; it does not presuppose the realm of Becoming. If we deem a flower beautiful, it is because it participates fleetingly in the Idea of Beauty. And although our flower will fade and wither, the Idea of Beauty will remain.

While Plato later modified his views, thus giving grounds for the quip that Plato was the first Neoplatonist, the ontology of Forms of the Middle Dialogues and the ontological function of participation were invoked by later traditions, both in philosophy and in theology. Various Christian writers, for example, identified God the Creator with Being and creation with Becoming, and they explained the continuing existence of the latter by positing its continuing participation in the former.

Participation figured into the debate that occupied the Council of Nicaea in 325 A. D. Alan Kolp (1975: 101), indeed, remarks that „Without noting it the Arian controversy is a struggle over the correct use of Platonic philosophical categories." Thus while Alexander and Athanasius maintained that the Son is God by nature rather than by participation, „true God from true God," Arius denied it. He is charged with claiming that although the Son is called God, he „is not truly so (οὐκ ἀληθινός ἐστιν), *but by participation of grace* (ἀλλὰ μετοχῇ χάριτος), he, as others, is God only in name" (Athanasius, *Orations Against the Arians* 6 [PG 26: 21–24], emphasis added).

Other examples of such Platonic uses of participation could be cited. And, to be sure, various divergences from Platonic formulations by mystics and others can be noted. Mainstream Western philosophy and theology nevertheless maintained certain core uses. But these differ in important respects from the participation that Lévy-Bruhl attributes to so-called primitive peoples.

First, in mainstream Western traditions, one normally forms representations of two or more distinct things or elements, and then one positis a participation between them. But according to Lévy-Bruhl, this is not what happens among „primitives." For such peoples, he tells us, participation „does not come after these representations, it does not presuppose them; it is before them, or at least simultaneous with them. What is given *in the first place* is participation" (1975 [1949]: 2, emphasis in original). For the „primitives," he goes on to claim, what is given is a complex, not elements between which one may come to see relations.

Second, in mainstream Western traditions there is always a recognized difference, and often an explicitly attributed inequality, between participating things. This crucial awareness of difference is put succinctly by Justin in his *Dialogue with Trypho* (6 [PG6, 489]): „that which partakes of anything is different from that of which it partakes." But „primitive man," according to Lévy-Bruhl, „feels ... a participation that forms for him a duality-unity of which, *first and foremost*, he feels the unity" (1975 [1949]: 4, emphasis in original).

Third, in mainstream Western philosophical and theological traditions, efforts are made to put participation on a rational footing. That is, at a minimum, analytical distinctions are specified among elements, and such conceptual exercises are often implicitly or explicitly related to, just as they are requisite for, attentions to the fundaments of standard logic. And even where certain of the details of posited participations are so exceptional as to escape the normal limitations imposed by what we deem the logical and the rational – as, for example, in the case of Cyril of Alexandria's doctrine of *communicatio idiomatum*, whereby predicates pertaining to each of Christ's two participating natures apply to the other, – efforts are typically made to explain exceptions in such a way as to preserve the structure of rationality that they might otherwise subvert. But in „primitive mentality," according to Lévy-Bruhl, concerns for rationality, and even considerations that we would enter respecting conceptualization, symbolization, and experience, are of little or no consequence. Participation, he writes, „is not represented by felt" (1975 [1949]: 158).

That point of view, reaffirmed in the *Notebooks*, is put in an interesting way in the 1910 book. In a concluding chapter entitled „The Transition to the Higher Mental Types," Lévy-Bruhl maintains that among such peoples as the Arunta and the Bororo, where participations are directly felt, all life might be said to be „religious," and yet we do not really find what we understand by „religion." He writes:

> Our own way of thinking makes us imagine the objects of their thought in the attitude of divine beings or objects, and that it is by virtue of this divine character of theirs that homage, sacrifice, prayer, adoration and all actual religious belief is directed towards them. But to the primitive mind, on the contrary, these objects and these beings become divine only when the participation they guarantee has ceased to be direct. The Arunta who feels that he is both himself and the ancestor whose *chiringa* was entrusted to him at the time of his initiation, knows nothing of ancestor worship. (1985 [1910]: 367–368).

With the development of individual consciousness prompted by changes in social institutions, Lévy-Bruhl supposes, mentality becomes more sensitive to experience, collective representations become truly cognitive, and participations, now realized rather than directly felt, become ideological. It is among peoples such as the Huichol, Zuñi, and Maori, who have made such a transition, Lévy-Bruhl claims, that we find such things as ancestor-worship, hero cults, gods, sacred animals, and so forth. „The ideas which we call really religious," Lévy-Bruhl holds, „are thus a kind of differentiated product resulting from a prior form of mental activity" (1985 [1910]: 368).

Affectivity in Thought

Jean Cazeneuve (1972 [1963]: 14) opines that „Lévy-Bruhl brings an important modification into philosophy which, since Aristotle, has limited categories of thought to the intellect, disregarding whatever comes from affectivity."

While this statement may be somewhat overblown, it does call our attention to possibilities beyond the conventional reach of traditional Western theories about „categories of thought" and related matters of „rationality."

It has long been a convention in Western traditions to distinguish between thought and emotion. While both thoughts and emotions are viewed as similar in some respects – both, for instance, are said to be private until expressed – they are for the most part distinguished, and Western languages normally include well established vocabularies for doing so.

This occasioned some difficulty for Lévy-Bruhl in his attempts to conceptualize, and to convey to us, what he deemed distinctive of the so-called primitive mentality. Thus in the 1910 book he tells us that the collective representations of „primitive" peoples are not really representations as we understand them. That is because our classificatory system distinguishes between the „emotional," the „motor," and the „intellectual," and we place „representation" in the last category. But representations for the „primitives" are more complex affairs, „in which," he writes,

> what is really „representation" to us is found blended with other elements of an emotional or motor character, coloured and imbued by them, and therefore implying a different attitude with regard to the objects represented. (1985[1910]: 35–36)

However critical we may be of some of the things that Lévy Bruhl claims, I think it fair to say that in these passages he prefigures some contemporary anthropological findings. Ethnopsychological research – that is, the systematic exploration of the psychological theories and classifications of diverse peoples – demonstrates that at least some non-Western peoples do not make the distinctions that we do between the cognitive and the affective. Rather, like Lévy-Bruhl, and to borrow an expression penned by Cazeneuve, they make great allowance for „the role of affectivity in thought." Unni Wikan, for example, reports that the

> Balinese regard feeling, thought, will, and desire as inextricably linked, truly one concept. In their native language they do not distinguish among them; all are summed up in the concept *keneh*. (1990: 95)

Wikan glosses *keneh* 'feeling-thought'. She remarks, moreover, that „Balinese laugh when they hear that some Westerners regard feeling as 'irrational'" (1990: 36).

Catherine Lutz reports something similar for the Ifaluk, a Micronesian people. She writes:

> At the core of Ifaluk ethnopsychology is a set of beliefs about the structure of persons which portrays them as basically undivided entities. In marked contrast to Western ethnopsychology, sharp distinctions are not made between thought and emotion, between the head and the heart, or between a conscious and an unconscious mind. (1988: 91)

Wikan and Lutz are among a growing number of anthropologists now studying emotions in novel and promising ways. Many of them suppose, as does Lutz, that

> concepts of emotions can more profitably be viewed as serving complex communicative, moral, and cultural purposes rather than [be viewed] simply as labels for internal states whose nature or essence is presumed to be universal. (Lutz 1988: 5)

Viewing emotion as, in Lutz's words (1988: 5), „an emergent product of social life," some anthropologists focus on how people talk about emotions, how discourse constitutes emotions as social objects, and how people employ or deploy emotions in social interactions. This orientation is part of a larger orientation, one that marks a shift from an emphasis on language as semantics to an emphasis on language as social action (Lutz 1988: 8). Among other things, it assigns hermeneutical functions to emotions, whereby emotions are viewed, in part, as interpretations that people put on situations.

The orientations sketched above, while sometimes offered as correctives to narrow conceptualizations of the emotions as largely or entirely precultural, psychobiological phenomena, do not always incorporate well informed distinctions between Western folk theories of the emotions and Western scientific understandings. The latter are decidedly more complex and nuanced than the former. Charles Darwin (1872), for example, deemed learning to be of some importance for expressions of the emotions, and he touched on the idea that emotional displays may constitute interpretations of situations, and scientists who followed after him widened and deepened his insights as well as going beyond them in various ways. Members of the more traditional scientific community (e.g., Spiro 1984; n.d.) have offered thoughtful and informed criticisms of some constructivist claims about the emotions, and a healthy debate has ensued. But in attending here to the question of what we might mean by rationality, particularly in the light of other understandings that often accompany widespread notions of rationality, studies of Western folk discourses about the emotions seem relevant.

In analyzing Ifaluk folk theory about emotions, Lutz compares it to a broadly conceptualized Euro-American or Western folk theory. Not only does the Western theory tend to associate thought with rationality, and emotion with irrationality, but it loads thought and emotion – and rationality and irrationality – with other associations as well. Focusing on emotion, Lutz describes this contrast set:

> Emotion is to thought as energy is to information, heart is to head, the irrational is to the rational, preference is to inference, impulse is to intention, vulnerability is to control and chaos is to order. Emotion is to thought as knowing something is good is to knowing something is true, that is, as value is to fact or knowledge, the relatively unconscious is to the relatively conscious, the subjective is to the objective, the physical is to the mental, the natural is to the cultural, the expressive is to the instrumental or practical, the morally suspect is to the ethically mature, the lower classes are to the upper, the child is to the adult, and the female is to the male. (Lutz 1988: 56–57)

Lutz also describes another Western contrast set, one that puts a higher valuation on the emotions. It values emotion as „the seat of the true and glorified self" (1988: 56), and as standing „against estrangement or disengagement" (1988: 57). There are thus two folk contrast sets regarding emotions in the West, and they speak to an ambivalence in Western discourse about emotion, and a perduring cultural paradox respecting the place of thought and emotion and, *inter alia*, rationality and irrationality, in Western life.

Exploring Affectivity

In his final reflections in the *Notebooks*, Lévy-Bruhl attempts to clarify his earlier claims that the „primitive mentality ... is not conceptual like ours" by affirming that at one and the same time it is both conceptual and affective (1975 [1949]: 127–128), though he continues to emphasize its affectivity. And he insists that he has long believed that although a mystical mentality „is more marked and more easily observable among 'primitive peoples' than in our own societies," it is nevertheless present in every human mind (1975 [1949]: 101).

Despite what some of us might regard as overstated or unnuanced formulations, Lévy-Bruhl begins to suggest the resolution of an old problem. Examining the affirmations of so-called primitives solely in cognitive or intellectual terms tends to nurture questions such as these: Why do „primitive" peoples seem to affirm seemingly irrational beliefs? Why, indeed, do they not test their beliefs against evidence or subject them to reasoned analysis? These can prove to be invidious questions, for they may well suggest a sharp divide between „us" and „them" – to the detriment of „them," to be sure, but perhaps also conducing to a unidimensional (and therefore misleading) consideration of „us." To the extent, moreover, that we dwell on the presumed falseness and irrationality of beliefs, we may sometimes loose sight of more interesting avenues of research. In advising sociologists of knowledge, for instance, Barnes and Bloor (1982: 23) suggest that inquiries into why something is „believed" may prove more rewarding than a focus on whether or not the purported belief is true.

Lévy-Bruhl's efforts to transcend the gratuitously invidious take this form: he begins by affirming that the beliefs of „primitive" peoples are largely social. They are, or they crucially pivot on, „collective representations." And collective representations among „primitives," he affirms, should not be thought of as primarily intellectual. Rather, they are in great degree affective. As such, they answer to the emotional needs of those who affirm them. Since, moreover, Lévy-Bruhl claims that a mystical mentality is present in every human mind, he suggests that our thought, too, is sometimes colored by affectivity. If we accept his suggestion, we may conclude that a purely intellectualist approach to our thought would also be inadequate. As Spiro (1984: 338) suggests, „Many apparently arbitrary cultural propositions make sense in terms of emotion."

The obvious and immediate conclusion to be drawn is that scholars should attempt to explore the affective as well as cognitive significance of beliefs for those who affirm them. For brevity of exposition I pose the matter in terms of the still regnant categorical distinction between cognition and affectivity, although we have increasing reason to suppose that the border between those analytical domains is unstable or fuzzy. Such exploration would include, to the extent possible, the probing of experiences and ideas associated with statements that we take to be statements of belief, for those experiences and ideas are contextualizing and so affect how the affirmers understand – and respond to – their affirmations.

The study of affect, to be sure, is difficult. Many suggest that sympathy and empathy are important, on the supposition that emotions are precultural and universal, and that we can come to recognize the emotional expressions of others on the basis of their similarities to our own. But putting aside the question of the universality of emotions, ethnographic and psychological testimony strongly suggests that the expression (and, indeed, control or repression) of emotions relates to cultural considerations and individual variables. While monitored and judicious empathy and sympathy can be useful in research, more is clearly required.

Insofar as the cultural exploration of affect is concerned, efforts should be made to learn local category terms for emotions and local cultural theories about their nature and expression. While in some situations it will prove as difficult to be certain about how a given individual may actually feel as it is to be certain about what that individual „really believes," we can have more confidence in our abilities to determine what people say about feelings and the expression and experience of them in different circumstances. Further, case studies, to the extent that such can be made, will be useful. One technique, by way of an ethnographic example, is to ask different informants to analyze some social transaction with respect to the possible deployment and probable experiences of emotions; while there is no guarantee that informants will be accurate, there is a good likelihood that what they say will prove culturally informative.

The above relates to what I deem a potentially rewarding set of methodological strategies and tactics for exploring the affective significance of cultural propositions. But now we might ask what larger lesson respecting our overall scholarly perspective on the study of religions might be drawn from Lévy-Bruhl's insights about the role of affectivity in thought. That question becomes even more intriguing when we couple it with a growing recognition that talk about „rationality" is likely to be freighted with the baggage of multiple homologies.

Rationality, Reflexivity, and Experience

The „modes of thought" problem addressed by Lévy-Bruhl was inspired in large measure by reports of seemingly odd „beliefs": that, for example, some individuals can be in two places at the same time, that rain dances bring rain, that certain people are both human beings and parrots, that the sun is a white cockatoo, and that while a cucumber can be an ox, an ox is never a cucumber.

A question was raised about the rational status of such assertions. Like the first question about rationality that introduces this paper, that question was an obvious and easy one for Western scholars to pose, yet difficult for them to answer in a manner that inspired wide agreement. Some attempts at answering are iterated or reiterated in three widely known anthologies edited, respectively, by Bryan Wilson (1970), by Robin Horton and Ruth Finnegan (1973), and by Martin Hollis and Steven Lukes (1982). But there are other attempts also. These include (but are not limited to) the so-called paleologic of Ernst von Domarus (1954) and Silvano Arieti (1974), David E. Cooper's (1975) invocation of the tri-valued logic of Jan Lukasiewicz, C. R. Hallpike's (1979) appropriation of Piaget's schema of cognitive developmental stages, Richard Shweder's (1977) essay on the wide distribution of „magical thinking," and the classicist G. E. R. Lloyd's book, *Demystifying Mentalities* (1990).

The wide fan of interpretations advocated in those sources testifies to a lack of scholarly consensus about the rational status and significance of many expressions of conviction and other behaviors among the peoples of the world. But that has had some positive consequences. Awareness of the lack of consensus has been one of several factors prompting some of us to develop greater sensitivity to the roles that our own categories and discourses play in attending to the world. And as we have become reflexively aware of our hitherto unrecognized commitments, commitments disposed and supported by those same categories and discourses, many of us have sought to transcend their limitations.

Current anthropological thinking about the socio-cultural roles, including the hermeneutical functions, of the emotions, is an example of such efforts at transcendence. In rethinking the matter of emotions, indeed, some anthropologists have not only begun to reconceptualize the category, in an effort to understand „emotion" in fresh ways, but to recognize and reflect critically on the categories and assumptions that tend to be conventionally associated with more traditional understandings of affectivity and cognition. This has not only promoted significant alterations in their views, resulting, for example, in a blurring of traditional boundaries between „thought" and „emotion," but it has made them all the more aware of intellectual options. Partially in consequence of the observations of their critics, indeed, they have become increasingly aware of some of the consequences of choosing to attend to the world through a set of emerging categories as compared to adhering to more traditional alternatives.

There is a wider lesson to be drawn from this respecting reflexivity and the matter of rationality in the study of religion. The philosopher Theodore Schatzki (1995: 154) characterizes reflexivity in terms of „self-knowledge, openness to self-criticism and change, and dialogue." These are qualities that he chooses to view as constitutive of objectivity and as hallmarks of rationality in intellectual practices. They ought to be, I believe, of crucial importance for our concern with rationality in the scholarly study of religion.

Rationality, as I prefer to conceptualize it with specific reference to scholars, is not the property of one theoretical or methodological approach as contrasted to some other. Rather, it is expressed above all in our critical monitoring of what we do and in our willingness to make serious efforts to understand and evaluate alternative possibilities. Rationality in that sense is realized in the actualized conjoining of openmindedness with critical dispositions in the pursuit of knowledge. And in pursuing knowledge, a rational humility suggests that we acknowledge that what we offer the world are knowledge-claims rather than fixed and eternal verities. In pursuing knowledge, moreover, the exposure and elimination of error in standing knowledge-claims are at least as important as the formulation of novel claims (Popper 1962).

Rational intellectual practices require us, in my opinion, to acknowledge that there is a world that exists independently of the self. We might well endorse a long-standing claim: that when we close our eyes in sleep, the world does not disappear. And just as we sometimes test our claims about the world, so, too, in a manner of speaking, does the world test us (and sometimes awards us flunking grades, as when we seek to transcend with inadequate means its physical realities).

But while there is a vast world that exists independently of the self, our access to that world is inevitably mediated by our categories and by our sensitivities and insensitivities. We cannot understand the world in any profundity or sophistication, nor can we convey our understandings to our fellows, outside of language. And language, semioticians cogently argue, is incapable of full transparency. At the very least,

> in any rule-governed sign system arbitrariness, the principle that expressive vehicles are not formally determined by the meanings they stand for, is constrained by systemic motivation, the principle that meaning combinations are predictable from sign combinations (regular grammatical proportionality, for example). As a result, no sign system can be internally cohesive and still be transparent to the meanings it is created to express. (Parmentier 1985: 372)

Some may nevertheless suppose that experience, when coolly considered, could provide the touchstone for an objective overview, one that offers the possibility of transcending the colorations of culture and their encodings in language. There are, I believe, serious arguments against such a view. Given the subject matter of this essay, however, it must suffice to consider only one such argument here: that of Lucien Lévy-Bruhl.

In his sixth book, *L'Expérience mystique*, Lévy-Bruhl considers the question of why so-called „primitives" might impress Euro-American observers as sometimes taking for „experience" what we identify as „belief." This, he remarks, is partially explainable by the ambiguity inherent in our usual uses of the terms „belief" and „experience" (1938: 125). While the distinction between them seems clear to us, it is nevertheless a convention „gradually acquired by our psychology and our theory of knowledge," and it thus bears „the mark of our civilization." To impose it on the study of „primitive mentality," he adds, is to render it a source of both hinderance and error. To do so, indeed, is to suppose imprudently that there is „a definition of experience that is uniquely and universally valid" (*ibid*).

Rodney Needham appreciates the importance of Lévy-Bruhl's point. He explicates it as suggesting that

> The concept of experience, which is commonly treated as though it denoted a constant possibility of apprehension and a permanent background to the varieties of categorical thought, is itself an idiocratic and problematical construct. (Needham 1972: 171–72)

That is, it is a complex concept for us, and it is „not a neutral and undifferentiated background against which cultural concepts can be set up for inspection" (Needham 1972: 172). In support of that position, Needham quotes (1972: 172, n. 9) Alfred North Whitehead's remark that „The word 'experience' is one of the most deceitful in philosophy"

(Whitehead 1927: 16). For Lévy-Bruhl, Needham notes, our concept of experience is prepossessingly „cognitive" (1972: 173). But such a concept, he points out with respect to Lévy-Bruhl's views," cannot be applied as it stands to the experience of primitives, which is predominantly 'affective'" (1972: 173). Lévy-Bruhl, Needham opines, has successfully invalidated our own concept of experience as a universally applicable instrument for „the comparative analysis of alien concepts" (1972: 175).

In short, then, there is no escaping the problems posed by language and culture in attending to the world. This need not be a cause of despair, however, even when we take into account the impossibility of achieving utter transparency in language and the complexities and vagaries of our categories. Taking those considerations into account, indeed, is the beginning of wisdom. And with wisdom, we may hope to improve our categories and, through their instrumentality, our claims to knowledge. We may hope to do so even though the world to which we attend is inescapably a participated world.

We are saddled with an irony that the admirably reflexive Lucien Lévy-Bruhl helps us to appreciate: that for those of us who aspire to a rational account of the world, the most troubling participation is the participation of the observer in the observed.

Notes

1. Lévy-Bruhl (1975 [1949]: 108–112) distinguishes between two major sorts of participation. First, a „community of essence," whereby an identity is felt between things, as between an animal and its footprints, an image of a person and the person, or, broadly put, „between symbol and what it represents." Second, a participation that equals an imitation, as when Australian aborigines, in order to bring rain, imitate what occurs when they are in the midst of a downpour. This, says Lévy-Bruhl, „is not a prefiguration of the rain;" rather, the imitation „effectively realizes the rain which will fall soon ... the imitation is a felt participation, and, as such, independent of time" (111). This second sort of participation, he remarks:

> has a metaphysical significance: it does not express a relationship between given things and objects; it founds an existence (legitimation, as we have seen in so large a number of myths of the aetiological sort [Volume V]. Imitation (μίμησις) is the *raison d'etre*, not by way of causality but by way of

consubstantiality, that is to say of essence, communicated and divided; in brief it is a participation (μέθεξις) and from this point of view it is nearly no longer distinguishable from the first sort. (112)

In declaring on the same page, and in classical Greek, that μίμησις equals μέθεξις, imitation equals participation, Lévy-Bruhl, we may suppose, was aware that he was not the first to equate those two Greek terms. The French scholar, whose Chair at the Sorbonne was in the History of Philosophy (Leenhardt 1975 [1949]: xii), and who in 1880 published an edition of The Nicomachean Ethics, was very likely to have known that Aristotle also pointed to a connection between them. According to Aristotle, when Plato maintained that sensible things exist by participation in the Ideas that share their names, „Only the name 'participation' was new; for the Pythagoreans say that things exist by 'imitation' of numbers, and Plato says they exist by participation, changing the name" (*Metaphysics* 1.6.10). In this additional sense, then, imitation equals participation.

One wonders what, if anything, Lévy-Bruhl might have made of this had he written the seventh book for which the Notebooks were a preparation. Pythagoras, a legendary and influential pre-Socratic, was both mathematician and mystic, and something of a transitional figure in the history of Greek philosophy and science.

Note that in Peter Rivière's 1975 English translation of the Notebooks, μέθεξις (methexis) is consistently misprinted as μέθεζις (methedzis). Rather than faithfully reproduce that error while condemning it with a „sic!," I have taken the liberty of correcting it above, and noting what I have done here.

2. Von Domarus and Arieti regard the „paleologic" as a distinctive form of reasoning, a precursor to our „normal" secondary process or „Aristotelian" logic. Secondary process logic is called Aristotelian, Arieti (1974: 229) writes, because „Aristotle was the first to enunciate its laws." According to the Principle of Von Domarus, while in Aristotelian logic identity is accepted on the basis of an identity of subjects, the paleologician accepts identity on the basis of an identity of predicates. Thus in a case cited by Arieti (1974: 230–231), a psychotic patient reasons, „The Virgin Mary was a virgin; I am a virgin; therefore I am the Virgin Mary." Von Domarus and Arieti attribute paleological reasoning to schizophrenics, who adopt it, they claim, as a matter of teleologic regression, in order to shield themselves from an unbearable

awareness of reality and ego-destructive anxiety. The psychotic, they maintain, will focus on all sorts of coincidences, in a veritable „orgy of identifications." More broadly, they hold that the Principle of Von Domarus lies behind Freudian symbology. Thus, for example, a cigar might symbolize the penis because the same general shape can be predicated of both. And in a case cited by Arieti (235), a cigar symbolized Jesus, for the patient predicated „encirclement" of both (cigars are usually banded by a ring of paper, and in images of Jesus halos often encircle his head — as, I might add, do crowns of thorns). Von Domarus and Arieti also attribute the „paleologic" to young children and to so-called primitive peoples. But, they hold, while young children and „primitives" have a propensity to reason paleologically, they are not driven to doing so by internal compulsions, as are schizophrenics.

Anthony Wallace (1961: 136) points out that the force of Von Domarus's distinction between Aristotelian logic and the paleologic depends on the analysts's ability to posit at least one predicate distinctive of one of two compared objects but not the other. If the analyst could not, then formally speaking the two objects would indeed be identical. Wallace concludes that the paleologic appears to be „the same old [Aristotelian] formal logic, operating in psychotic thinking with a drastically limited range of predicates," and he deems the attribution of it to children and to „primitives" to be „even less justified than its attribution to schizophrenics" (Wallace 1961: 136).

3. Jan Lukasiewicz (1878—1956), a Polish logician, developed a three-valued logic in 1917, the values being „true," „false," and „possible." He built on this work, as did various of his students (e.g., Mordchaj Wajsberg and Jerzy Slupecki), devising multi-valued logics, and so demonstrating that in propositional logic there are viable alternatives to bivalent „standard" logic (Aristotelian logic). Lukasiewicz's work (e.g., 1964, 1974) has proven useful to a diversity of persons, including the physicist Hans Reichenbach in dissolving certain apparent anomalies in quantum mechanics, the electrical engineer Lofti Zadeh in developing fuzzy set theory, and the mathematician Iván Guzmán de Rojas in writing algorithms for the computer-aided analysis and modeling of Aymará grammar. David E. Cooper, a British social anthropologist, also makes use of Lukasiewicz's three-valued logic, and argues that „Primitive magico-religious thought incorporates an alternative logic to our 'standard' one within the terms of which the apparent inconsistencies

[noted by anthropologists in certain famous statements made by non-Western peoples] are not inconsistencies at all" (1975: 241).

In a Reichenbachian variant of three-valued logic, Lukasiewicz's third value, „possible," is conceptualized preeminantly as indeterminate. Propositions that are indeterminate cannot be either verified or falsified logically, although we may know or believe them to be true or false on other grounds. Thus, for instance, in accordance with the quantum principle of complementarity, some paired propositions complement one another because determining the truth of one renders it impossible in principle to determine the truth of the other. Where verification and falsification are ruled out in principle, a proposition must be assigned some value other than true or false. Cooper holds that when applying three-valued logic in an effort to dissolve anomalies in magico-religious thought, two conditions must be satisfied: First, it must be demonstrated that if „primitive" thought does incorporate this alternative logic, the anomalies do indeed disappear. Second, it must be shown that „primitive" thought actually does incorporate it. If we fulfil the first but not the second condition, we only show that certain troublesome propositions can be interpreted by us in such a way as to render them less troublesome, but we do not save the authors of those propositions from the charge of being inconsistent (and thus, perhaps, irrational). Cooper then goes on to argue in favour of this claim:

> The magico-religious thought of a people is a highly theoretic explanatory system, within which propositions occur that, while meaningful in terms of the system, are not capable of any verification or falsification within it. Such propositions are not counted by the people in question as being either true or false, but as having a third truth-value. The anomalies arise because the people explicitly reject the consequences of propositions they appear to accept. However, in every such case, we find that at least one of the propositions is counted by the natives, in virtue of its untestability, to be neither true nor false – hence, despite appearances, the people do not regard as true a number of inconsistent propositions. (Cooper 1975: 244)

Cooper's thesis elicited a small number of published responses, for the most part negative. His major examples of non-Western propositions are those that others have also given opinions about, thus lending support to a complaint voiced by Michael Kenny:

> The recent contributions to the rationality discussion have a pronounced lack of empirical referent, and depend rather heavily on the question of the logic of Azande witchcraft and on Nuer propositions that „twins are birds." (Kenny 1976: 116)

Cooper's interesting thesis, I think, deserves evaluation in fieldwork specifically intended to explore it. Insofar as I am aware, such evaluation has not been undertaken.

4. Jean Piaget (1896–1980), biologist turned psychologist, and self-styled „genetic epistemologist," played a major role in establishing developmental psychology as a scientific enterprise. He continues to be respected for his efforts even though many contemporary developmental psychologists – probably, indeed, the great majority of them – reject various of his claims about cognitive ontogeny and deem certain of his experiments to be flawed. Piaget holds that children creatively struggle for cognitive mastery. They are, in fact, cognitive constructivists, engaged in actively developing their abilities to understand, their capacities to abstract, and their other cognitive skills. He concludes, moreover, that the European children whom he and his associates studied go through four distinct stages of cognitive self-development: the sensori-motor, the pre-operational, the concrete operational, and the formal operational. These stages, he maintains, form sequential phases in the normal cognitive trajectory of the children studied (Piaget 1929; 1972; 1977)

The British social anthropologist, C. R. Hallpike, applies Piaget's developmental stages on a societal level, even though Piaget and various of his followers warn against going from findings about the development of individuals to characterizations of social groups or, alternatively, going from crystallized cultural products to claims about the cognitive skills of individuals. Hallpike, however, holds that collective representations must reflect the cognitive development of adults in small-scale or so-called „primitive" societies. Grounded in that assumption, he goes on to argue that the collective representations of nonliterate, non-Western peoples in a number of small-scale societies indicate pre-operational processes of thought. That is, the thought processes of at least some „primitive" peoples are of the sort that Piaget attributes to European children between the ages of two and seven. Hallpike attempts to account for the reason why many „primitive" peoples would remain at a pre-operational level of cognitive skills. Accepting Piagetian constructivism, whereby increasing cognitive sophistication is largely a matter of progressive self-development, Hallpike suggests that the socio-cultural enviroments within which many „primitives" grow up and live do not stimulate or challenge them to develop other cognitive skills.

Hallpike's thesis has been attacked strongly by anthropologists and psychologists. One of the most well informed critiques was penned by the anthropologist Richard Shweder (1982). (See also Shweder's 1981 comments on a paper by Allan Young that makes use of Hallpike.) Shweder (1982) maintains that Hallpike takes little or no notice of some important post-1966 developments in the field of cognitive developmental psychology. These break with Piagetian psychology: they move away from the advocacy of broad stages in thinking, they hold that various operational structures are available to young children, and that individuals are not frozen at some one level of thought for all of their tasks. They suggest, moreover, that the contents of what people think about are of great importance for how they think.

5. Like many others, Shweder addresses the possibility of a significant distinction between contemporary Western science and some other extant mode of thought. But his essay differs from number of such exercises in three ways: (1) Shweder is personally skilled in, and lucidly explicates, an important form of mathematical/statistical reasoning in the sciences; (2) he draws on a richness of experimental and clinical studies accomplished by psychologists who address the matter of how people actually think; and (3) he argues that „primitive" peoples, and most of the rest of us most of the time, think „magically," basing our inferences on perceptual or conceptual likeness, whereas scientists *qua* scientists attempt to base inferences on co-occurrent likelihood (probability assessments, as modeled by the four-celled contingency table). The latter cognitive effort, he points out, is normally achieved only after sustained tutoring; most of us are neither trained to use it nor are we motivated to do so.

6. Lloyd analyzes various weaknesses in the idea of „mentalities," the notion that distinct modes of thought can be attributed to social collectivities of persons. He finds reasons to advocate that we move away from efforts to characterize mentalities as such. Rather, we should consider the contexts of communication, the natures and styles of different sorts of interpersonal exchanges, and the explicit categories available to persons and the ways those resources are used. „The all-important contrast," Lloyd argues, is not between different mentalities, but between „situations of communication where certain types of challenge, concerning meaning or belief, are possible and expected, and others where they are not" (1990: 15). Individuals in any society, he maintains,

may exhibit diverse modes of reasoning, and those modes of reasoning, not mentalities, should constitute the focus of our investigations (1990: 145).

Lloyd faults Lévy-Bruhl for, among other things, never acknowledging „that the uniformity of primitive thought is a mirage, the product of the distance from which it is viewed" (1990: 144). And in considering the development of argumentation among the Greeks, from whom we have derived many of our analytical categories, he draws on his considerable erudition as a classicist to argue that developing Greek philosophy and science favoured polemical contrasts, and that such contrasts were often overdrawn (1990: 8). Thus, for example, the contrast between the literal and the metaphorical arose out of polemic, and we ought not to impose it on the statements of non-Western peoples, Lloyd maintains, unless we find that they make use of a similar contrast.

Culture in Phylogenetic Perspective: An Appreciation of the Contributions of A. I. Hallowell[4]

Abstract: A. Irving Hallowell was an American anthropologist. Two of his views are likely to be of special interest to contemporary proponents of the cognitive science of religion who value intellectual history: (1) Hallowell argues that self-awareness is crucial not only for individual human functioning, but also for the functioning of human social orders, in that all human social orders operate as moral orders. Individuals must be able to compare their behavior to a socially supported moral canon. Self-awareness, moreover, is culturally influenced. Culture provides humans with five basic orientations that facilitate successful individual maneuvering in a „culturally constituted behavioral environment." (2) Culture is not a sudden emergent, but the result of a long history of evolutionary developments, developments that can be glimpsed by viewing culture in phylogenetic perspective. While Hallowell did not explore the possibility that culture may underdetermine many of our concepts, his focus on positive relationships between culture and cognition, and his emphasis on evolutionary continuities between humans and non-human animals, render him a pioneer and predecessor worth reading.

1

In their „Call for Papers," the organizers of our Conference, Armin W. Geertz and Jeppe Sinding Jensen, invite us to „explore the interstices of religion, cognition and culture in an attempt to bring culture back into cognitive study." Various attempts „to understand the origins of humanity," they note, „have raised fundamental questions about the complex relationship between cognition and culture." Their invitation, as I read it, is forward looking. In the last couple of decades, scholars working within the frameworks of the contemporary cognitive and evolutionary sciences have taken appreciable strides in coming to understand our humanity in general and religion in particular. But much

---

4 „Culture in Phylogenetic Perspective: An Appreciation of the Contributions of A.I. Hallowell." Unpublished paper read at a conference on „Origins of Religion, Cognition, and Culture" at Aarhus University, January 6, 2006.

remains to be done. We can better consolidate and extend our understandings by looking more closely at culture both in phylogenetic and in functional perspectives. How does culture contribute to a human level of existence? And how did it arise?

Those questions are not new. But we are better equipped to answer them than were our predecessors. And we are better able to use our answers in theorizing about religion. The general approach to religion that many now gathered in Aarhus endorse is actually synthetic, for it draws upon a variety of disciplines and fields. We are the beneficiaries of the contemporary cognitive and neural sciences, of evolutionary biology, and of developmental and evolutionary psychologies. Our predecessors were not so advantageously endowed and situated. They did not – indeed, they could not – put things together in the ways that we can. Despite that, however, some of them were remarkably shrewd in their sense of problems. And they were often insightful in their theorizing, especially about culture. It would be blind-sided of us to ignore their history. And so, and especially since our Conference is forward-looking, I invite you to look back a moment in celebration of a predecessor whose inquiries and intellectual grasp remain relevant and instructive.

I refer to A. Irving Hallowell, who was born in 1892 and who died in 1974. Hallowell identified himself as a cultural anthropologist. But while he accorded culture very important roles in what he called „the human situation," he distanced himself from extreme assertions of cultural autonomy and determinancy. Hallowell came to suppose that culture needs to be explained in several ways and on several levels. He maintained that human psychology, human social orders, and culture not only interpenetrate and support each other, but that we can best understand them by seeking to comprehend their emergence in phylogenetic perspective.

Hallowell was educated at the University of Pennsylvania, and he was a member of its faculty for most of his academic career. He became an important figure in what some call „The Culture and Personality Movement in Anthropology". But while he selectively made use of various components of Freudian theory, he never became an ardent Freudian or Neo-Freudian, unlike certain other Culture and Personality anthropologists. Indeed, at different times he experimented with Thorndike's learning theory and various other psychologies in efforts to enhance our understandings of the human condition.

Hallowell was a pioneer in the use of the Rorschach Test in anthropological fieldwork. He became, moreover, an important figure in the development of ethnohistory. He used the Rorschach Test as a tool, along with more traditional ethnographic methods, for inferring what he supposed to be the typical personality sets of twentieth century Northern Ojibwa among whom he did fieldwork. And he employed ethnohistorical research in an attempt to reconstruct the configurational or culturally-deduced personality of Ojibwa of earlier centuries — that is, the personality dispositions analytically posited to be most congruent with the presumptively dominant configuration of Ojibwa culture. While that interest allied him with Ruth Benedict, Margaret Mead, and other Culture and Personality strategists, he was comparatively cautious and nuanced in his claims.

In one of his earliest published papers, „Some Empirical Aspects of Northern Saulteaux Religion," Hallowell remarks that „discussion of religious phenomena cannot be profitably carried on except in terms applicable to all races, periods, and cultures" (Hallowell 1934: 389). The significance of that statement as it relates to Hallowell's maturing views is well put by one of his students, Dennison Nash:

> The movement of American anthropology in the 1930s and 1940s was towards narrowly conceived, functionally oriented studies of cultural diversity. There were few if any attempts to apply grand evolutionary schemes or sweeping generalizations to humanity. For Hallowell, this movement, which is expressed in his Ojibwa studies, appears to have terminated when he began to ask questions about „human nature and the human mind" (see Hallowell 1947, 1950) and to put these questions in an evolutionary perspective. The turn from human diversities to universals was within the scope of the Boasian „program" in that it occurred only after adequate data had been gathered to permit valid generalization; and it was true to the main thrust of the „program" in which the ultimate questions came to be psychological ones; but it was Hallowell who took the initiative in this turnaround, and it was he who played an important role in developing a more theoretical American anthropology. (Nash 1977: 5—6)

Some understanding of Hallowell's views can be achieved by considering three of his essays: „The Self and Its Behavioral Environment" (1955 [1954]), „Self, Society, and Culture in Phylogenetic Perspective" (1960a), and „Ojibwa Ontology, Behavior, and World View" (1960b).

2

In „The Self and Its Behavioral Environment," Hallowell emphasizes the importance of *self-awareness* in human life. He deems it „a psychological constant, one basic facet of human nature and of human personality" (1955: 75). It underwrites the likelihood that every normal human being, in the course of ontogenetic development, will learn to conceptualize his or her self as a distinctively recognized object in a world of objects variously conceptualized as other than one's self. And, Hallowell maintains, „it seems necessary to assume self-awareness as one of the prerequisite psychological conditions for the functioning of any human social order ..." (1955: 75).

All normal human beings everywhere, Hallowell argues, develop self-concepts. Such concepts are strongly influenced by a constellation of five „basic orientations" provided by culture. The *contents* of those orientations vary from culture to culture, but their provision is pan-cultural. Because these cultural orientations play important roles in the constitution of self concepts, Hallowell writes, „the nature of the self, considered in its conceptual content, is a culturally identifiable variable" (1955: 76).

The first orientation is *self-orientation*. In coming to view one's self as a distinctive object in a world of other objects, language plays important sociopsychological roles (1955: 89). Personal pronouns, personal names, and kinship terms all serve to mark off the self from others. And, of course, various aspects of culture tend to flesh-out self concepts. Thus, for example, culturally supported beliefs in life after death are, in effect, beliefs about the likely future careers of selves, and they can be accounted components in self-orientation.

Object orientation, Hallowell declares, is „A *second* function of all cultures ..." (1955: 91). It has to do with „the orientation of the self to a diversified world of objects in its behavioral environment, discriminated, classified, and conceptualized with respect to attributes which are culturally constituted and symbolically mediated through language" (1955: 91). Thus, for instance, „... if we assume the outlook of the self as culturally oriented in a behavioral environment with cosmic dimensions and implicit metaphysical principles, a great deal of what is ordinarily described as 'religion' is seen to involve the attitudes, needs, goals, and affective experience of the self in interaction with certain classes of objects in the behavioral environment. These classes of objects are typically *other* selves – spiritual beings, deities, ancestors" (1955: 92)

Spatiotemporal orientation is the third basic orientation afforded by culture. It prepares the self for action within „some kind of spatiotemporal frame of reference" (1955: 92). It is likely, for instance, to eventuate in the self's conscious use of culturally constituted reference points respecting space and time.

The fourth orientation provided by culture is *motivational orientation* (1955: 100). Hallowell characterizes it as „orientation of the self towards the objects of it behavioral environment with reference to the satisfaction of its needs" (1955: 100). „Motives at the human level," Hallowell writes, „are peculiarly complex because they are essentially acquired rather than innately determined. In consequence, their range and variety is very great" (1955: 101). Drawing on the literatures available to him in mid-twentieth century, he further remarks that „Many attempts to reduce human motives to constant biological attributes of the organism, or physiological determinants, have proved inadequate" (1955: 101). We can now do better in that regard, as recent experimental and theoretical work in the cognitive science of religion indicates. At the same time, however, I think that we should pay attention to Hallowell's insistence that some degree of cultural understanding can be requisite for correctly inferring motives. He gives an illuminating example from his own fieldwork among Northern Ojibwa. Those hunters often share food beyond their immediate family circles. While it may not be incorrect to raise the possibility of motivations suggested by terms such as „unselfishness, generosity, affection, kindness, and love" (1955: 102), to say no more would be misleading. Ojibwa culture supports the idea that sorcery is a real and ever-present danger, especially for those who anger others by refusing to share food. Hence, Hallowell writes, „one of the most potent motivations in food-sharing and hospitality is apprehension or fear of sorcery" (1955: 102). A sophisticated interpretation of Ojibwa motivations in this case therefore requires an understanding of „relevant cultural facts" (1955: 103).

Normative Orientation, in Hallowell's schema, „is the *fifth* orientation" that culture provides the self (1955: 105). It has to do with values, ideals, and standards. Hallowell deems them „intrinsic components of all cultures;" some are implicit, others explicit (1955: 105). He adds that „motivational orientation in man cannot be fully understood without normative orientation, since values are an integral aspect of needs and goals" (1955: 105). At the same time, Hallowell states, „without normative orientation, self-awareness in man could not function in one of its most characteristic forms – self-appraisal of conduct. For the individual would have no standard by which to judge his own acts or those of others, nor any ideals to which he might aspire" (1955: 103).

Now, in summarizing part of what Hallowell affirms in the 1954 paper, I have quoted some of his uses of the expression „behavioral environment," the environment in which the individual self operates. Hallowell describes that environment as „culturally constituted" (1955: 87). His employment of that modifier, unfortunately, has led some persons to suppose him to be more of a cultural determinist than he actually was. While Hallowell clearly emphasizes the importance of culture in human life, he also credits significance to psychodynamic variables and to evolved constitutional structures and processes. The expression „culturally constituted behavioral environment" must be understood not only as assigning importance to culture for a warranted understanding of human behavior, but also as a mediating construct in the section of his essay where it is most fully discussed.

In that section, Hallowell acknowledges claims that our contemporary Western science and epistemology encourage us to describe in a putatively „objective" fashion an environment that, so to speak, stops at the human skin. But identifying such an „external" and „objective" environment, he opines, „has a limited usefulness even in the observation of animals at the subhuman level" (1955: 86). Thus, for instance, whether or not a species has color vision can affect its relation to an „environment" with certain physical properties, But this, of course, means that a supportable understanding of the situation would involve some understanding of the capacities of organisms as well as some understanding of the constitutions of extra-somatic environments (1955: 86). Hallowell evinces somewhat more enthusiasm for George Herbert Mead's claim that an organism „determines the environment" (quoted in Hallowell 1955: 86). He supposes, nevertheless, that it is necessary to do better than Mead in conceptualizing what is involved on the human level.

The idea of „behavioral environment," Hallowell writes, „takes account of the properties and adaptational needs of an organism in interaction with the external world as constituting the actual behavioral field in terms of which the activities of the animal are more thoroughly intelligible" (1955: 86). On the human level, as his discussion of the „basic orientations" provided by culture indicates, that behavioral environment is filled with culturally supported objects, some of which may not be deemed objective realities by Western scientific epistemology. Spirits are one of many examples. The conceptualization of such objects, nevertheless, characteristically affects human behavior in significant ways. In advancing his conceptualization of „the culturally constituted behavioral environment" as both mediating and transcending the different truths glimpsed by the externalists (the environment stops at the skin) and by G. H. Mead (the organism determines its environment), Hallowell might more appropriately be labeled a cultural realist than a cultural determinist.

3

In his 1960 paper, „Self, Society, and Culture in Phylogenetic Perspective," Hallowell attempts to outline „a conjunctive approach to human phylogeny in which the organic, psychological, social, and cultural dimensions of the evolutionary process are taken into account with reference to the necessary and sufficient conditions that underlie a human level of existence" (1960a: 318). In doing so, he observes that numbers of other anthropologists have been so preoccupied with culture that they have *re*-created

> the old gap between man and the other primates which, it was once thought, the adoption of an evolutionary frame of reference would serve to bridge. The repeated emphasis given to speech and culture as *unique* characteristics of man sidestepped the essence of the evolutionary problem... For unless culture and speech be conceived as sudden and radical emergents, they must be rooted in behavioral processes which can no more be considered apart from the general framework of behavioral evolution than the distinctive structural characteristics of man can be considered apart from morphological evolution. (Hallowell 1960a: 316–317)

In that regard, Hallowell raises the question of how far an emphasis on distinctive attributes credited to human beings may advance our understanding of humanity's „evolutionary position in the animal series" (1960a: 317). He cites examples such as man the rational animal, man the tool-making animal, and man the symbol making animal. In their Call for Papers, the organizers of our Conference supply still more examples, and they invite us to contemplate them. Hallowell takes a dim view of such characterizations, for, as he puts it, they „stress man's differences from other living creatures. Like the criteria of culture and speech, they emphasize discontinuity rather than continuity, which is likewise inherent in the evolutionary process" (1960a: 317).

Hallowell holds that „A cultural level of adaptation could not arise *de novo*" (1960a: 359). He supposes that at least some other animals evolved to an adaptive condition that he characterizes as „protocultural" (1960a: 323). But he sees human culture as more richly endowed by our evolved psychology. In keeping with ideas that he expressed in his 1954 paper, he calls our attention to humanity's great capacities for self-awareness and self-objectification. Those capacities and the basic orientations provided by culture make for the distinctive functioning of human societies „through the commonly shared value-orientations of self-conscious individuals, in contrast with the societies of non-hominid and probable early hominid primates, where ego-centered processes remained undeveloped or rudimentary" (1960a: 357). From the standpoint of this „peculiarity of man," Hallowell writes, „culture may be said to be an elaborated and socially transmitted system of meanings and values which, in an animal capable of self-awareness, implements a type of adaptation which makes the role of the human being intelligible to himself, both with reference to an articulated universe and to his fellow men" (1960a: 357)

4

In the third of the three papers under discussion, „Ojibwa Ontology, Behavior, and World View" (1960b), Hallowell analyzes selected Ojibwa concepts, especially as they relate to what he calls the „person" category implicit in Ojibwa thought. Human beings in Ojibwa metaphysics are but one type of person. There are many others: dream visitors, thunder birds, humanlike curers who live in rocky places, and so on. These other-than-human persons overlap with humans in various ways. They have consciousness, will, purpose, and speech or other communicative abilities. Further, other-than-human persons, as well as some humans, have powers of metamorphosis, albeit humans receive such powers from other-than-human patrons. Thus, for instance, human sorcerers may sometimes turn into bears, just as persons who usually have animal form may sometimes turn into humans, thus contributing to what Hallowell (1960b: 40) terms „the deceptiveness of appearances" in the Ojibwa worldview. „Outward appearance," Hallowell writes, „is only an incidental attribute of being," for in Ojibwa sensibilities „neither animal nor human characteristics" in their outward manifestations „define categorical differences in the core of being" (1960b: 35). For the Ojibwa, he tells us, „What persists and gives continuity to being is the vital part, or soul" (1960b: 38).

> Although not formally abstracted and articulated philosophically, the nature of „persons" is the focal point of Ojibwa ontology and the key to the psychological unity and dynamics of their world outlook. This aspect of their metaphysics of being permeates the content of their cognitive processes: perceiving, remembering, imagining, conceiving, judging, and reasoning ... „Persons," in fact, are so inextricably associated with notions of causality that, in order to understand their appraisal of events and the kind of behavior demanded in situations as they define them, we are confronted over and over again with the roles of „persons" as *loci* of causality in the dynamics of their universe. For the Ojibwa make no cardinal use of any concept of impersonal forces. (Hallowell 1960b: 43–44)

Hallowell adds that „With respect to the Ojibwa conception of causality, all my own observations suggest that a culturally constituted psychological set operates which inevitably directs the reasoning of individuals towards an explanation of events in personalistic terms. *Who did it, who is responsible*, is always the crucial question to be answered" (1960b: 44–45).

My brief summary of some of the points that Hallowell makes in this paper is inadequate for conveying the ethnographic and analytical richness of his essay. It does, however, give you an indication of the consistency and flowering of his perspective. Some of the ideas advanced in the earlier essay, „The Self and Its Behavioral Environment," are now ethnographically actualized in his analysis of Ojibwa ontological concepts. He shows us how those concepts situate Ojibwa selves in an Ojibwa culturally constituted behavioral environment. And, in keeping with the perspective found in the first two papers, he emphasizes the role of culture in not only creating a world of meaning but in facilitating adaptations that are more or less gratifying to human actors.

5

Hallowell's point of view, to be sure, is not fully congruent with that of many proponents of the contemporary cognitive science of religion. While not explicitly endorsing the notion of human infants as so many blank slates, Hallowell seems to take it for granted that culturally parochial socialization and enculturation, in tension with panhuman psychological processes, will produce the cognitive contents of adult minds. Culture, for Hallowell, is preeminently something learned. His theorizing does not adequately provide for the possibility that in some cases culture may actually underdetermine our concepts, and that conceptual enrichment is likely to occur because our multiple inferential systems typically operate on cultural fragments in orderly (and discoverable) ways. He nevertheless does make an impressive case for the importance of culture in the constitution of human behavioral environments, particularly with respect to self-orientation. And, of course, he differs from most of his anthropological contemporaries by cogently arguing that a greater understanding of culture is to be gleaned from viewing it in phylogenetic perspective. Because of his measured and analytical treatment of culture and its emergence, Hallowell is a predecessor whom we can continue to read with appreciation and profit.

Part III Beliefs

On What We May Believe About Beliefs[1]

Abstract: This essay describes two major theories of belief offered by philosophers (belief as mental state and belief as disposition), and it discusses what appears to be a newer conceptualization of belief emerging from the cognitive and neurological sciences. Anthropologists, for the most part (with the exception of Rodney Needham and some others), do not appear to have accessed the philosophical literature on belief. The author regards that as unfortunate, since at the very least philosophers apprise us of certain complexities and subtleties likely to be encountered in talk about belief. The essay also briefly considers Pascal Boyer's distinction between the „cognitive" and the „epistemic," and long-standing invocations in anthropology of an „emic" approach to beliefs.

I begin with certain claims that may stimulate some of you to disbelief. Surveys accomplished by well known polling organizations suggest that about one in four adults in the United States „believes" that intelligent beings from outer space have been in contact with humans (Gallup and Newport 1991: 138; TIME, June 23, 1997: 66). And Jon D. Miller's surveys, which asked U.S. adults whether or not they believe that „some of the unidentified flying objects reported are really space vehicles from other civilizations," elicited affirmative replies from 54% of the respondents in 1985, 57% in 1988, and 54% in 1990 (Frazier 1992, 346).

Extrapolations from the polls suggest that millions of people in the United States „believe" that extraterrestrial beings have actually contacted earthlings, and that even larger numbers affirm the reality of at least some unidentified flying objects as spacecraft from distant worlds. These figures, as one may expect, are welcomed by members of the UFO community. Thus, for instance, Robert J. Durant, a ufologist writing in the *International UFO Reporter* of November/December, 1993, exults as follows:

> UFO proponents have won the war for public opinion. For every fundamentalist Christian there are five UFO believers. Roman Catholics comprise by far the largest Christian denomination in the United States,

---

1 „On What We May Believe About Beliefs." In Jensine Andresen (ed.), *Religion in Mind: Cognitive Perspectives on Religious Belief, Ritual, and Experience*, 47–69. Cambridge: Cambridge University Press, 2001.

and UFO believers outnumber them by a ratio of better than two to one. UFO believers outnumber the voters who placed Reagan and Bush and Clinton in office ... That UFOs are real is a solidly mainstream belief (Durant 1993: 22–23).

Now, there are serious questions that can and should be raised about these polls. They typically solicit information by telephone from sample populations of between nine hundred and fourteen hundred people, and the pollsters estimate sampling errors of between three and six percent. We may well criticize the contents of the questions posed, the lack of explication and follow-up, and the pollsters' apparent supposition that what people say in such cases stands in an uncomplicated relationship to what they think. What, indeed, does it mean to say that roughly one-fourth of the adult population of the United States „believes" not merely that „Intelligent beings from other planets" exist, but that some of those extraterrestrials „have been in contact with human beings?" That question relates to a larger one: What does it mean to say that anyone believes anything?

„Belief," to be sure, is a matter of concern to members of the UFO community. Insofar as I am aware, however, it is not a problematical construct for them. Something similar may be said about some anthropologists. While statements about what their informants „believe" are crucial to their ethnographies, and while they may argue about how we are to understand local beliefs, numbers of anthropologists do not raise fundamental questions about the nature of belief. Their failure to do so reminds me of David Hume's remarks about that „operation of mind which forms the belief of any matter of fact, [which] seems hitherto to have been one of the greatest mysteries of philosophy: tho'," he adds, „no one has so much as suspected that there was any difficulty in explaining it" (1896 [1739]: 628). „For my part," Hume goes on to say, „I must own, that I find a considerable difficulty in the case; and that even when I think I understand the subject perfectly, I am at a loss for terms to express my meaning" (1896 [1739]: 628). This chapter attempts to sketch part of what constitutes „a considerable difficulty in the case," and it suggests that we may advance the study of religions by taking that difficulty into account.

Anthropologists have had much to say about beliefs. But most have talked about them as if their elicitation were less problematical than the interpretations to be put on their contents. With certain exceptions, moreover, numbers of anthropologists appear to have neglected much of what philosophers have written about belief. That, I think, is a serious failing. At the very least, philosophers apprise us of certain complexities and subtleties likely to be encountered in talk about belief.

Philosophical Traditions

Three broad observations on the work of philosophers concerning belief are relevant to our interests in cognition and the study of religion. First, and depending on one's classificatory preferences, we can point to two or three major theories of „belief" that have commanded the attention of philosophers in the twentieth century. The first, chronologically speaking, is the mental state theory. To distinguish it from a third theory, should we agree that there are three, we may call it the classical mental state theory. It has its roots in past centuries, and it was the dominant perspective on belief up until the 1930s. The second major theory may be called the disposition theory. It commanded the allegiance of most English-speaking philosophers in mid-century and up until perhaps two or three decades ago. What we may term a third theory is a new variant, or set of variants, on the mental state theory. I prefer to treat it as a separate theory, both because it differs from the classical mental state theory in several significant ways and because doing so carries certain expository advantages. It may be called the cognitivist theory.

Second, philosophers committed to either the classical mental state or disposition theory frequently refer to conventions of language use; supporters of the cognitivist theory often do so, but such references on their part are less critical for their theorizing. Regardless of how they may otherwise differ in their theories of language and meaning, classical mental state and dispositional theorists commonly acknowledge constraints imposed by natural language uses, and they frequently refer to such conventions in their analyses and arguments. They are emulated in this by some anthropologists. Thus, for instance, Rodney Needham (1972) considers how the verb believe is utilized in English, and Jean Pouillon (1982 [1979]) likewise considers the French verb *croire*.

Third, and restricting ourselves to English, the philosophical literature associated with the three aforementioned theories attests strongly to the complex polysemy of believe and the noun belief, both in common uses and in various philosophical formulations. Numbers of philosophers note and analyze discriminations such as those between „believing in" and „believing that," between believing propositions and believing persons, between first person and third person uses of the verb believe, between strong and weak senses of the noun, and so forth. These discriminations, founded on the richness of natural language conventions, conduce to the conclusions that no single, simple model, and no monolithic definition, will suffice for either the noun or the verb.

Perhaps the oldest Western philosophical tradition respecting „belief" is the effort to distinguish it from, and relate it to, „knowledge." Plato associates genuine knowledge, *episteme*, with the Intelligibles, the immutable and eternal Forms or Ideas that can only be apprehended by the mind, while associating „opinion" or *doxa* with the Sensibles, the unstable and transitory particulars of experience that we bring into awareness through the senses. While later Western philosophers take varying positions respecting Plato's ontology of Forms, many follow him to the extent of distinguishing knowledge from belief and privileging knowledge over belief. While such privileging is salient in Plato and Aristotle and among twentieth century positivists, it is also the case for numbers of Christian philosophers who extol certain sorts of belief in the form of „faith" (see below). Nowadays, there is a strong proclivity to reduce knowledge to belief. But not many years ago numbers of epistemologists commonly held that propositional knowledge − „knowing that," as distinguished from „knowing how" − is defined conjunctively „in the strong sense" by three conditions: belief, evidence, and truth (Scheffler 1965: 21).

The „belief condition" holds that knowledge entails belief. One presumably believes what one claims to know. The „evidence condition" maintains that one ought to have evidence for what one claims to know. Numbers of philosophers, however, allow that one can have knowledge in the absence of evidence, albeit knowledge in a „weak" sense. The „truth condition" requires that knowledge be incompatible with error. Thus, for instance, the Trobriand Islanders may believe that a human pregnancy is caused when a spirit enters any of several orifices in a woman's body. And they may believe that while sexual intercourse can be a facilitating factor, it (or, by modern extension, human sperm) is not necessary for a pregnancy to occur. On Malinowski's testimony the Trobrianders can be said to *believe* these things. But according to Western science and a strict reading of the classical Western epistemological tradition, they cannot properly be said to *know* them.

In a paper critical of various claims advanced by Edmund Leach (1967) respecting ideas about procreation reported by ethnographers for certain Australian aborigines and the Trobriand Islanders (and critical as well of Leach's interpretation of the doctrine of the Virgin Birth in mainstream Christianity), Melford Spiro (1968: 244) uses the expression „false knowledge." In doing so, he breaks with the classical epistemological tradition (which deems „false knowledge" to be an oxymoron), but not with current practice, which reduces knowledge to belief. He does so in refuting Leach's assertions that claiming that a native is ignorant is tantamount to saying that s/he is „childish, stupid, superstitious," for, according to Leach (1967: 41), „Ignorance is the opposite of rationality." Spiro retorts:

> ignorance is the opposite not of rationality, but of knowledge; irrationality, not ignorance, is the opposite of rationality. To be ignorant of something, i.e., to have no knowledge (or false knowledge) is not necessarily to be irrational (or, for that matter, childish, stupid, superstitious, etc.) (Spiro 1968: 244).

Now, while the coupling of „knowledge" and „false" is acceptable to many of our contemporaries, it does not accord with the general perspective that we associate with postmodernism. The postmodernist may avoid imposing the judgment „false," on the ground that truth is authorized by a discourse. The coupling of „knowledge" and „false," however, accords well with certain conventions of high modernism. Those conventions elevate reported assertions to the status of theoretical claims and treat them as constituting a distinctive „knowledge," thus according them dignity within a relativist framework. At the same time, however, the modernist steps outside of that framework and identifies the claims as errors because they depart from what s/he deems to be objective facts.

My preference is to speak of „knowledge claims" rather than knowledge. By so doing, we recognize the provisional status of all such claims, our own included. Further, as Barnes and Bloor (1982, 23) suggest, research directed to why people may voice certain beliefs may prove more rewarding than concentrating on the truth or falsehood of what is purportedly believed.

Mainstream Christian Traditions

While Western philosophical traditions generally treat belief as inferior to knowledge, mainstream Christian traditions sometimes accord certain sorts of belief a special dignity and importance. They do so, that is, in the case of beliefs that are claimed to derive from God and to be crucial for the possibilities of human salvation. Such beliefs are to be accepted largely or entirely on faith.

A stereotype (if not, indeed, a caricature) of the aforementioned point of view is given in a phrase of broken Latin widely but mistakenly attributed to Tertullian: „*credo quia absurdum.*" What Tertullian actually wrote is, „And the Son of God died; it is believable because it can't be grasped" („*credible est quia ineptum est*") (*De carne Christi* 5.4). In that regard, Augustine of Hippo exemplifies a popular subtradition, one that suggests the transformative powers of belief: „Understanding," he writes, „is the reward of faith. Therefore seek not to understand so that you may believe, but believe so that you may understand" (*On the Gospel of St. John*, 29,6). And Thomas Aquinas gives voice to another subtradition, one that holds that certain divine truths – the Trinity and the Incarnation are the examples that he gives – are supernatural mysteries that we cannot understand in this world. They are revealed to us by God, he writes, „not, however, as something made clear to be seen, but as something spoken in words to be believed" (*Summa contra Gentiles*, Bk. IV, 1: 5).

Within the Christian tradition there has long been argument over the relative weightings that may be assigned to faith and to reason. Thus, for example, Origen declares of *pístis*, „belief" not deemed to be the product of reasoned conviction, „We accept it as useful for the multitudes, since, partly owing to the necessities of life and partly owing to human weakness, very few people are enthusiastic about rational thought" (quoted by Dodds 1965, 122). In short, differing opinions exist within the Christian camp. On balance, however, Christian theologians celebrate certain sorts of belief, and by so doing they produce something of a subtext to traditional epistemological considerations of belief as it relates to knowledge. This, however, often lends reinforcement to the classical distinction between knowledge and belief. Faith that corresponds to divinely revealed truths, numbers of Christian theologians and philosophers maintain, *is* knowledge, and it can produce within the believer a sense of certitude that transcends the certainties implicated by other forms of knowledge. As a famous line in Handel's *Messiah* (and in an Anglican prayerbook) puts it, „I know that my Redeemer liveth" – not merely, „I believe that my Redeemer liveth."

Belief as a Complex Analytical Phenomenon

Now, in addition to considering belief with reference to knowledge, philosophers also look at belief as a complex phenomenon meriting particularized analysis. As is generally the case with efforts at characterization and explication, they invoke a vocabulary of other terms, some of the more prominent among them being opinion, conviction, entertainment, assent, acceptance, faith, disposition, doubt, and suspicion. A global treatment of belief would consider these and other terms. Here, however, it must suffice to foreground just two of them: assent and disposition.

Assent pertains with special relevance to the (classical) mental state theory or occurrence analysis of belief (Price 1969), and disposition pertains with special relevance to the disposition theory, or dispositional analysis, of belief. Both of these theories admit of variants. The line between them, moreover, is far from sharp. Occurrence analysts acknowledge a dispositional sense of belief, though treating it as derivative or secondary (Price 1969: 244–245). And dispositional analysts concede that when a person is disposed to use a proposition as a premise for making a conscious and explicit inference, that person must assent both to the proposition and to the inference drawn from it; such assentings can be described as mental occurrences (Price 1969, 296).

The (Classical) Mental State Theory

The mental state theory holds that when one believes, something happens. That is, an alteration in mental state occurs. In this view, one entertains a proposition in the mind and believing, construed as a mental act or event, occurs when one mentally assents to that proposition. John Locke maintains that there are degrees of assent, ranging from full confidence or conviction to doubt or distrust (1959 [1689]: Bk. IV, Sect. 2, Ch.15). John Henry Newman (1913 [1870]: 124–137), however, disagrees with Locke. He holds that assent is a matter of yes or no: that while there are degrees of inference, assent is unconditional. Locke's view, I think, is closer to what most of us suppose.

Yet while many may tend to think that there are degrees of assent, they do not always represent beliefs in that way. The polls about extraterrestrial spacecraft and alien encounters that I referred to earlier typically solicit assent to, or dissent from, voiced propositions, with narrow allowance for expressions of „no opinion." In writing up the results of polling, moreover, assent and dissent are often represented as if they were unconditional. But on more extensive interview, self-declared „believers" evince diversity in their statements, ranging from hedged affirmations to strongly affirmed convictions.

The mental state theory generally holds that the believer can introspect his or her beliefs, and by introspection can come to know the degree of belief (Price 1969: 248). According to this view, the believer is privileged over all others — for while others may make shrewd inferences about what the believer believes, only the believer can know what is believed with full warrant. But this is not the case for the disposition theory. According to that account, the believer is not advantaged over others, for, as Price (1969: 249) puts it, „Any knowledge he can have about his own dispositions is as indirect as the knowledge which other people can have about them."

The mental state theory, I think, began as a folk theory about beliefs. Philosophers suggested various refinements, refinements often based on close attention to how people generally speak about beliefs or how they speak in averring what it is that they do or do not believe. It is my impression that the mental state theory, in elemental form, continues to be the prevailing folk theory of belief in our society. It is, moreover, part and parcel of folk belief-desire psychology, a powerful assemblage of existential assumptions and understandings that underwrite a host of operative expectations about human behavior.

The Disposition Theory

According to the disposition theory, when we say that someone believes something, we are claiming that that person has a tendency or readiness to act, feel, or think in a certain way under appropriate circumstances. This may include verbally and publicly affirming a proposition on occasion. Disposition analysts agree with (classical) mental state theorists that entertaining a proposition is an occurrence. Further, acquiring (or loosing) beliefs, on this view, are occurrences, and beliefs are likely to manifest themselves in occurrences, but those occurrences are not acts of believing, and belief is not an occurrence (Price 1969: 20).

The argument between classical mental state theorists and disposition theorists over the nature of belief did not, insofar as I am aware, become a widely diffused issue in anthropology. Most of the ethnographies that I have read incorporate statements about what the natives believe. Such statements for the most part seem to accord with the classical mental state theory, i.e., they accord with the regnant folk theory of belief widespread in our society. Further, there are relatively few explicit definitions of belief given in the anthropological literature. But up until the last decade or two, those few that were obviously influenced by the philosophical literature tended to express a dispositional viewpoint, while others suggested the folk theory. Thus, for example, Robert Hahn defines beliefs as „general propositions about the world (consciously) held to be true," and he goes on to say that „*Holding a belief* is here explicated as exhibiting a disposition to behavior symbolic of that belief" (1973: 208). In contrast, Ward Goodenough defines beliefs simply as „propositions that people accept as true ..."(1963: 155).

It is my impression that anthropologists for the most part did not enter into the arguments among philosophers respecting beliefs. While treating beliefs as mental states, anthropologists also sometimes gave them a dispositional sense, without apparent awareness of contested issues in philosophy. Disposition is a powerful concept, and it is made use of in personality theory and in other strands of theorizing that are of interest to anthropologists, particularly by anthropologists who specialize in psychological anthropology.

The disposition theory, endorsed in one form or another by such famous philosophers as Ludwig Wittgenstein and Gilbert Ryle, was itself part of a larger intellectual perspective that dominated Anglo-American psychology and philosophy in the mid-twentieth century. Most commonly referred to as „behaviorism" in psychology, that perspective was unsympathetic to the idea of mental states and to the Cartesian dualism of mind and body. Behaviorism as a coherent intellectual program in psychology, however, could not withstand its critics, one of the most powerful of whom was Noam Chomsky, whose famous review (1959) of B. F. Skinner's *Verbal Behavior* called attention to some of the conceptual weaknesses of behaviorism. Yet while behaviorism as a persuasive research agenda within psychology was damaged, philosophical objections to the idea that mental states are real (as distinct from being fictional posits) persisted. They did so not under the tattered banners of

„behaviorism," but under the rubrics of „eliminative materialism" or „eliminativism."

Eliminativism, in its strongest form, is the claim that beliefs, desires, and various other mental states do not exist except as fictional posits deriving ultimately from the mistaken assumptions of folk psychology (Churchland 1981; Stich 1996: 3–4). Those who do battle with eliminativists are sometimes called realists, for they affirm, to one extent or another, the reality of mental states.

The Cognitivist Theory

In a work published in 1969, H. H. Price (1969: 243) writes that the occurrence analysis of belief, the classical mental state theory, „is now almost universally rejected, at any rate in the English-speaking philosophical world." Those lines were written in the declining but still potent years of behaviorism. Today, however, we witness the development of new theories that make unashamed, positive use of the expression „mental state." But rather than term these theories „New Mental State Theories," the designation „Cognitivist" seems more appropriate, given the importance of the cognitive sciences both as locus and as framework for their development. Cognitivism embraces a number of alternative and competing views, but for expository purposes it is useful (if a bit risky) to generalize to some extent.

The (generalized) cognitivist theory differs from the classical mental state theory in a number of ways. It is, to begin, thoroughly physicalist or materialist in orientation. While the classical mental state theory tolerated or made room for what Gilbert Ryle called a „ghost in the machine" – the notion that a non-physical object, the mind, could act upon and move a physical object, the body – the cognitivist theory disallows such a possibility. When cognitivists talk about „the mind," they are talking about many of the functional aspects of a physical object, the brain, and they may sometimes use such conventions as „mind-brain" or „mind/brain" to drive home the point.

Second, arguments between those who affirm the reality of mental states (the realists) and those who deny such reality (the eliminativists) may sometimes turn on the expectations or bets of the latter that neuroscience eventually will liberate us from the last vestiges of folk psychology, which supposes beliefs to be mental states. Or so, for example, Daniel Dennett suggests of Paul Churchland, whom he credits with appreciating the predictive powers of „the intentional stance" (a strategy for interpreting the behavior of an entity by treating it as if it were a rational agent that is guided in choices by beliefs and desires). Yet while Churchland appreciates the intentional stance's utility, he also holds that it will eventually end up on the trash heap of discarded constructs and theories. Why? Because, Dennett (1998: 119) writes, Churchland „anticipates that neuroscience will eventually – perhaps even soon – discover a pattern that is so clearly superior to the noisy pattern of folk psychology that everyone will readily abandon" folk psychology in favor of neuroscience „except, perhaps, in the rough-and-tumble of daily life."

Third, the cognitivists do not attach the same importance to ordinary language conventions for talking about belief as did the classical mental state theorists. This is not to say that they ignore such conventions. Given their interest in folk theory, total disinterest would hardly be likely. But they do not allow ordinary language conventions to constrain their theorizing to the same degree as did the classical theorists.

Forth, the cognitivists sometimes evince a phylogenetic interest and sensitivity that were not much in evidence among the classical theorists. The latter generally restricted their interests in belief to the human. Some of the former, however, raise questions about whether or not animals can be said to believe – and some even play with the notion that belief in some sense may be attributed to non-living things (Dennett, for example, is fond of the thermostat).

As Dennett (1998: 324) points out, some (but not all) cognitivists ascribe „a special, non-ordinary sense" to belief, using „belief" as „the *generic*, least-marked term for a *cognitive* state." By doing so, indeed, „whatever information guides an agent's actions is counted under the rubric of belief," at least in applications of the term in English (1998: 324). Dennett, in adopting a realist position, rightly recognizes different degrees of realism. He opines, moreover, that „a mild and intermediate sort of realism is a positively attractive position" (1998: 97), and in accordance with his preference for the mild and intermediate, he claims that „beliefs are best considered to be abstract objects rather like centers of gravity" (1998: 97). He remarks, further, that „the maximal leniency" of his position „is notoriously illustrated by my avowal that even lowly thermostats have belief" (1998: 327). But not all philosophers accept that position. Donald Davidson (1975), for instance, prefers to restrict belief to language-using animals that have – and that distinguish between – concepts of truth and falseness. In any case, the generalized cognitivist theory certainly allows for what the folk (and most anthropologists) generally mean by belief. That on the theorizing of some philosophers it may also allow for a good deal more ought to stimulate cerebration among cultural anthropologists, even though we ordinarily stop well short of doing research among dogs and cats, let alone thermostats.

Fifth, unlike classical mental state theorists, but rather much like disposition theorists, cognitivists do not privilege the believer as having the best knowledge of what s/he believes. Cognitivists sometimes explicitly allow that there can be beliefs of which the „believer" is unaware. Such, of course, is always the case for thermostats and other non-living entities the behaviors of which, according to some philosophers, can be rendered intelligible (patterned) through invocations of a widened idea of belief. But it may sometimes be the case among human beings as well.

Sixth, and unlike both classical mental state theorists and disposition theorists, cognitivists make significant use of the vocabulary that we ordinarily use for talking about computers. Some of that language, to be sure, is taken metaphorically. But a good deal of it (e. g., „computation," „processing," „default assignment") is applied non-metaphorically. Indeed, to verge briefly on the technical, the „computational model" is important in the theorizing of many cognitivists. In drawing parallels between the operations of the brain and the operations of a computer, however, cognitive theory generally employs a far more sophisticated understanding and appreciation of computers than do many ordinary computer users. A computer, in cognitivist applications, is a physical instance of a formal system (Jones n.d.: 15). A formal system consists of the stipulation of elements and the stipulation of a set of rules for operating on those elements. Viewing the operations of the brain as the expressions of formal systems is both an analytical and a theoretical ploy for many cognitivists. It should be noted, however, that the „classical" cognitivist view of the mind-brain as a general device and/or a set of „modules" for computation, for the manipulation of symbols in accordance with a set of rules (the so-called „Rules and Representations" account of cognition), has come under increasing criticism. That is especially so with respect to the idea that cognitive processes can be adequately and revealingly simulated by computer programs of the sorts presently available. In addition to a number of specific complaints, there is the overall charge that, as Horgan and Tienson (1996: x) put it, „The cognitive processes of natural cognizers are too rich to be captured by programmable rules." That conviction, in tandem with certain other considerations, has stimulated the rise of what are variously viewed as alternative approaches or varietal extensions and supplements. Those include, for instance, connectionism, which Steven Pinker (1997: 114) describes as a variety of the computational theory. In any case, the newer developments, insofar as I can judge, do not compel us to alter radically our uses of the term „belief," and I shall say no more about them here.

Now, while I have been generalizing (perhaps overgeneralizing) above, I do not want to leave the impression that there is a well-formed cognitivist theory the details of which command the allegiance of most cognitivists. Cognitivism embraces an expanding universe of emerging theories. While they are well beyond the primordial chaos that we associate with the Biblical *tohu v'vohu*, they are still in development. Further, their protagonist-developers differ strongly among themselves on numbers of points, some of them quite technical. But if cognitive realists were to search for a Manifesto to express the core of the consensus that they have thus far reached, they may do well to adopt these words of John Searle:

> On my view, mental phenomena are biologically based: they are both caused by the operations of the brain and realized in the structure of the brain. On this view, consciousness and Intentionality are as much a part of human biology as digestion or the circulation of the blood. It is an *objective* fact about the world that it contains certain systems, viz., brains, with *subjective* mental states, and it is a *physical* fact about such systems that they have *mental* features. The correct solution to the „mind-body problem" lies not in denying the reality of mental phenomena, but in properly appreciating their biological nature (Searle 1983, ix).

Belief and The Ethnographer

Immersion in the ethnographic field tends to implicate a number of problems respecting beliefs. One of the most salient, of course, is the problem of translation. As W. G. Runciman (1969, 150) succinctly puts it, „Although beliefs of any sort may be legitimately *explained* in categories foreign to the subjects themselves, they can only be *identified* in the subjects' own terms." But even where the ethnographer has mastered the local language and achieved profound understandings, there are still likely to be general problems in effecting translation – problems having to do, for instance, with mapping correspondences (glosses) across languages, preserving (if we deem it a desideratum) truth values, and so forth.

Problems of translation are especially difficult when it comes to ideas that we associate with religion. Suffice it here to mention briefly two of the several reasons. First, as Pascal Boyer (1994) notes, religious ideas are likely to incorporate some counter-intuitive elements, and counter-intuitivity can exacerbate the difficulties of translating. How does one convey non-intuitive formulations encountered in the ethnographic field to readers – academics, say – whose own non-intuitive adventuring may take a different direction? Second, important terms may be used in a variety of contexts and pertain simultaneously to different domains of interest, and informants may have difficulty in explicating them. Learning and then conveying their complexities and nuances is not easy.

Various belief assertions recorded in the ethnographic literature – statements, for example, that some people are parrots, that twins are birds, and that the sun is a white cockatoo – pose something of a challenge for many anthropologists. What are we to make of those statements and many more like them? In attempting to answer that question, however, some anthropologists devote more ingenuity to explaining away the troublesome assertions than to explaining them. In so doing, they engage in a distinctly anthropological version of „saving the appearances"– they attempt to save the natives, to save them, that is, from charges that they are childlike, irrational, or worse. Such efforts, I suspect, are often motivated in part by ideological commitments.

In any case, efforts to save the appearances, native division, are diverse. Virtually all are clever, and they are often plausible to some extent. Thus, for instance, it is sometimes suggested that the troublesome beliefs are not really existential claims, that they are not general statements about the world, so much as they are emotional or evocative declarations. That suggestion can command our partial endorsement in that beliefs often function in multiple ways; but once we acknowledge multiple functions we must also allow for their intellectual contents and potential consequences. Other ploys are to argue that various belief statements are not really full propositions in the logician's sense (Sperber 1982), or that they are deployed in accordance with the canons of some non-Aristotelian logic, such as Hans Reichenbach's adaptation of Jan Lukasiewicz's tri-valued logic (Cooper 1975), or something of the sort. But the best known and most widely used strategy is subsumed under the rubric „symbolism" (Skorupski 1976).

The symbolist tends to treat religious statements that may otherwise prove troublesome as symbolic affirmations about social relations and social structure. While generally admitting that such statements have „literal" meanings – a sometimes facile admission that G. E. R. Lloyd (1990) warns us against – symbolists tend to gloss over or ignore their own admissions in favor of focusing on another level of meaning: what the utterances purportedly say, in coded form, about social life. This level of meaning, symbolists suggest, is the real significance of many religious beliefs. Thus, for instance, according to Edmund Leach (1967), the reported Trobriand beliefs to which I referred earlier are not to be understood as components of an erroneous or defective theory of human procreation, as Spiro supposes. Rather, they are cultural dogmas that make sociological sense, for they are symbolic affirmations and justifications of certain realities in Trobriand social life. Their significance is not bio-theoretical but sociological.

One potential problem with such an attempt to save the appearances is put in this way by John Skorupski (1976: 13): „a metaphorically or symbolically expressed thought is a thought expressed in a form which *does* have a literal meaning ... and ... the literal meaning of the words must be grasped if one is to 'decode' the meaning which *is* to be understood." The „meaning which is to be understood," of course, is the meaning that the anthropologist is to understand. Lloyd (1990), a classicist who traces the literal/metaphorical distinction to the polemical interests and conventions of the ancient Greeks, warns that not all peoples may make a similar distinction, and that we need to find out whether or not they do rather than facilely impose a literal/metaphorical distinction on them. If in fact some people do not recognize such a distinction, what is it that they do understand when they make assertions that we interpret to be belief declarations?

If the reported assertions are empty clichés, then their presumptive significance must be evocative, emotional, and/or nostalgic. But if they do have some intellectual meaning for those who affirm them, it is something of a stretch to claim that the believers themselves deem them coded claims about social reality. The believers may conceivably *use* the reported beliefs as premises for drawing inferences about social structure, but on occurrence, dispositional, and at least some cognitivist accounts of belief, that would mean that the reported beliefs have an intellectual value in keeping with what they affirm existentially.

As difficult as it may be to sustain the symbolist perspective in the Trobriand Islands, it is even harder to make a cogent case for it among my friends in the UFO community. To the extent that members of that community affirm strong convictions – and numbers of them do – the asserted beliefs, I have been given to understand, are not intended by those who assert them to be „symbolic" of anything. Rather, they are proclaimed to be statements of cold, hard fact, or irresistibly logical conclusions, or sober and plausible inferences. And if you or I do not openly acknowledge them as such, it is because we are ignorant, or dupes, or agents of an obstinate conspiracy orchestrated by the federal government and the scientific and military establishments (Saler, Ziegler, and Moore 1997).

In research now in progress, I am attempting to find out why numbers of persons who do not claim to have been abducted by aliens profess belief in alien abductions. Those who profess belief most commonly supply two reasons for their profession: (1) the abductees (or „experiencers") impress them as being sincere in their claims, whether the claims be voiced under hypnosis or furnished seemingly from conscious memory; and (2) experiencers give very similar accounts of their experiences, and in light of geographic and other diversities, collusion in so large a group of persons is implausible.

I concede that the apparent sincerity of experiencers can sometimes be striking. But the second reason, I think, is not as strong a reason as those who profess it often appear to suppose. First, the accounts given by experiencers are not all that similar – there are numbers of significant differences. Second, those who profess belief in the abductees' accounts strike me as often underestimating the extent to which the media (TV especially) have cultivated and widely diffused both ideas about alien abductions and a vocabulary for talking about them. Abductees and others draw on those ideas and vocabulary. And third, some theoretical considerations and claims recently advanced by Pascal Boyer can contribute to our understandings of how the experiencers and those who profess to believe them (as well as numbers of media writers, producers, editors, and others) draw upon similar intuitive ontologies, how they are constrained as to what sorts of counter-intuitive claims they might accept or proffer, and why, indeed, the experiencers often impress others as sincere.

Pascal Boyer

In accounts rendered by people who claim to have been abducted by aliens, the aliens are usually described partly in anthropomorphic terms. At the same time, however, they are often credited with doing certain things that human beings do not „naturally" do. They are reported, for instance, to pass through locked doors or other solid impediments. Not only that, but the people whom they abduct, the abductees or experiencers, are made to pass through closed windows, walls, the roofs of cars, and other solid substances. Passage is not „supernatural" but is made possible by an alien science and technology that are superior to those of earth. Such alien technology, moreover, is even understandable to some extent, though not in sufficient detail as to be patentable. The „transporter" in *Star Trek,* first and second generations, is something of a model that can guide our understanding.

This matter of passing through solid matter is very similar to one of Pascal Boyer's examples of counter-intuitive claims. Boyer says nothing of aliens and experiencers, basing his examples instead on more traditional religious fare: Gods, spirits, and ghosts.

Boyer's 1994 book, *The Naturalness of Religious Ideas,* is concerned both with explaining the transmission of religious ideas from generation to generation and with accounting for the recurrence in different human minds of similar religious assumptions, such assumptions being taken as examples of mental representations. Focusing for the moment on transmission, Boyer argues that in the competition among ideas for a place, so to speak, in the human mind, those ideas that strike an optimal cognitive balance between the intuitive and the counter-intuitive are most likely to be given attention, to be remembered, and to be passed on to succeeding generations. Gods, spirits, and ghosts, for instance, are often depicted as anthropomorphic in various ways, and their conformance to our expectations respecting human capacities, purposes, and behavior renders them plausible. But it is the counter-intuitive capacities and qualities assigned to them – their invisibility, their ability to pass through material barriers, and so forth – that render them memorable. People, moreover, are likely to know more about religious beings than is transmitted through socialization and enculturation. Indeed, the richness and saliency of religious ideas are likely to be underdetermined by culture. That is largely because, Boyer argues, people make inferences on fragmented material, basing their enrichments of religious ideas on prior ontological assumptions. Individuals tend in many cases to rework ideas rather than simply accept them.

All of this, I think, is very much the case for abductees and for those non-experiencers who profess to believe them. Boyer's insights and arguments help us to account both for similarities in the contents of avowed convictions and narratives and for some of the differences. Abduction stories for many persons in our society, believers and disbelievers alike, are simultaneously intelligible, novel, and familiar. Yet while an appreciation of commonalities in attending to the intuitive and to the counter-intuitive helps us in beginning to understand why persons who positively cathect such stories might impress others as sincere (intelligibility being something of a condition for judgments of sincerity), we are still a long way from cogent and non-superficial explanations of why some accept abduction accounts and others reject them. Heterogeneity both in belief and in cathexis of belief remains an issue that deserves study.

I turn now to what Boyer (1994: 287) describes as „the central question" of his book, „How can we account for the recurrence, in very different cultural environments, of particular aspects of religious ideas?" Such recurrences, he makes it clear, are not recurrences of identities. Beyond our minimal recognition that in many human groups there are ideas „concerning non-observable, extra-human agencies and processes[,] ... the similarities between religious ideas are a matter of family resemblance rather than universal features" (1994: 5).

Now, in attempting to answer his „central question" about the recurrence in different cultural environments of similar religious representations, Boyer proposes a number of hypotheses that are far too complex to summarize here. He writes, for instance, about constraints on the acquisition of religious ideas, constraints that are themselves constrained by domain specificity („There is no reason to think that all types of mental representations are amenable to the same constraints." 1994: 287). And he posits certain widely encountered psychological conditions and considerations, such as an almost universal preference for essentialism, a wide-spread use of abductive thinking in the enrichment of religious representations, the common attribution of belief-desire psychology to posited sentient beings, and so on. In proposing a complex solution to the question posed, moreover, Boyer criticizes a number of positions that have been espoused by many anthropologists. These include what he deems to be an exaggerated notion of the powers and inclusiveness of culture (a notion entertained by anthropologists,

Boyer maintains, at the expense of developing a rich psychology). Two others are of particular interest to us here, given the general topic of this essay. One is termed „theologism;" the other pivots on a distinction that Boyer draws between the „epistemic" and the „cognitive."

Theologism, Boyer writes, combines two mistakes:

> One is to take the connections between religious assumptions for granted, as a self-evident or necessary aspect of religious representations. The other is to think that they can be best described by postulating some abstract intellectual entities („symbol systems," „webs of meaning," „cultural theories," etc.) that supposedly underpin the connections. Theologism, in its various guises, begs the question of systematicity by positing that religious representations *necessarily* constitute shared, integrated, consistent sets of assumptions, often in the face of less than perfect empirical confirmation (Boyer 1994: 229).

Boyer's point, one that various other writers also make, is well taken. It is worth cautioning, however, that in addition to guarding against the facile assumption that religious representations constitute well-integrated systems, we ought also to guard against the facile supposition that they do not. In either case, theoretical commitments to necessity could productively be bracketed in favor of detailed investigations.

Boyer's characterization of the „epistemic" approach to religious ideas, in contrast to the „cognitive," appears to overlap to an extent with what he says about the theologic fallacy. His „cognitive" approach is dedicated to describing the processes that can be said to lead people to entertain the thoughts or ideas that they actually do entertain. The epistemic approach, in contrast, views ideas as attempts to say something about the world (1994: 50), and it encourages the analyst to describe what people may intellectually support if they tried to make sense out of what they actually do and say (1994: 51). This, he warns, can lead to mistakes, as when certain properties that may be attributed to „the mental representations actually entertained" are, instead, „properties of their idealized (epistemic) description" (1994: 236). The investigator, Boyer correctly notes, does not actually observe idea-systems or worldviews. Rather, the investigator observes people asserting various statements (1994: 114–115).

Now, if, by „idealized (epistemic) description," Boyer means description that cannot be adequately supported by the data in hand, then he is right to adopt a pejorative stance regarding the epistemic. I think, however, that Boyer taints the epistemic approach with too broad a brush in his book. First, beliefs, as Boyer himself recognizes, do not occur in vacuums. They are surrounded by other beliefs, and people typically render beliefs in subsets interactive. This is an understanding that is widely incorporated into cognitivist theory. Stephen Stich, for example, who advocates that we redirect attention away from a focus on the semantic contents of beliefs to a concentration on their syntactic relations, writes of „surrounding beliefs, the doxastic neighborhood, in which a belief is embedded" (1983: 93). Indeed, some cognitivists who view beliefs as mental states maintain that they are individuated by their interactions with other mental states.

Second, while Boyer is correct in pointing out that in the field we directly encounter people making assertions rather than belief systems, informants (sometimes without much prompting) often do explicitly connect various of their belief assertions. Further, people do not just „have" beliefs. They frequently *use* or deploy them in social interactions, in keeping with desires and interests, and there is meaning in that use.

Boyer's cognitive approach is important and useful. It is such not only with respect to understanding the transmission and recurrence of religious representations, but also with respect to pointing out various sorts of self-constructed traps that we may fall into in pursuit of „the native's point of view." But if we take – as I think that we should – Boyer's caveats seriously, an epistemic approach may be improved and thus better warranted.

Anthropologists have long desired to achieve what some call „emic models." They express, however, divergent opinions about what such models may actually be. Many suppose that an emic model is an „insider's model," or a model of certain aspects of „what goes on in the native's head." As I understand it, in contrast, an emic model is always an analyst's model. The analyst observes people saying and in other ways doing things. People typically make various distinctions and discriminations in doing what they do (saying, it should be remembered, is a form of doing). An emic model is the analyst's effort to make sense of those distinctions and discriminations. If the model can accurately predict them back, then it has structural reality; but structural reality may not constitute psychological reality, especially if more than one model can predict back with equal power (Wallace and Atkins 1960). In any case, an „emic" model, as I view it, is an effort to understand the making of presumptively orderly discriminations among cultural events, just as a „phonemic" model is an effort to understand the making of presumptively orderly discriminations among phonic events. In neither case should we suppose that informants are consciously aware of the details. In my opinion, moreover, analysts interested in constructing emic models should pay close attention to considerations of scale. While emic models may be defensible and useful for subsets of beliefs, beliefs in doxastic neighborhoods, I very much doubt that they are warrantable in cases of alleged overarching or large scale „belief systems."

The epistemic approach can be understood as an effort to achieve emic models (emic models in the sense endorsed here). Although I take seriously Boyer's strictures concerning the epistemic approach, including his caveats about conflating the cognitive and the epistemic, I nevertheless think that the cognitive and the epistemic can be rendered complementary where scale is circumscribed and modest. In my opinion, moreover, the line between them is not quite as sharp or as stable as some of Boyer's discussion may lead us to suppose. Analysts working within the classical mental state and disposition theories, as well as more than a few cognitivists, deem belief propositions to be potential premises from which further belief propositions could be inferred. It is here, I think, that the epistemic and the cognitive converge. Both Boyer and epistemologists recognize that belief does not beget belief. Procreation, so to speak, requires psychological intervention. And the uses to which beliefs may be put can have something to do with procreation – or, at any-rate, with desire and with birth-control.

Epilog

Some years ago I wrote that belief is „a can of worms that many anthropologists do not seem to recognize as a can of worms" (Saler 1993: 92). That one-liner now strikes me as being as harsh as it is colloquial, and I welcome the opportunity to soften it a bit. We can, I think, believe of beliefs some of what we have ample warrant to believe of worms: that they have multiple functions, that it is specious to suppose them to have simple natures, and that they are part and parcel of life as we know it.

Finding Wayú Religion[2]

Abstract: This essay begins by addressing the question, „Do beliefs constitute systems?" The answer, „sometimes, but not always," is explored with reference to two anthropological classics, E. E. Evans-Pritchard's Witchcraft, Oracles, and Magic among the Azande and Godfrey Lienhardt's Divinity and Experience: The Religion of the Dinka. It then proceeds to consider the case of the Wayú or Guajiro Indians of northern Colombia and Venezuela, among whom the author did fieldwork. Various missionaries, anthropologists, and others describe Wayú religion as pivoting on belief in named, godlike characters described in Wayú myths. The myths include a creator (who, in different narratives, creates by transforming different substances into human beings). But no one worships, propitiates, sacrifices to, or prays to the creator or to any of the other godlike figures in the myths. In what sense, if any, are these personages religious objects? The author argues that they are not religious figures so much as they are tropes, and that Wayú religion is to be found elsewhere (in the mortuary and shamanic complexes), and that it falls well short of Whitehouse's criteria for doctrinal integration. One conclusion suggested in the essay is this: if Westerners (scholars included) entertain narrow, ethnocentric ideas about the nature of religion, they have an enhanced likelihood of misunderstanding religions among people such as the Wayú.

Belief „Systems"

Do beliefs constitute systems? It seems safe to say „sometimes." But I think that it would be a mistake to say „always." In any case, it would be useful to specify the extent of systematization that one has in mind. Thus, for example, beliefs that mutually pertain to some relatively circumscribed ideational domain may relate systematically to one another in what Stephen Stich (1983: 93) calls a „doxastic neighborhood," that is, a „neighborhood" of „surrounding beliefs … in which a belief is embedded." But what of larger scale phenomena, where, say, our interest devolves on beliefs in several different such „neighborhoods?" Do they usually or characteristically align into some overarching system?

---

2   „Finding Wayú Religion." *Historical Reflections/Réflexions Historiques* 31 (2): 255–270, 2005.

It is my impression that many anthropologists who write about religious or magical beliefs facilely suppose that such beliefs typically constitute „belief systems." To assume systematicity, however, is to beg the question of systematicity (Boyer 1994: 229). Further, even where an ethnographer is alive to the dangers of question begging, and is generally sensitive to complexities and subtleties that may be involved in writing about systematicity, s/he may deal with the matter in ways that could well strike some readers as equivocal or otherwise perplexing. E. E. Evans-Pritchard's 1937 classic, *Witchcraft, Oracles, and Magic Among the Azande* (abridged 1976), provides an example.

Among the Azande, Evans-Pritchard tells us, „Witchcraft, oracles, and magic form an intellectually coherent system" (1976: 201). He writes, indeed, that

> I hope that I have persuaded the reader of one thing, namely, *the intellectual consistency of Zande notions.* They only appear inconsistent when ranged like lifeless museum objects. When we see how an individual uses them we may say that they are mystical but we cannot say that his use of them is illogical or even that it is uncritical ... Once the idiom is learnt the rest is easy, for in Zandeland one mystical idea follows on another as reasonably as one common-sense idea follows on another in our own society. (1976: 222, emphasis added)

Evans-Pritchard affirms not only that Zande „mystical notions are eminently coherent" (1976: 150), but that the Azande often explain away existential or experiential failures to conform to them by invoking „secondary elaborations of belief" or rationalizations. Further, the Azande

> reason excellently in the idiom of their beliefs, but they cannot reason outside, or against, their beliefs because they have no other idiom in which to express their thoughts. (1976: 159)

The above and similar assertions suggest a case for what Evans-Pritchard himself terms „the intellectual consistency of Zande notions." But Evans-Pritchard makes other statements that appear to raise problems for untroubled or unmodified acceptance of a case for consistency.

Thus, for instance, Evans-Pritchard advises us that insofar as the Azande are concerned,

> each situation demands the particular pattern of thought appropriate to it. Hence an individual in one situation will employ a notion he excludes in a different situation. The many beliefs I have recorded are so many tools of thought, and he selects the ones that are chiefly to his advantage. (1976: 162–163)

Armed with that understanding, we are better able to assimilate Evans-Pritchard's accounts of how he understands the Zande situation and of how he has presented it to the reading public:

> Throughout I have emphasized the coherency of Zande beliefs when they are considered together and are interpreted in terms of situations and social relationships. I have tried to show also the plasticity of beliefs as functions of situations. They are not indivisible ideational structures but are loose associations of notions. When a writer brings them together in a book and presents them as *a conceptual system* their insufficiencies and contradictions are at once apparent. *In real life they do not function as a whole but in bits.* A man in one situation utilizes what in the beliefs are convenient to him and pays no attention to other elements which he might use in different situations. Hence a single event may evoke a number of different and contradictory beliefs among different persons. (Evans-Pritchard 1976: 221, emphases added)

From Evans-Pritchard's own account, it seems reasonable to come to this conclusion: Zande beliefs do not actually constitute an overarching, well integrated, and stable intellectual system, despite some statements in Evans-Pritchard's book that may seem to suggest otherwise. At best, the many Zande beliefs described by Evans-Pritchard constitute a more or less pragmatically successful aggregate of ideas. Those ideas pertain, respectively, to different domains. The Azande, as Evans-Pritchard presents them, have little interest in producing and defending overarching theories. They are concerned, rather, with immediate situations and with solutions deemed appropriate to them, and they are not given to abstracting beliefs from the social contexts in which they are relevant. The „coherence" of which Evans-Pritchard writes is largely a pragmatic coherence. And the „consistency" he affirms is constrained by Zande disinclinations to transcend contexts and a complementary absorption in the pressing social, emotional, and intellectual specifics of real-life situations.

What we have in the Zande case appears to be a complementarity of beliefs *within* „doxastic neighborhoods" and the lack of a *doctrinal* (but not necessarily a *pragmatic*) systematicity *between* „doxastic neighborhoods." That is something that we can discern even more clearly among the Dinka as they are described for us in Godfrey Lienhardt's classic work, *Divinity and Experience: The Religion of the Dinka* (1961).

„Dinka religion," Lienhardt tells us, „is a relationship between men and ultrahuman Powers encountered by men" (1961: 32). But that religion-constituting relationship, he tells us, „is rather phenomenological than theological, an interpretation of signs of ultrahuman activity rather than a doctrine of the intrinsic nature of the Powers behind those signs" (1961: 32). Lienhardt emphasizes the lack of overarching doctrine and orthodoxy:

> Statements about the divinities, as represented in hymns, are imaginative and creative, not dogmatic or doctrinal. There is no formal orthodoxy, and any imaginative association which does not contradict the general configuration of associations for particular divinities in the mind of the Dinka can be accepted as an insight into the nature of Divinity. (1961: 91)

Lienhardt, indeed, affirms that it would be misleading „to attempt to produce an account, however lucid and ingenious, of a kind of Dinka 'creed' and pantheon ..." (1961: 96).

Religion for the Dinka, as Lienhardt describes it, is to a great extent experiential. Indeed, in that regard he enters an arresting claim, one that may strike some readers as remarkable though not, perhaps, self-evidently persuasive:

> The Dinka have no conception which at all closely corresponds to our popular modern conception of the 'mind', as mediating and, as it were, storing up the experiences of the self. There is for them no such interior entity to appear, on reflection, to stand between the experiencing self at any given moment and what is or has been an exterior influence upon the self. So it seems that what we should call in some cases the 'memories' of experiences, and regard therefore as in some way intrinsic and interior to the remembering person and modified in their effect upon him by that interiority, appear to the Dinka as exteriorly acting upon him, as were the sources from which they derived. Hence it would be impossible to suggest to Dinka that a powerful dream was 'only' a dream ... They do not make the kind of distinction between the psyche and the world which would make such interpretations significant for them. (1961: 149)

It is not, Lienhardt maintains, „a simple matter to divide the Dinka believer, for analytic purposes, from what he believes in, and to describe the latter then in isolation from him as the 'object' of his belief" (1961: 155). Furthermore, even when we piece together the various assertions that Dinka make about the Powers, Lienhardt warns us, we should not expect those assertions „to have the connectedness and logical consistency of reflective thought." (1961: 156).

Now, while some readers may be inclined to question or contest some of the statements given above (my own included), I suspect that most will nevertheless agree that neither Zande beliefs nor Dinka beliefs, as we glimpse them in the accounts quoted, represent doctrinal codifications. Such codifications are crucial to Whitehouse's (2000: 1) characterization of a „doctrinal mode" of religious organization. While it is moot as to how far we may go in regarding Evans-Pritchard's monograph as a description of Zande „religion," there is no comparable difficulty in identifying Lienhardt's treatment of Dinka beliefs and practices. In any case, both accounts give us reasons to be wary of facile presumptions about the intellectual or doctrinal systematicity of belief.

Religion and The Anthropology of Religion

Many 19th and 20th century Western students of religion have emphasized „belief systems" as important for conceptualizing and identifying religion, with various allowances made for the significance of ritual. Numbers of scholars, moreover, have looked for central myths as revelatory (with appropriate interpretation) of the presumptive organizing doctrines of religions. That they should have done so is no mystery. Nor does it suggest a distinctive scholarly psychology. Rather, many Western scholars of religion did what people everywhere tend to do: to use the familiar as a template or set of established expectations, and to search newly encountered situations or phenomena for analogies to what is familiar.

Religion is a contemporary Western folk category that scholars appropriate and attempt to refine. It is not a traditional folk category in numbers of non-Western societies. Nor was it a folk category in Western classical antiquity, even though the Romans popularly employed the term religio (Benveniste 1969; Fowler 1908; Saler 1987; 2000 [1993]: 64–68; Smith 1962). Western scholars tend to find religion in non-Western societies and in classical antiquity by creatively discerning analogies to phenomena that they elsewhere associate with the clearest or best examples of what they mean by religion. Those best-example phenomena typically include central or organizing narratives. Further, the adjudged clearest or best exemplars of what numbers of Western scholars mean by religion – that is, the Western monotheisms – typically emphasize what Whitehouse calls the „doctrinal" mode or principle of religious organization. This both expresses and reinforces the disposition of numbers of scholars to accord a certain primacy to belief and meaning in the study of religions. Some observers call this a „Protestant bias," or, as Talal Asad (1983) would have it, a „Christian" bias.

The disposition of which I speak also finds expression in proffered monothetic definitions of religion that focus on beliefs in spiritual beings, supernatural agencies, the numinous, the sacred, and so forth. I argue elsewhere (Saler 2000a [1993]) that our scholarly model of religion ought to transcend such definitions. Our scholarly model, I hold, should be constructed of a pool of elements that we deem *typical* of religion without any one of them, or any specific conjunction of them, being necessary to establish the existence of a religion. Religion, in my view, is not some specific this or that. It is best thought of as a congeries of many different things. Historically, however, many Western scholars have been inclined to emphasize what they have variously supposed to be the essence of religion.

One of the important services that anthropology can perform for religious studies, I think, is the documentation of examples of religiosity that do not place comparable emphasis on belief and its systematization. If religions such as Judaism, Christianity, and Islam constitute what many Western scholars deem the clearest or best examples of religion – the central or „most prototypical" exemplars –, then many non-Western religions constitute more peripheral examples of the category (Saler 2000a [1993]). While they differentially exhibit some of the typicality features (Jackendoff 1983: 139) that we associate with our clearest or best cases, numbers of them do not give prominent place to overarching systematizations of belief.

Whitehouse's analytical distinction between „imagistic" and „doctrinal" principles of organization could have been developed in the library. I doubt, however, that his treatment of the distinction would have been as inclusive, as cogent, and as elegant as it is had he not personally engaged in ethnographic fieldwork. Day to day experience of local life-ways over some appreciable period of time not only may wean one away from stereotypes, but it can effectively promote the apprehension and appreciation of alternatives to what was once the accepted familiar. Such possibilities, however, must be exploited by appropriate field methods and cultivated analytical sensitivities if they are to be realized.

In the remainder of this paper, I deal with the history of efforts to find and describe the religion of an Amerindian population in lowland South America. The Amerindians about whom I write, the Wayú or Guajiro of northern Colombia and Venezuela, have a substantial myth corpus, and numbers of those myths have been recorded. Further, the myths often involve godlike personages. Various scholars use some of those myths to lay out what they suppose to be the central beliefs or doctrines of Wayú religion. I argue, however, that they are wrong to do so. Until recently, I maintain, some scholars have made misleading use of the myths largely because of facile assumptions about what religion is and how one goes about finding religion in unfamiliar settings.

The Wayú

Wayú is the autodenomination of the largest distinct Amerindian population in both Colombia and Venezuela. I do not have reliable, up-to-date population figures, but I guess that people who identify themselves as Wayú now number well over 200,000. There are large clusters of Wayú resident in Maracaibo, Venezuela's second largest city, and there are Wayú populations in various other cities and towns in both Venezuela and Colombia. The cultural heartland of the Wayú, however, is the Guajira Peninsula, the northernmost extension of the South American land mass. Bounded on the north and west by the Caribbean Sea, and on the east by the Gulf of Venezuela, the peninsula is credited with a surface area of 15,380 square kilometers (Matos Romero 1971: 38). Approximately 80% of that territory belongs to Colombia, the remainder to Venezuela.

The Guajira Peninsula is a semi-arid landscape. That is, for approximately eight or nine months of the year evaporation in the Guajira exceeds precipitation. During the intense rainy season, however, savanna grasses cover sizeable areas, and the xerophytic plants, many of which retreat into desiccation during the dry season, renew themselves. Wayú traditions maintain that the ancestors of the present population originated in a well-watered region, and eventually migrated to the peninsula where they engaged in hunting, fishing, collecting, and, in some places, limited horticulture. Subsistence activities altered significantly, however, when contact with Europeans and Africans introduced pastoralism in cattle, sheep, goats, horses, donkeys, and mules.

Pastoralism spread widely but unevenly among the Wayú, and it contributed to the development of marked and socially significant inequalities of wealth, which is one of the factors that distinguish the Wayú from most other Amerindian populations in the South American lowlands. The Wayú, moreover, strongly emphasize uterine kin connections, and much of the literature on them describes them as „matrilineal," a complex subject that I cannot go into here (see Goulet 1980; Saler 1988). While increasing numbers of Wayú have learned to converse in Spanish, especially in the last several decades, many of them continue to speak their own language, a member of the Arawak family of languages.

Finding God (Mistakenly)

Wayú myths generally relate stories about four kinds of beings: named, godlike personages; humans (some of whom are heroic); individuated shades of the dead (*yolujas*); and anonymous spirits (*wanülü*) who shoot disease-causing arrows at humans and livestock. The narratives often include, moreover, references to wild and domestic animals, wild and cultivated plants, and topographical or other markers found in the peninsula. Quite a few myths deal with hunting, albeit hunting today is largely a recreational sport rather than a significant subsistence activity.

One of the godlike characters of myth is a being known as Maleiwa. In some narratives he created the ancestors of the Wayú. He formed them, in some stories, out of clay, rather like a potter. In others narratives he transformed them out of animals, thus establishing the identification of each Wayú clan with one or more animals. And in still other myths he fashioned ancestors out of sea foam. Maleiwa, moreover, has a mother, a personage known as Boronka or simply referred to as „the mother of Maleiwa." In some myths she was impregnated by a clap of thunder during a lightening storm.

Roman Catholic missionaries have long tended to see in Maleiwa something of a crude analog to the Christian creator (Goulet 1980). The several Italian Capuchin monks who staffed the boarding school for Wayú children in Nazareth in the Upper Guajira did so during the time of my fieldwork. None of them spoke the Wayú language, but they used „Maleiwa" as a gloss for God in sermons that they delivered in Spanish and in their conversations with me. Indeed, they also glossed the Wayú term yoluja, which is primarily used by the Wayú to mean an individuated shade of the dead, by the Spanish term „diablo" ('devil'). They were supported in those usages by small numbers of Wayú who have associated themselves in various ways with the missionaries.

They thus affirmed in Wayú terms an arresting but, according to the conventional language uses of many Wayú, a mistaken opposition, one that they intended to be between God and the devil. They were imitated in that error by three Protestant missionaries of the South American Indian Mission whom I interviewed. Further, some bilingual mestizos who served as culture guides to anthropologists as well as to government agents appeared to endorse the opposition by repeating it. Yet although shades of the dead, as I point out in more detail below, have their unpleasant or sinister aspects, they are by no means traditionally equivalent to the devil of Christian traditions. Nor does Maleiwa approximate to the Christian god.

The European creation of the Maleiwa-Yoluja opposition has had some interesting consequences. As the Canadian anthropologist Jean-Guy Goulet (1980) points out, it has supported the notion of some Wayú that Christian baptism can be an effective magical cure for disease.

In Wayú traditions, individuated shades of the dead, motivated both by loneliness and by love for their living kinsmen, may try to cause their kinsmens' deaths by afflicting them with fever and/or psychic trauma. The traditional Wayú treatment for yoluja-induced sickness is to bathe the afflicted person with a locally produced rum-like drink. But some Wayú, Goulet (1980) found, have come to suppose that Christian baptism can be more efficacious, especially since the missionaries preach that baptism separates man from the yoluja, a preaching that the missionaries understand in one way and many Wayú in another. Some Wayú, indeed, have sought multiple baptisms for themselves or their sick kin. Magical cures, I should add, are not the only reasons that numbers of Wayú seek baptism. My own informants emphasized other things, such as the utility of a baptismal certificate for facilitating the acquisition of other identity markers that have payoff values with respect to medical services made available to Indians, acquiring voting rights (which they are sometimes paid to exercise), and so on. Virtually none of the baptized Wayú whom I interviewed about baptism and related matters seemed seriously interested in Christianity as a religion of salvation.

In any case, a focus on Maleiwa narratives, particularly as they may remind us of familiar Judeo-Christian doctrines, is by no means restricted to missionaries. The French anthropologist Michel Perrin, whom I regard as the first European to have accomplished a really good study of Wayú myths in the last 400 years, analyzed 43 narratives published between the years 1883 and 1968 by 12 of his predecessors, at least six of whom have advanced degrees in anthropology. He reports that „Most of these tales concern the Maleiwa cycle and are generally limited to the episodes concerning the origin of humankind" (Perrin 1987 [1976]: 163). Perrin, who collected more than 400 stories in different parts of the Guajira Peninsula (1987: 75), describes Maleiwa as a „Culture

Hero." He reports, moreover, that when he spoke to his Wayú informants about Maleiwa,

> many fell silent ... This lack of interest in Maleiwa surprised me, as all the works written about the Guajiro had assigned the utmost importance to him. But by the end of my investigation I was convinced that his preeminence reflected the inadequacy or the strongly slanted character of these previous studies. Today Maleiwa is of little importance to the Guajiro. (Perrin 1987: 74)

Godlike Beings and Cultus

Wayú myths collectively include a wide cast of godlike beings. Perrin finds that the most prominent of such personages are a „hypermasculine" being named Juya and his wife, a „hyperfeminine" figure named Pulowi. In Perrin's structuralist analysis, Juya and Pulowi represent a fan of values in paired oppositions. Juya is male, a wanderer, a hunter, a warrior, and a seducer. He is unitary, and he dwells above, beyond the sun. Juya is the master of rain, and he is associated with rain and the rainy season, both of which are termed juya, and with fertility and life. Pulowi, in contrast, is female and fixed in place rather than a wanderer. But she is mysteriously multiple, for there are numbers of Pulowis associated with discrete places, on land and sea and under them, yet all Pulowis are Pulowi. Pulowi, moreover, like numbers of other Wayú mythic characters, has powers of metamorphosis, and she may sometimes even appear as a male criollo or as a European. She is associated with the dry season, aridity, drought, and death, albeit she is also associated with the reproductive powers of women. Specific places associated with her, known as pulowi places, are mysteriously dangerous to humans. The terms juya and pulowi, it should be noted, are polysemic, and their subtleties in meaning are context-related in Wayú discourse.

Perrin (1987: 120, emphasis added) writes that „Juya and Pulowi are the subject of *no prayer, no cult, no sacrifice*." That is, these godlike beings of myth are not worshipped or propitiated or entreated. In what sense, then, may they be deemed religious objects?

To enlarge the scope of considerations affecting an answer to that question, I add some additional information from my own fieldwork. I had tape-recorded a long myth in the Wayú language, and the bilingual myth-teller then proceeded to translate his narrative into Spanish from the tape. Since I was learning the Wayú language, I paid close attention to the translation process. At one point I raised a question about some detail. My question, I thought, was about syntax and vocabulary. My informant, however, apparently understood it differently and supposed that I was trying to get the existential facts right, for he said to me in Spanish, „Do you believe that?" I sensed one of those glorious moments in ethnographic fieldwork when a window unexpectedly opens on a topic of considerable importance, and I thought deeply about how I should reply. Apparently, I thought deeply for too long a time, for the myth-teller punctuated my silence by declaring, „We don't believe that these things happened."

In a follow-up discussion the myth-teller stated flatly that Maleiwa, Juya, and other godlike beings in the traditional narratives don't actually exist. It is entertaining and instructive to tell stories about them. Further, the multiple meanings of some of the terms used to name them lend themselves to rhetorical artifice. But the godlike beings of myth are what we would call fictional characters. They do have a certain truth to them, however, for the themes and conditions expressed in stories about them – drought, sickness, death, grief, desire, fecundity, and so on – are real enough, and the narratives often capture in poignant and dramatic ways the existential realities of Wayú experience. The godlike characters of Wayú myth, in short, are very meaningful tropes.

Other informants with whom I subsequently discussed this matter for the most part supported the myth-teller. Without further laboring the point, let me give it as my opinion that the godlike beings of Wayú myth are not themselves religious objects. They do serve, however, as discursive devices for talking not only about Wayú religion but about many aspects of Wayú life, and particularly the cognized and experienced tensions and contrasts of that life.

My View of Wayú Religion

Wayú religion, in my opinion, mainly consists of two complexes of activities and a congeries of diverse ideas that relate to those activities in specific ways. The complexes to which I refer can be labeled the mortuary complex and the shamanic complex.

Central to the mortuary complex are, ideally, two funerals and accompanying wakes accorded to the dead, the first shortly after death, in which the body is interred in the ground or placed in a tomb, and the second when the flesh has largely rotted from the bones and the bones are removed from their resting place, „cleaned," and placed in an ossuary or in a large pottery jar.

The shamanic complex pivots on the efforts of shamans, most of whom are women, to cure sickness, mainly by chanting, shaking a rattle, sucking out disease objects, and invoking the help of the shaman's spirit „husband" who is sometimes described as a wanülü spirit. Shamans may also find lost objects, divine, and do other things.

Rituals in both complexes are not regularly scheduled but are *ad hoc*, performed when there is need. In a shamanic curing ritual the patient and the shaman are normally the only two persons present. Shamanic curing ritual *qua* ritual may therefore be said to implicate a constituency but not a congregation.

Mortuary rituals are public and normally include sizeable numbers of people. They are major forms of gathering in Wayú society, and the sequence of events normally follows a well known and widely known script, and in that sense suggests Whitehouse's doctrinal mode of religious organization. But they may involve intensely personal, and intensely memorable, „imagistic" experiences. In any case, it should be noted that mortuary rituals are complex and involve sociocultural subtleties. Thus, for instance, when funeral guests wail in the presence of the corpse, they maintain their status as guests but now add a new status: litigant at law. The deceased has caused them sorrow by dying, and, as the Wayú say, „tears have their price." The close kin of the deceased must compensate them, usually by paying each litigant a goat or sheep or a portion of beef, the worth of the animal or portion varying to some extent with judgments made by the payers about the social status of the person paid (Saler 1986). The latter's memory of the funeral is likely to be influenced by what he or she receives relative to self-evaluation.

Ideas or „beliefs" associated with the two complexes of activities are harder to describe parsimoniously and fairly. That is because not all Wayú affirm or harbor them, they vary from person to person, and they are not explicitly and systematically related to one another in some overarching perspective. To some extent, however, domain-specific ideas tend to have relationships to one another.

In briefly describing certain beliefs, I draw on the works of three ethnographers who have taken pains to use the local language and to employ relatively sophisticated eliciting and analytical procedures: Michel Perrin, Jean-Guy Goulet, and myself. I must note, however, that all three ethnographers have indulged in what Pascal Boyer calls „the epistemic approach." As Boyer (1994: 50–51) characterizes the epistemic approach, it treats belief statements as efforts to say something about the world, and it encourages an analyst to go beyond actual informant statements by describing what people may intellectually support if they tried to make sense out of what they say and do. This, as Boyer points out, can lead to misattributions, where the ethnographer or historian mistakes his own filling in of interstices and context for what his informants actually believe. While Boyer's point is well taken, I elsewhere (Saler 2001: 65–67) suggest that an epistemic approach can be improved and thus better warranted. In any case, the works of the three ethnographers I draw on have tried to fill in contexts to the point of attributing certain tacit ideas and perspectives to the Wayú. In doing so, the ethnographers have moved the fruits of their analysis in the direction of what Whitehouse calls „the doctrinal" mode of religious organization by suggesting or implying certain systematizations that may not be there in their entirety.

Basic to Wayú religious ideas is a notion that virtually all Wayú whom I questioned accept: that every individual has an *ain*. Ain means, among other things, heart, and in colloquial use it is also widely employed to mean the essence of a person: those enduring qualities or personal characteristics that make the person the individuated being that he or she is.

When a person dies, many Wayú affirm, his or her essence leaves the body and travels to Jepirra, the Land of the Dead. In Jepirra the ain becomes a yoluja, a shade of the dead. Early in its career the yoluja looks very much as it did in life. Scars, broken teeth, or other features of an individual close to the time of death are found on the yoluja. The yoluja can be seen and heard by its adult kin in dreams. Human infants, dogs, horses, mules, and donkeys, however, can see yolujas when awake, owing to a liquid substance in their eyes that makes such vision possible. (In some myths, human heroes poke their fingers in a dog's eye and then transfer the fluid to their own eyes so that they can see a yoluja.)

Over time, a yoluja's features will become progressively blurred, and the yoluja will become increasingly more anonymous. (I regard this idea as psychologically astute, for the longer the time from death, the more likely it is that survivors will loose rich and vivid memories of the deceased. And, of course, buried or entombed corpses, the material remains of persons, will loose recognizable features as they decay.) Finally, the yoluja will die in the Land of the Dead – we die twice, some Wayú say – and it will become totally anonymous, either becoming rain that fecundates its kinsmen's lands or becoming a wanülü spirit that shoots disease arrows at living humans and livestock.

As Michel Perrin (1987: 109) points out, however,

> I did not meet a single Indian who had a clear-cut awareness of the cycle referred to. Although the Guajiro commonly claim that „the dead go to Jepira" or that „the rains and the wanülüs are Indians who have long been dead," they seldom speak of the transition ... and even less do they allude to the circumstances surrounding such a transition.

Perrin nevertheless holds that the cycle that he depicts can be inferred from Wayú funeral rites and the articulated conceptions of the beyond that are commonly associated with those rites (Perrin 1987: 109). And Goulet (1980) and I (Saler 1988) agree with him.

The History of the Search for Wayú Religion

From Colonial times to our own day a diversity of persons have published works ranging from short anecdotes to long monographs that deal with what the authors suppose is Wayú religion (for bibliographies, see Goulet 1980, Perrin 1987, and Saler 1988). For the most part, these works emphasize two things. First, they supply a congeries of beliefs purportedly entertained by the Wayú about malignant spirits, potentially harmful behaviors, and magical possibilities for achieving desires, as well as related descriptions of prophylactic, remedial, or other magically instrumental acts. The Colombian anthropologist Roberto Pineda Giraldo (1950) supplies us with the most exhaustive inventory of such beliefs and practices. Second, the literature deals with what some authors seem to suppose is a more cerebral or elevated form of religiosity, a set of beliefs and philosophical perspectives that pivot on, or otherwise connect to, myths (e.g., Caudmont 1953; Chaves 1946; 1953; Paz 1973; Pineda 1947; Wilbert 1962).

As I indicated earlier, numbers of people who wrote about Wayú religion not only accorded prominence to Maleiwa myths, but, in particular, those Maleiwa narratives or sections of narratives that seem relatively familiar to persons who find religion in exotic locales by establishing analogies to Judeo-Christian religions. And more recent and more sophisticated students of Wayú religion, while avoiding the uninformed and crude emphasis on Maleiwa tales exhibited by their predecessors, nevertheless favor the epistemic approach that Boyer warns us against.

Now, in the Wayú case, beliefs that relate to particular domains and interests often do have some systematicity to them, if only because they pertain to specific „doxastic neighborhoods." Overall, however, Wayú religion falls short of doctrinal integration. That is, it is hard to make an empirically grounded case for what Whitehouse (2000: 1) characterizes as a „tendency ... for revelations to be codified as a body of doctrines, transmitted through routinized forms of worship, memorized as part of one's 'general knowledge', and producing large, anonymous communities."

Whitehouse persuasively maintains that both imagistic and doctrinal tendencies may exist within the same religious tradition. Historically, however, students of Wayú religion have privileged systematicity and leaned in the direction of the doctrinal.

The above observations conduce to an important consideration. Whitehouse is concerned with tendencies within religions, tendencies making for „particular patterns of codification, transmission, cognitive processing, and political association" (2000: 1). His prepossessing internalist orientation is nicely illustrated by the subtitle of his *Arguments and Icons* book: *Divergent Modes of Religiosity*. Figuring and identifying divergent modes, however, depends in significant measure on the sophistication and acuity of the researcher. This is not to say that there is nothing out there to identify. Rather, it recognizes the likely importance of bias. As I put it elsewhere, „If we were to insist on regarding an ethnographer as a recording instrument, then we would be well advised to realize that all recording instruments exhibit biases and, to the extent that we might calibrate and measure them by using other instruments, greater or lesser distortion curves" (Saler 2000a [1993]: 233).

The history of the study of Wayú religion clearly shows bias and distortion. Happily, however, it also shows improvement, for now we recognize some of the bias and distortion. One of the most important things that can be done to promote further improvement in the study of religions is to broaden the understandings and enlarge the sensitivities of students of religion.

Virtually everyone recognizes that religions differ considerably in content. But there is not enough understanding of how they may differ in form. Whitehouse's work addresses that important topic, particularly with respect to organizational tendencies, and by so doing it expands our conceptualization of religion. We cannot do without templates. But we can hope to fabricate templates that will allow for more variety or alternatives in that complex human enterprise that we call religion.

On Credulity[3]

Abstract: To the extent possible, this essay attempts to divest the word credulity of its pejorative senses in order to look at some of the informational functions that may attach to the term. It offers a stipulative definition of credulity: the justification or acceptance of belief largely or entirely on the basis of human testimony. So defined, credulity is widespread in human life. As a panhuman phenomenon, credulity promotes the accessing and utilization of information stored outside of any given individual, it facilitates the development of cognitive complexity, and it makes for the co-ordination of cognitive resources within social groups. Among the potential costs are the possible dissemination of misinformation, the narrowing or closing off of avenues of potentially useful cognizing, and unproductive diversions of energies and other resources because of faulty information. On the whole, however, the benefits outweigh the costs on individual and societal levels and in evolutionary perspective.

In everyday speech the word „credulity" normally has a pejorative sense. Credulity means a readiness or willingness to believe on the basis of little or no evidence. A person deemed credulous is thus someone who, in the judgment of another, is credited with a disposition, or a realized disposition, to believe too readily or too easily. Judgment is often rendered on the basis of observing someone appear to accept belief where, in the opinion of the judger, there is dubious or insufficient ground for acceptance.

Credulity is widespread in human life. Indeed, if we divorce it from its pejorative connotations and look at the fundamental phenomenon involved, credulity is quite important in human life. In terms of a cost-benefit analysis, its benefits greatly outweigh its costs. Further, credulity is of considerable evolutionary significance. In order to argue those claims expeditiously, however, we need a less judgmental sense of credulity than that normally encountered in everyday speech. So in order to strip the phenomenon down to basics while minimizing any immediate judgmental evaluation of it, I offer. this stipulative definiti-

---

[3] „On Credulity." In Timothy Light and Brian C. Wilson (eds.), Religion as a Human Capacity: A Festschrift in Honor of E. Thomas Lawson, 315–329, Leiden: E.J. Brill, 2004.

on: Credulity is the acceptance or justification of belief largely or entirely on the basis of human testimony.

If you accept that stipulative definition, then we are all credulous to a great extent. Much that we claim to know or believe is based largely or entirely on what we have heard or read. I, for instance, believe in the germ theory of disease (at least to the extent that I understand it). But I have never attempted to justify my belief by systematic efforts to look for and evaluate evidence. All of my friends say that germs cause disease, as do my primary care physician and other authority figures. They all seem to suppose, moreover, that competent people have checked it out, and so, too, do I. A great many of my other knowledge claims or beliefs depend on similar sources. I think it very likely, moreover, that that is also true of the reader.

Widespread and habitual credulity on the part of just about everyone carries both benefits and costs for the individual. On a greater plane of abstraction, moreover, credulity can be said to be both functional and dysfunctional for human societies. We can argue, furthermore, that both credulity and the development of what we may call skeptical constraints have been of importance for the evolution of humankind. Let us take each in turn.

Credulity and the Individual

An obvious benefit of credulity for the individual is that it facilitates the accessing of information stored elsewhere. Reciprocally, one of its more obvious costs is that it facilitates the acquisition of misinformation.

Throughout our lives we depend on others for much of the information that we utilize. We learn from others not only in what they say (or write), but in observing what they do and in hearing about them from third parties. In the course of benefiting cognitively from others, however, we sometimes suffer by appropriating their errors and follies. In any case, the vast amount of information that we process and utilize derives in great measure from our fellow human beings. The individual, in short, is cognitively or informationally dependent on others.

Dependency is the condition of looking to others for the satisfaction of one's needs and wants. As we mature we usually become less dependent on our parents or other early caretakers for subsistence, and there is likely to be an emotional weaning as well. For most of us, however, there is likely to be an increase rather than a decrease in informational dependency as we mature. Not only does cognitive dependency typically increase, it widens with respect to the informational sources accessed. Beginning with parents or early caretakers, the maturing individual increasingly accesses other informational sources, it being important for multiple kinds of competency to acquire and process new information of increasingly diverse kinds.

Most individuals do not simply receive information from others. They re-work what they receive in keeping with their established representations and understandings. Even if the information acquired is not distorted by noise in the initial transmission, significant alteration of the information processed may take place through enrichment or de-emphasis. Indeed, there are screening or editing mechanisms of various sorts that ordinarily come into play. Information that strongly conflicts with our established ideas and expectations about the world may be rejected outright or accepted only provisionally or conditionally. Further, evaluations of sources may well play a role, even if the individual doing the evaluating cannot explicitly or consciously formulate all of the factors that enter into the evaluation. The channeling of purported information is very important, and appraisals of the characteristics of channels are likely to play significant roles in whether or not, or how readily, or how conditionally, information may be accepted. Account may be taken of such things as the social status and credentials of the source, beliefs about the track record of the source, whether or not the informational transmission is accompanied by reassuring body displays (eye contacts, facial expressions, and/or other valued stimuli), wide social support for the putative information, and so forth.

We humans employ a multiplicity of evaluative criteria, some of them rather subtle. At the same time, however, we sometimes readily or precipitously accept information because we have no alternative sources of information or because we are strongly disposed to do so by fervent wishes, desperation, social pressures, or a host of other possible motivating factors. And, it needs to be said, some persons may be less evaluative or more accepting of what is proffered than are others. All of us, nevertheless, are credulous to significant extents. Two salient (and partly overlapping) expressions of credulity are suggested by the terms „trust" and „faith."

Trust, in the sense that concerns us, is reliance on another person's, or on other people's, veracity, integrity, or predictability. We may, for instance, trust a certain person to do a certain thing. Or we accept the information that someone supplies on trust. Trust, so conceived, is a positive restatement of credulity. As such, it is vital factor in the conduct of social life. We commonly trust in others to do various things, to behave in expected ways, and to supply information on which we can rely.

Trust is of great significance in science as well as in much else. Contemporary science in our society is deservedly famous for its skeptical epistemology, its celebration of the idea that claims to knowledge should be systematically tested rather than facilely accepted. In actual practice, however, skeptical epistemology is not thoroughgoing. It is impossible to monitor everything or to attempt to review all claims. In consequence, scientists are obliged to take much on trust. They do, however, make efforts to safeguard that trust. Part of their structure of safeguards can be discerned in such prophylactic measures as rigorous professional training, demanding requirements for advanced degrees, apprenticeship to senior scientists, and so on. Graduate and „post doc" training in the sciences is intended to do more than enhance the knowledge and skills of the person undergoing it; it is also intended to weed out weak candidates and to produce credentialed scientists upon whom other scientists can rely.

The importance of trust in the sciences is instructive because of the explicit importance that scientists accord to skeptical epistemology. In much else in life we are less consciously or explicitly skeptical, and we are even more dependent on implicit trust. Every time we cross a bridge without care or worry we implicitly trust the engineers and builders who designed and constructed it. Every time we drive without concern through a tunnel we implicitly trust its builders to have. done their jobs properly. (I am indebted to Charles A. Ziegler for these examples.) When regulatory agencies and manufacturers establish safety standards for an electrical appliance that will be used by the public, they trust that people will use the appliance in anticipated ways, for otherwise safeguards would have to be so complex and costly that the product would be unviable, commercially and perhaps functionally. In these and in many other ways trust is implicitly, and sometimes explicitly, widespread.

Despite trust's importance in our lives, however, widespread dependence on it can have its downsides. While individuals often depend on the trust of others to engage in mutually satisfying interactions, sometimes trust is abused. Con men, hoaxers, and practical jokers, to say nothing of terrorists and serial killers, frequently depend on the trust of others for their own satisfactions. Trust can and often does facilitate the acquisition of misinformation, sometimes with unfortunate consequences, regardless of whether the misinformation is disseminated intentionally or not. Trust, even when deemed a positive expression of credulity, is thus multifaceted.

Faith implies confidence in propositions, persons, or the likely occurrence of envisioned events. The term, moreover, is often used in contemporary English to indicate a confidence that need not rest on „evidence" or „facts," at least in the most common acceptations of those terms. Faith suggests an inner certainty or confidence. It need not depend on outer validation. This does not mean, however, that it is never ascribed a source outside of the person.

In a fairly extreme example, that of certain Christian theological traditions, which assign great importance to faith, faith in the doctrines of Christianity is declared to come ultimately from God. Individuals, numbers of theologians assert, attain their faith by God's grace. That faith, moreover, is held to transform the individual, cognitively and in other ways. In Augustine of Hippo's admonitory expression of this tradition,

> Understanding is the reward of faith. Therefore seek not to understand so that you may believe, but believe so that you may understand. (On the Gospel of St. John, 29.6)

Christian theological traditions respecting faith constitute what numbers of Westerners deem to be some of the clearest or best examples of what they understand by that term. It is important to note however, that popular parlance does not restrict faith to a religious context. Among the many uses of the term, some of the more prominent include faith in persons to whom we attribute various qualities (honesty, probity, conscientiousness, whatever), faith in „human nature" (claimed confidence, for instance, that individuals or collectivities of persons will behave in expected ways), or faith that events will transpire in some predicted sequence. These uses, moreover, do no exhaust actual and possible applications of the term. Its association with religion is nevertheless important and instructive, even if not exhaustive.

A strong argument has been made that religious ideas typically include some counter-intuitive elements (Boyer 1994, 2001b; Pyysiäinen 2001). That is, the objects posited in religious ideas – gods, ghosts, spirits, etc. – to some extent either violate expectations that we have about prototypical members of the macro category to which they pertain or they are credited with one or more features that we normally associate with some other category. Thus, for instance, in many religions the gods neither eat nor die, whereas more prototypical exemplars of the macro category person normally do both. And in various parts of the world witches are depicted as having, and exercising, the power to fly, although they are neither birds nor aviators. Yet while the objects posited in religious ideas typically depart in some ways from expectations grounded in our intuitive ontologies, they nevertheless conform to them in other respects. Thus, for example, gods typically are credited with will, purpose, and various other important qualities and capacities associated with the person category (Guthrie 1993; Boyer 1994). As Boyer (1994; 2001b) persuasively argues, conformation to our ontological intuitions and expectations renders posited religious objects plausible and easy to learn, while their „attention-getting" departures from those intuitions and expectations make them memorable.

Faith in the existence and persistence of posited religious objects thus signals acceptance of the reality of the counter-intuitive. One may argue that much the same thing could be said about modern science, since it, too, often suggests the counter-intuitive. What could be more counter-intuitive than quantum mechanics? But there is a difference. The constructs of science are recognized to be constructs. They are provisional, in keeping with the skeptical epistemology discussed earlier. Ideally, they should not be taken on faith. Efforts should be made to test them and to find something better. Posited religious objects and narratives, however, even when in principle refutable, are usually not subject to systematic refutational efforts, nor is there an institutionalized imperative to find something better. If they are plausible because they accord to a significant extent with already established understandings and expectations albeit departing from them in some arresting particulars, and if they appear to answer in significant fashion to interests and desires, they may become part of one's archive of ideas.

Cognitively, faith is not extraordinary. It includes a motivated and prioritized storage of ideas that have survived filtration and are marked as authoritative. Typically, moreover, those ideas are strongly affect-laden relative to desires, and their positive cathexis often serves as a barrier to subsequent refutation – albeit in the right combination of circumstances cathexis may sometimes eventually prove to be an emotional door to loss of faith. When ideas originate outside of the individual, we could choose to characterize faith in them as an intensified form of credulity. But inasmuch as all ideas are framed by a language of ideas and, if expressed, are expressed within such a framework, faith is always a matter of credulity, if only contextually.

Credulity and Society

In 1950, a committee of anthropologists and sociologists – David F. Aberle, Albert K. Cohen, Arthur K. Davis, Marion Levy, and Francis Sutton – published a paper entitled „The Functional Prerequisites of a Society." Influenced to a significant extent by the theoretical and analytical perspectives of the sociologist Talcott Parsons, Aberle et al. supply a list of supposedly necessary basic conditions for the existence, functioning, and continuation of human societies. The list includes „shared cognitive orientations" and a „shared, articulated set of goals."

At first glance, the above two „prerequisites" may seem reasonable or perhaps, in the judgment of some, even obvious. One can, however, raise questions about the meaning of „shared." Does it suggest identity in orientations and goals or only some sort of approximation? How indeed, except by citing colloquial conventions (which may be out of place in anything as solemn as an exercise in formulating „functional prerequisites"), do we justify the notion that individuals, the loci of cognitive orientations and goals, „share" them? Voicing or publicly endorsing orientations and goals that are articulated by others signals public agreement. But can two people actually share what we normally regard as internal mental phenomena? Even if this question is resolved, however, there is a further difficulty that inhibits our acceptance of the requirements proffered by Aberle et al.

In a masterful criticism of the idea that human society could not exist and persist unless there were a sharing of cognitive orientations and goals, the anthropologist Anthony F. C. Wallace (1961a, 1961b) demonstrates formally that individuals with different understandings and different goals may nevertheless support and sustain mutually satisfying social transactions. What is necessary, Wallace argues, is not „sharing" but, rather, what he terms „mutually facilitating equivalence structures." That is, social actors must entertain complementary expectations that if they behave in certain ways others will act in a predictable manner. If I do x, alter will do y. Such expectations, of course, must be realized more often than not lest they become extinguished. But the actors need not actually „share" cognitive orientations and goals for satisfying relations to occur and to be reinforced. Nor need they know the cognitive orientations and motives of other people. Indeed, Wallace argues, they need not even know the social identities of those with whom they interact.

One of Wallace's examples is the „tooth-fairy" scenario: a child looses a tooth, places it under its pillow at night, and awakens to find the tooth gone and money in its place. The child supposes that she has interacted with the tooth-fairy, whereas in reality, of course, it was a parent who made the switch. The parent's goal, we may suppose, was different from the child's. Further, the parent and child have different understandings of the transaction, and the child is ignorant of the identity of the actual actor who took the tooth and replaced it with money. But the expectations of child and parent, though different in cognitive content, were mutually facilitating.

Wallace (1961b: 40) goes on to argue that cognitive „non-uniformity" can be deemed „a functional desideratum" of human societies. All human societies, including those considered to be relatively „small-scale," typically include a considerable diversity of roles. Competent performance of those roles involves a great deal of knowledge. If we were to measure the complexity of societies in terms of the diversity of roles, then the cognitive complement of that measure would be a measure of cognitive complexity on a societal level. Contemporary American society, for example, is very complex in both. But even so-called „primitive" societies (i.e., typically and classically, small-scale societies of non-literate persons) exhibit a good deal of role diversity and a corresponding cognitive complexity.

As Wallace points out, if everyone in a human society were obliged to know everything requisite to competent discharge of all social roles, the complexity of roles would be drastically constrained by the cognitive capacities of most individuals. But nowhere that I know of is that actually the case. Roles are numerous and the continuance of all societies depends on knowledge that exceeds the knowledge of any individual. As Wallace (1961b: 40) puts it, „ ... cognitive non-uniformity subserves two important functions: (1) it permits a more complex system to arise than most, or any, of its participants can comprehend; (2) it liberates the participants in a system from the heavy burden of knowing each other's motivations."

Various other social scientists had made points that support Wallace's view. Thus, for instance, in a paper on „Some Social Functions of Ignorance," Wilbert E. Moore and Melvin Tumin (1949) argue persuasively that in human social orders successful role playing sometimes requires cognitive inequality between actors. Indeed, as in the case of typical physician-patient interactions in contemporary American society, the authority of one role-player rests on an assumption of special knowledge and a complementary ignorance on the part of the other. But Wallace's treatment, in my opinion, goes beyond the contributions of his predecessors both in its global perspective and in the elegance of its formal proofs.

„Evidently," Wallace writes, „groups, as well as individuals, can integrate their behaviors into reliable systems by means of equivalence structures, without extensive motivational or cognitive sharing" (1961b: 40). Allowing, then, for the likelihood of a good deal of motivational and cognitive diversity in a human society – a diversity, indeed, in personality variables as well as in cognition – Wallace suggests that the task of the social scientist is to comprehend how such diversity is organized. His major answer, as already indicated, is by the establishment of partial, mutually facilitating equivalence structures, „a system of equivalent behavioral expectancies" (1961b: 41). These constitute an „implicit contract," in the general sense of the term „contract," and, Wallace contends,

> society is, as Rousseau intuited, built upon a set of continually changing social contracts which are possible only because human beings have cognitive equipment adequate to their maintenance and renewal. Culture can be conceived as a set of standardized models of such contractual relationships, in which the equivalent roles are specified and available for implementation to any two parties whose motives make their adoption promising. The relationship is based not on a sharing, but on a complementarity of cognitions and motives. (Wallace 1961b: 41).

Culture, in Wallace's view,

> shifts in policy from generation to generation with kaleidoscopic variety, and is characterized internally not by uniformity, but by diversity of both individuals and groups, many of whom are in continuous and overt conflict in one sub-system and in active cooperation in another. Culture, as seen from this viewpoint, becomes not so much a superorganic thing *sui generis*, but policy, tacitly and gradually concocted by groups of people for the furtherance of their interests; also contract, established by practice, between and among individuals to organize their strivings into mutually facilitating equivalence structures. (Wallace 1961b: 28)

Adopting and adapting that perspective, we can characterize a human society as constituting, at any one moment, a pool of information to which social actors have differential, and differently motivated, access.

Credulity facilitates both the flow and appropriation of information while other mechanisms (such as social proprieties conventionally related to distinctions in age, sex, and, more broadly, social identity and role playing) serve to inhibit or channel its diffusion.

A human society is characteristically strengthened by the richness of its informational pool, without the necessity of that information being equally available to everyone. Indeed, as pointed out earlier, informational complexity beyond the cognitive capacities of individuals is made possible by the differential participation of those individuals in the pool. At the same time, however, the social value of an informational pool would be compromised or subverted unless there were mechanisms to facilitate appropriation. Credulity is one such mechanism.

Evolutionary Considerations

One sometimes hears this complaint about commercials on television: the advertisers and/or stations, it is alleged, increase the sound level of commercials above the level used for ordinary program transmissions in order to get the auditor's attention. That allegation is probably false in many (but perhaps not all) cases. Sound level is regulated by code, and it is usually in the interests of most television stations to adhere to code. If one were to measure sound level in decibels, program materials and commercials would often be found to be about the same. The impression of greater loudness in ads is, in a number of cases, an artifact of the care (and expense) that some producers of television advertisements devote to reducing background noise in their commercials. Signal to noise ratios are sometimes higher in TV ads than in TV programs, and that, indeed, may get the auditor's attention.

Now, signal to noise ratios ought to be taken into account in certain sorts of evolutionary studies. The phylogenetic scale evinces, as it were, diverse strategies for distinguishing signals from background noise in cases of locating food, finding mates, avoiding predators, and in other important activities. Signals, of course, are quite diverse and include more than sonic signals. But whether signals be auditory, visual, tactile, olfactory, kinetic, thermal, or combinations of these, their utility or effectiveness is often related to their experienced strength relative to the experiential capacities of living things. In brief, their adaptive significance rests not only on the signals themselves but on the discriminative powers of organisms.

On the human level, the diversity of potential signals and the diversity of potential background noises increase greatly. Complexity, moreover, is expanded by considerations relating to the reliability of signals. Reliability may be compromised or enhanced not only by factors directly affecting cue discriminations, stimulus generalizations, extinctions (e.g., „The Boy Who Cried Wolf"), and the like, but by subtle rhetorical, kinetic, and other ploys that may, as it were, italicize signals and messages in ways that further stimulate the receiver to productive actions or that effectively subvert her attentions and energies by deceptions. Deception, of course, is encountered elsewhere in the phylogenetic scale. The diversity of animal camouflages is one sort of example, and „playing dead" is another. But humans have – and often exercise – greater capacities to deceive than do other animals.

Deceiving by word, by deed, by body posture, by facial features, by vagueness or ambiguity, by silence, and by other means, is common among humans. Sometimes it is inadvertent. But often it is intentional, and it may be diversely motivated (as we suppose in English by employing such expressions as „white lie," „noble lie," „damn lie," and so forth). Scanning or monitoring devices for detecting deceptions in the conduct of human life can be useful if effective. Indeed, we are disposed by evolutionary endowments to make efforts to assess reliability, if only subliminally. At the same time, however, we are disposed to be credulous, and that, too, is a disposition with an evolutionary foundation. I shall take up each in turn. But before doing so, it is worth noting (based on informal observations made in my own society and in others) that some individuals may be more given to skepticism than various of their fellows, while some appear to be rather more credulous than others. Stronger or weaker dispositions in either case may relate to the personal experiences of different individuals and to a myriad of variables such as childhood socialization, education, employment, and so on. Considered more abstractly, however, variable intensities of dispositions in a population respecting skepticism and credulity hint at polymorphism, and that also suggests an evolutionary consideration.

Reliability

Human reliability assessments are rooted in genetically transmitted sensitivities and dispositions that have adaptive significance. Charles Ziegler furnishes an example that spills over to an ironic contemporary application:

> Most higher vertebrates produce specific sounds (e.g., cries that attract mates or warn of predators). Although the production of, and response to, such sounds might be considered a form of communication, there is no need to assume that the animals recognize it as such. It is only necessary to assume that the animal is programmed genetically to make a certain sound when, say, the mating „drive" is experienced, and that conspecifics of the opposite sex are programmed to respond to that sound with mating behavior ...
>
> By introspection and inference from observing others, we know that phylogenetic responses to certain sounds are still with us and that information conveyed in this way has a high „believability quotient." Those of us who have heard, say, piercing screams of fear or rage can testify that the same information sonically conveyed by speech (e.g., „I am afraid" or „I am angry") has much less impact. Why is this so?
>
> Using „reverse engineering" it is possible to describe – at least at the level of systematics – how the „instinctive" response to certain sounds occurs .... In the case of input sensed as sound, a neural „shunt" must exist that performs rudimentary signal processing wherein the incoming sound pattern is compared with phylogenetically stored patterns. If a match occurs the „shunt" bypasses the neural mechanisms that constitute the usual intervening cognitive steps and triggers the appropriate emotion (e.g., fear or anger) which is followed by „the assignment of action" ...
>
> In effect, if a certain internal state prompts an animal to make a certain sound, that sound „automatically" induces an appropriate internal state in conspecifics. In humans, the response produced by the „shunt" can be ignored, but the response itself is „automatic." Indeed, this is why the most banal horror movie can „work" if it includes loud and convincing screams of fear. This sound will always induce in us a frisson of fear despite the banal plot and the knowledge that we are safely sitting in a theater. We can consciously repress „the assignment of action," (i.e., flight), and remain in our seats, but the „shunt" insures that „the assignment of affect" (i.e., fear) occurs, however momentarily, as an involuntary response. (Ziegler n.d.: 53–54)

There are various other sensitivities and excitations that negatively or positively affect the „believability quotient" and that appear to be genetically disposed. Among the more popularly recognized – as sometimes described by novelists in portrayals of character in social interactions – are eye behaviors in face-to-face contacts (e.g., pupil dilations and alterations in blinking behavior), other aspects of facial expressions (e.g., smiles, frowns, lip tremors, eyebrow arching, etc.), facial pallor or blotches or colorations, body postures and tics, vocal tremors or other vocal behaviors that affect the evaluation of messages transmitted in speech, and so forth. These are often involuntary on the part of the signaler. Further, those who „read" or „audit" them may not be consciously aware that they are taking them into account in assessing the reliability of information proffered.

While the above can be regarded as genetically disposed, there are also, of course, learned modalities of reliability assessment respecting the credentials of informational sources and the plausibility and probability of truth claims. These latter, which are culturally variable, are related in complex and subtle ways to the former, which constitute natural resemblances among human beings.

In exploring ethno-epistemological traditions in the ethnographic literature, for example, we find that different cultures, while tending to support similar evaluative sensitivities relating to face-to-face informational transmissions, also accord importance to different modalities for receiving and validating different sorts of information. Thus, for instance, seventeenth century and some later Iroquois value and make efforts to obey what they take to be imperatives delivered in certain ways in dreams (Wallace 1958), Azande maintain that the poison oracles of their princes are infallible (Evans-Pritchard 1937), and other populations are variously reported to repose a generalized confidence in seers, divinations, omens, astrological computations, and so forth, while often being prepared to explain, or to explain away, discrete failures in the truth claims and predictions entered in specific cases. Further, as Pascal Boyer (1994; 2001b) cogently argues, the entertainment, elaboration, and cultural transmission of religious ideas are crucially affected by inference systems that are supported and constrained by the pan human architecture of the human brain and common existential experiences. This means, he points out, that not everything goes insofar as the successful transmission of religious ideas is concerned, and it helps to explain why there are broad family resemblances in various religious ideas entertained by populations that differ culturally.

Credulity

I suggested earlier that credulity, as defined in this essay, promotes the accessing and utilization of information stored outside of any given individual, that it facilitates the achievement of cognitive complexity, and that it is generally a cost-effective way of enabling persons within a social group to coordinate their cognitive resources. The possible costs include dissemination of misinformation, the narrowing or closing off of avenues of potentially useful information and ratiocination, and the diversion of energies that might be gainfully employed elsewhere. On balance, I think that the likely benefits outweigh potential costs, all the more so since dispositions to credulity are ameliorated to some extent by dispositions to skepticism and reliability assessments.

If one accepts the several components of the view expressed above, then we can go on to argue that credulity has been a phenomenon of immense evolutionary and societal importance. Indeed, human life as we know it could not have emerged or persisted without it.

Impressive arguments have been made to the effect that the architecture of the human brain evolved to its present state during the Pleistocene, and that that architecture is adapted to a Paleolithic lifestyle, a life-style in which humans lived in small groups that depended on hunting and gathering (Barkow, Cosmides, and Tooby 1992; Mithen 1996). Such small groups were loci of cooperation and nurturing, and that includes informational exchanges.

Means for distinguishing between insiders and outsiders were important for husbanding and distributing resources and channeling nurturing. Such means would facilitate and support social solidarity. They may have included language markers, so that even in territories where speech was mutually intelligible groups could nevertheless be distinguished by perhaps slight but recognizable sonic variations. Other distinguishing devices may have included variations in dress or adornment, odors, traditions, and so forth. And, of course, the memories of group members were important for distinguishing between insiders and outsiders. Further, sensitivities and traditions that discouraged and perhaps punished freeloaders or cheats could also have had social and survival value. Another factor making for solidarity in the in-group and enhancing survival prospects may have been a willingness or readiness to accept information proffered within the group.

Just as credulity can enlarge an individual's informational resources and facilitate cognitive coordination within groups, so, too, can it be something of a condition for group membership and social solidarity. That is, an individual affirms and validates group membership by accepting – or appearing to accept – much of the information seemingly endorsed and proffered by the group. Too much overt skepticism would subvert group solidarity. Hence the realization of dispositions to credulity is not only typically accomplished within a social framework, but such realizations and the dispositions that fund them are themselves factors making for human sociability.

We can readily imagine how this was the case in small-scale Paleolithic societies, but we can also comprehend how it is the case in our complex contemporary world, with its increasing requirements for information. An arresting problem is how our Paleolithic mindbrain and its dispositions to credulity may cope with the dangers of our present condition. We cannot be free of credulity. Happily, however, evolution has also endowed us with critical (and inter-individually variable) faculties for evaluating many informational claims, faculties that, with appropriate cultivation, can be applied to the assessment of still more claims. Ultimately, it is our probable polymorphism that may preserve us as we increasingly face dangers of our own making.

Secondary Beliefs and the Alien Abduction Phenomenon[4]

Abstract: Numbers of persons with cultivated interests in UFOs and claimed alien abductions distinguish among „believers" (people who maintain that it is true, or probably true, that UFOs are spacecraft from distant planetary systems and that abductions have occurred), „skeptics" (those who doubt such claims), and „debunkers" (a subset of skeptics who actively and publicly attempt to refute believers). In addition to acknowledging and discussing these established distinctions, this essay adds another in the case of claimed alien abductions: a distinction between „primary believers" and „secondary believers." Primary believers are persons who assert that they were abducted and who supply „first-hand" details about their abductions. Secondary believers are people who do not claim to have been abducted but who maintain that they believe the claims of abductees (or „experiencers," as they are sometimes called). Most of the literature on so-called alien abductions focuses on abductees and their proffered beliefs. Secondary believers and their asserted beliefs receive much less attention. This essay helps to redress the balance. As we know from studies of somewhat analogous religious movements, secondary believers sometimes play important roles in organizing, disseminating, and enlarging the claims of visionaries or experiencers, and their functions in those regards are clearly deserving of study.

This chapter reports on some research now in process. My colleague, Charles Ziegler, and I are engaged in a complex project dealing with the nature and multifaceted significance of belief. Among other things, we are very much interested in the phenomenon of credulity, which we characterize as the acceptance or justification of belief largely or entirely on the testimony of other persons (Saler 2004).

Our stipulative definition of credulity does not necessarily connote something pejorative, despite a widespread, popular use of the word to mean an uncritical or unsophisticated readiness to accept belief. Credulity, as we conceive it, is a panhuman phenomenon of immense evolutionary significance. It promotes the accessing and utilization of

---

4   „Secondary Beliefs and the Alien Abduction Phenomenon." In Diana G. Tumminia (ed.), *Alien Worlds: Social and Religious Dimensions of Extraterrestrial Contact*, 128–137. Syracuse: Syracuse University Press, 2007.

information stored outside of any given individual, and it facilitates the achievement of cognitive complexity. It is often a cost-effective way of enabling persons within a social group to coordinate their cognitive resources, as well as to benefit from information derived from outsiders. However, there can be costs. Among them are the possible dissemination of misinformation, the narrowing or closing off of avenues of potentially useful investigation and ratiocination, and the diversion of energies that might be gainfully employed elsewhere.

Rather than discuss credulity and related matters mainly in abstract fashion, Ziegler and I attempt to explore them with respect to selected case studies. We are particularly attracted to situations that include expressed differences of opinion within the same society. That is, cases where some members of a given society express what seems to be strong, positive conviction, whereas others register skepticism or disbelief. For exploratory, illustrative, and comparative purposes, and confining ourselves to North America, we have chosen these primary case studies: the Salem witchcraft trials of 1692, a rash of trials in the 1980's alleging ritual or „Satanic" sexual abuse of young children, and the alien abduction phenomenon. While we depend entirely on published material and studies for our coverage of the first and the second, our exploration of the alien abduction phenomenon is based on interviews and a diversity of other sources of information. The alien abduction phenomenon is our central case study, and it constitutes our primary substantive focus for the investigation of what we call „secondary beliefs" as they relate to the matter of credulity. This chapter deals only with that case study.

The Modern Abduction Phenomenon

Persons who affirm the reality of alien abductions generally claim that „alien beings" have abducted contemporary residents of our planet. Numbers of people suggest or maintain that earthlings are kidnapped for medical examinations or experiments, and especially for examinations or experiments dealing with procreation. While most of those who assert this appear to believe that the aliens are extraterrestrial beings from distant solar systems, some suggest that the abductors either are from „parallel dimensions" or that they are time travelers from the troubled future of our own planet.

The modern abduction phenomenon contains elements that remind various of its interpreters of many other things. These include Celtic and other folklore accounts of fairy abductions, certain events in Greek, Roman, or other myths, Judaic and Christian references to angels, North American Indian captivity narratives, still other captivity stories, and a wide diversity of themes found in science fiction, ufology, and other expressions of contemporary Euro-American popular culture. Indeed, Terry Matheson (1998), Professor of Literature at the University of Saskatchewan, sees in them and in the analyses made of them by several authors a complex and subtle ambivalence toward technology, along with a related discourse on power. Elsewhere I attempt to relate abduction narratives to certain developments in the postmodern world as sketched by the postmodernists Frederic Jameson and Jean-François Lyotard. I believe that, „Common themes in abduction accounts are the powerlessness of the victims, their vulnerability to exploitation, and the indifference to human dignity and pretensions of autonomy that is a marked aspect of alien hegemony" (Saler, Ziegler, and Moore 1997: 143), albeit more recent accounts of abduction sometimes suggest more positive themes. The alien abduction phenomenon, to be sure, evinces continuity with a long and probably pan-human history of seeing mysterious or remarkable things in the skies, but one can also interpret it as resonating with much else. As a set of Euro-American narratives for our times, it blends in arresting ways power and sexual themes with interests in science, technology, and the occult.

One of the most famous cases of claimed abduction is that of Betty and Barney Hill, who were reportedly abducted from a highway in New Hampshire in September of 1961 and who later recalled their experiences under hypnosis. From the time of the putative Hill abduction, there have literally been thousands of cases of claimed abductions. No one knows precisely how many, but hundreds have been summarized in a growing literature accessible to the public (e.g., Brookesmith 1998; Bryan 1995; Bullard 1987; Denzler 2001; Fowler 1979; 1982; 1990; 1993; Fuller 1966; Hopkins 1981; 1987; Jacobs 1993; 1999; 2000; Lorenzen 1963; 1970; Lorenzen and Lorenzen 1977; Mack 1995; Randle et al. 1999; Randles 1988; Rogo 1980; Streiber 1987; 1989; Walton 1978). Still other accounts are stored in the private files and videotape archives of numbers of researchers. Some of the abductees tell their stories under hypnosis, but others furnish reports without being hypnotized.

It is important for scholarly purposes to distinguish between the accounts of people claiming to have been abducted — narratives that are often fragmentary and sometimes inconsistent — and the published or filmed versions of those accounts as fashioned by others. Some commentators have recognized the importance of this distinction. It is often recognized, indeed, in distinctions that are drawn between „contactees" and „abductees." So-called contactees are individuals alleging typically friendly personal contacts with aliens, whereas abductees are usually removed against their will. Randle et al. (1999: 90), for instance, remark that the contactee is the focus (and, usually, the expositor) of his or her tale, whereas in the case of abductions the „researcher" (the author or co-author of published accounts) is „the man in the middle" between the abductee and the general public, because the researcher is the person who „answers questions."

Terry Matheson (1998) makes analogous points in a critical analysis of the writings of several authors dealing with the abduction phenomenon. In his initial examination of the abduction literature, Matheson tells us,

> I made two discoveries regarding these narratives and their crucial role in determining how they were received. By and large, authors of most abduction chronicles favored one interpretive possibility that the experiences were taking place more or less as the abductees claimed — and relentlessly privileged that possibility even when the evidence pointed in other directions. I also noticed that the original evidence itself — the actual information provided by the abductees — was often less precise and coherent than was the material the public received. In fact, readers of such books were being manipulated to a significant extent, the writers having employed various strategies designed to enhance coherence and lessen the likelihood that alternative conclusions would be reached (Matheson 1998: 12).

Matheson goes on to make a point similar to those expressed by Carl Jung (1959), Curtis Peebles (1994), Saler, Ziegler, and Moore (1997), Thomas E. Bullard (2000a; 2000b), and others. As Matheson (1998, 13) puts it, „I began to suspect that what was occurring was the creation of a modern, secular myth that we were fortunate enough to be able to observe in the process of being formed and refined."

Causation and Belief

Proponents of the alien abduction phenomenon sometimes employ a trinomial vocabulary for distinguishing among persons who express opinions about the reality of abductions by aliens. „Believers" are those who accept such abductions as real or as highly probable. „Skeptics" are those who confess to harboring strong doubts. „Debunkers," a subset of skeptics, actively attempt to discredit the idea of alien abductions, sometimes proposing alternative explanations for the claimed experiences.

Proffered explanations alternative to actual abduction by aliens include deliberate lying, screen memories that mask sexual abuse, hypnogogic or hypnopompic states associated with „sleep paralysis," hysterical contagion, birth traumas, psychopathology, suggestions from hypnotists and others, wish fulfillment, confabulation, fugue states, temporal lobe epilepsy, and special cases of temporal lobe dysfunctions triggered by electromagnetic stimulation stemming from movements of the earth's crust.

Ziegler and I hold that the claims of abductees relate to a diversity of causes – that, indeed, the alien abduction phenomenon is best conceived to be multi-causal in origin. Allowance should be made for the very real possibility that different alleged abductees respond to different factors and that no one causal factor can be adduced for all cases. If this be accepted, then efforts to dismiss a possible alternative cause not only cannot be taken as significantly strengthening the case for alien abductions, but such efforts are unlikely to equate to a blanket refutation of the suggested alternative possibility. Various skeptics, for instance, have suggested a phenomenon termed „sleep paralysis" as an alternative explanation for the abduction phenomenon. In doing so, some have been inspired by the folklorist David Hufford's analysis (1982) of tales about a folkloric being known as „The Old Hag." Hufford argues that a textual approach to understanding Old Hag stories can be enriched by also considering an experiential dimension of such narratives, inasmuch as some people claim to have actually experienced the Hag. Such experiences often involve a sensation of being paralyzed soon before either waking up or going to sleep. Hufford suggests that those experiences may have enriched folkloric repertoires about the Old Hag. While physiological states by themselves, Hufford maintains, cannot account for either Old Hag folklore or for the meanings of experiences that people associate with that folklore, they and the narratives may sometimes be mutually reinforcing. Drawing on their readings of Hufford's nuanced analysis, some students of alien abductions hypothesize that some abductees may „see" aliens in consequence of their physio-mental states during the transition from wakefulness to sleep or during the transition from sleep to wakefulness (hypnogogic and hypnopompic states).

The historian David M. Jacobs (1993), however, attempts to discredit that explanation entirely, thus removing a causal possibility alternative to the extraterrestrial agency explanation that he favors. He points out that there are a number of reported abductions that occur in daylight when the reputed abductees are presumably in full wakefulness. If, however, we adopt a multi-causal perspective, Jacobs cannot legitimately champion a blanket refutation of the sleep paralysis possibility. Although that possibility cannot account for persons appearing to experience abduction in full wakefulness, hypnogogic and hypnopompic explanations remain as viable alternative explanations for at least some of those persons who reportedly encounter aliens in the bedroom either when going to sleep or when beginning to wake up.

Understandably, most of the literature to date focuses on reputed abductees. Abductees, who are also called „experiencers," relate dramatic tales: arresting stories that stimulate some to suppose that earthlings have been contacted by aliens, while motivating others to offer alternative conjectures as to why their fellow citizens might furnish such narratives. Ziegler and I call the affirmations of abductees *primary beliefs*. However edited and packaged they may be on their way to the public arena, they constitute the primary public „data" of the abduction phenomenon.

Yet, while we must take account of and seek to comprehend primary beliefs and those who affirm them, we also have a strong interest in what we call *secondary beliefs* and their proponents. Secondary beliefs are the affirmations of persons who do not claim to have had abduction experiences but who profess to accept and support the reports of those who do claim such experiences.

Secondary believers have not been adequately studied in the academic literature on alien abductions. For scholars of religion they can be as interesting, or perhaps even more interesting, than primary believers. In the histories of religious and secular movements, it is secondary believers, after all, who sometimes turn the claims of experiencers or visionaries into successfully diffused persuasions, and they deserve at least as much attention as the original sources of the narratives that they support and extend.

Considering secondary believers with respect to the alien abduction phenomenon, credulity in the stipulative sense offered earlier is salient. That is because secondary beliefs in the reality of the alien abduction phenomenon rest entirely on the testimonies of persons, whether hypnotized or not. For despite the efforts of dedicated secondary believers, such as Budd Hopkins (1981, 1987), to find unambiguous material evidence for abductions, no such evidence has been produced. Hopkins and others, for example, have explored the possibility that aliens may have „implanted" monitoring or control devices into some abductees. Hopkins showed me two albums of color photographs of skin colorations and other bodily markings that he deemed possible evidence of implants, but I saw nothing unusual in the photographs. And sensational rumors spread by other persons, to the effect that actual implants have been (or are soon to be) surgically recovered, have never, insofar as I am aware, been given credence by the scientific community. Neither claimed implants nor other claims of material evidence have been produced to the satisfaction of interested skeptical observers. Until claims of such evidence are authenticated, I feel obliged to conclude that what people say happened in abductions remains the basis for secondary beliefs.

Some Attractions of Secondary Beliefs

An obvious and immediate question that merits consideration is this: Why do secondary believers appear to believe in alien abductions? Why, indeed, in the face of challenges from skeptics and debunkers within their own society, do they persist in affirming what they affirm? Further, what might be the larger cultural, comparative, and perhaps even evolutionary implications of their affirmations? These are questions that Ziegler and I are addressing in our ongoing research, and it would be premature to attempt to answer all of them here. However, our project is well enough advanced to sketch some answers to the first question posed.

To begin, just as primary believers are best viewed within a multi-causal framework, so, too, is it necessary to entertain a variety of hypotheses for attempting to understand what may motivate secondary believers. It must be noted in that regard that not all secondary believers register the same intensity of belief. We have been struck both in our interviewing and in our reading by evidence of diversity in the profession of belief, as well as in the contents being professed. Some secondary believers so hedge their affirmations as to suggest lack of firmness in belief, whereas others give the appearance of strong conviction. In that regard, moreover, secondary believers mirror in opposition skeptics and debunkers, making for interesting comparisons. Some skeptics, in our experience, are not entirely skeptical, and they sometimes give the appearance of wanting to believe while not being willing to say that they do. Belief in the reality of aliens, after all, can stimulate, as well as be stimulated by, the imagination. We surmise that it is attractive to some people at least partly (or perhaps largely) on that score.

On the extreme, we have persons who are strongly committed either to affirming or to denying alien abductions and various other claims about UFOs, aliens, and the positions of the government and the military and scientific establishments respecting UFOs and abductions. Thus, for instance, one of the strongest proponents of the reality of UFOs as alien spacecraft, and one of the strongest claimants that there are government-supported conspiracies to suppress information about UFOs, is Stanton T. Friedman. Mr. Friedman has interviewed numerous witnesses to seemingly unusual events – certain of his interviews in the late 1970 s and thereafter, for example, were instrumental in making the so-called „Roswell Incident," the claimed crash of an alien spacecraft near Roswell, New Mexico in 1947, an important case in the UFO community's roster of cases (Saler, Ziegler, and Moore 1997). And, armed with the Freedom of Information Act, he has tirelessly (and sometimes successfully) petitioned US government agencies to release hitherto classified documents. Utilizing the purportedly eyewitness accounts that he and other researchers have collected, along with the documents that he has obtained, Mr. Friedman has devoted many years of his life to lecturing and writing about UFOs and conspiracies (his dedication in that regard is well captured in the Redstar Film documentary, „Stanton T. Friedman IS Real"). Mr. Friedman is matched both in zeal and in the allocation of much of his lifetime by the dedicated debunker, Philip J. Klass. Mr. Klass's numerous publications and many lectures over the years have been directed to rebutting what Mr. Friedman and like-minded others affirm. Karl Pflock, a ufologist who has moved from being a circumspect believer to being a sometimes outspoken debunker in the case of the Roswell Incident, has pointed out to me in a personal communication that Mr. Klass is as much a member of the UFO community as Mr. Friedman. I deem that an astute observation if by „community" we mean a set of persons who evince more that a casual interest in some topic. Much of Mr. Klass's identity is invested in topics of immediate interest to the UFO community.

What motivates such strongly committed persons as Mr. Friedman and Mr. Klass? As of this writing, Ziegler and I have not had the privilege of interviewing either, so I cannot answer the question that I pose. I do think, however, that it is an interesting one, and I hope that we may later attempt to answer it within a biographical framework.

In our interviews and in our readings, we have also been struck with the frequently expressed opinions of secondary believers respecting the apparent *sincerity* of many abductees or experiencers, a sincerity that secondary believers encounter either on personal contact or through reading accounts or viewing videotapes or films furnished by others. While secondary believers occasionally discount the testimonies of some persons who claim to be experiencers, dismissing them as lies or as suggestive of pathology, they often appear to be favorably impressed by narrations that meet certain standards of reportage. First, those standards include the deliverance of narratives that accord with those furnished by other experiencers. Something of a subculture on alien abductions has crystallized (largely with help from the media, Hollywood and television in particular), and, though still somewhat heterogeneous in details, it includes now a fair degree of consensus about what happens when one is abducted. Second, standards for judging abduction narratives dispose at least some secondary believers to favor stories that are related with shows of emotion that are judged to be convincing.

Emotional expressions adjudged especially convincing are shows of fear or terror. These are deemed appropriate and are accepted as integral elements in the primary narrations. Such expressions on the part of primary believers remind me of a radical form of psychotherapy known as abreactive therapy, which supposedly releases repressed emotions. In that form of treatment, the patient is encouraged to re-experience a trauma and accompanying emotional responses that triggered the disturbance. From the skeptic's point of view, however, abductees would be abreacting non-events (Holden and French, 2002; McNally et al, 2004). If the skeptics are correct, how then are we to explain the seemingly sincere expressions of fear or terror? As displacements? As false memories occasioned by traumatic stress? As play acting? Or as something else?

In any case, the emotional component that primary believers communicate to, or evoke in, secondary believers is a matter that deserves close scholarly attention. Sensitivity to emotive transmissions and triggers would be useful not only with respect to studying the dissemination of narratives of claimed alien abductions, but also for a wider understanding of the spread of what we conventionally term religious narrative.

In a 1973 paper dealing with the nature of belief, the anthropologist Robert Hahn proposed what he called „the ethnography of sincerity." Hahn was largely concerned with formal criteria for evaluating propositions. A widened sense of the ethnography of sincerity, a sense that includes attention to the emotions, could well strengthen and extend our scholarly engagements. People, after all, often make efforts to assess the sincerity of messengers as part of their more inclusive efforts to assess the reliability of messages.

Scholars, as we well know, generally seek to situate, analyze, and interpret messages. If they aspire to convincing explanations of why some messages are accepted and others rejected, and by whom, they also need to consider the messengers, their audiences, and the nature of, and constraints on, interactions between them. While we can be guided by general theoretical understandings, those cannot by themselves explain why, within the same society, some people are believers, others are skeptics, and still others are active debunkers. Yet, these are matters that need explaining.

Part IV Studying Religion: Some Conceptual Issues

Family Resemblance and the Definition of Religion[1]

Abstract: Most of this essay is taken up by an argument in favor of defining religion by combining the idea of family resemblance with insights derived from prototype theory. In consonance with that discussion, there are brief considerations of two other issues: (1) If we assign causality to religion in various arguments, to what are we actually assigning causality? (2) A caveat is entered respecting calls to do away with popular analytical categories because they are problem-plagued.

In this article I attempt to do three things. First, to express my views about the idea of family resemblance relative to the problem of defining religion. Second, to suggest a partial answer to a question posed by Luther Martin and his fellow panelists at the 1996 Annual Meeting of the Society for the Scientific Study of Religion: if we assign causality to religion, to what are we assigning it? And third, to enter a caveat respecting the replacement of popular analytical categories.

Fitzgerald and Byrne

The idea of family resemblance as it may relate to the definition of religion has recently been considered by Timothy Fitzgerald (1996, 1997). Fitzgerald adduces reasons to fault both essentialist and family resemblance solutions to the problem of defining religion. With respect to the latter, he claims that „the concept of religion must have some essential characteristic, and if it does not, then the family of religion becomes so large as to be practically meaningless and analytically useless." He maintains, moreover, that „the concept of religion has no distinctive theoretical property and therefore cannot supply the basis for an academic discipline." And he recommends that persons in departments of religious studies turn their attentions to „cultural studies," which he characterizes as „the analysis and interpretation of the values

---

1 „Family Resemblance and the Definition of Religion." *Historical Reflections/ Réflexions Historiques* 25 (3): 301–404, 1999.

institutionalized by different societies" (Fitzgerald 1996: 216, 232–233).

As a cultural anthropologist, I endorse Fitzgerald's call for the study of values. But I do so independently of his claim about family resemblance. Indeed, I reject that claim. And I deem the strategy that he adopted for justifying it to be dubious in principle and unfortunate in execution.

Fitzgerald chose to depend very largely on one effort to connect family resemblance and religion, that of Peter Byrne (1988) in an article of twenty-five pages. Fitzgerald's dependence on that one source is relieved only modestly by references to a book that Byrne published in 1989 on the legacy of deism, by brief allusions to a work by Ninian Smart (1973), and by a one-sentence quotation from A. J. Ayer describing what Wittgenstein meant by family resemblance (cited in Fitzgerald 1996: 216).

Fitzgerald does not quote, cite or otherwise engage Wittgenstein directly, perhaps supposing Byrne's reading of that philosopher to be adequate. Nor, in a paper in which the word philosophy is given a prominent place in the title, does he expand our understanding by invoking the views of other philosophers (save for Byrne) on the subject of family resemblance. He thus ignores such oft cited works, pro and con, as those of J. R. Bambrough (1960) and K. Campbell (1965). Nor does he consider the contributions of the recurrence theorist R. Aaron (1967) or such resemblance theorists as H. H. Price (1969) and A. D. Woozley (1967), philosophers whose views bear certain family resemblances to those of Wittgenstein but who offer their own distinct perspectives and advocacies.

Fitzgerald's declared justification for his strategy is that Byrne is „a competent Oxford-trained philosopher with a lucid style and a considerable ability to present systematic argument." Further, he notes that Byrne's article appears „in a major book edited and written by 40 or more religion scholars," so that we can check Byrne's argument about the definition of religion „against the actual usage of a large family of users" (Fitzgerald 1996: 216).

As Fitzgerald's analysis of Byrne's argument proceeds, he discerns weaknesses in that argument. Fitzgerald intimates that these are occasioned by application of the idea of family resemblance to the definition of religion. I, in contrast, deem them to be occasioned by Byrne's efforts to apply that idea. While Fitzgerald is prepared to reject family resemblance on the basis of his analysis of Byrne's essay, I am not. Byrne's paper makes some valuable points, but it also suffers from certain limitations. And, of course, it is only one of a number of efforts to apply family resemblance to the problem of defining religion.

Some appreciation of the problems involved can be gleaned from a consideration of two matters noted by Fitzgerald. First, Byrne writes that religious beliefs in his schema are concerned with „God, or the gods or more generally sacred things," and he opines that the „sacred" (in a more or less Durkheimian sense) can contribute to distinguishing religion from other things (Byrne 1988: 7, 9). Fitzgerald rightly observes that Byrne's use of the sacred moves in the direction of introducing a necessary condition for distinguishing religion (Fitzgerald 1996: 227). Byrne, on my reading, attempts to guard against such a charge by stressing that the sacred is „vague," that there is no „simple formula" that can give an adequate idea of its complexity, and that „fixing the object of religion" by using the sacred is advantageous because the object is then „broad enough to include religious realities (such as nirvana) which are none the less not divine" (Byrne 1988: 7). In part, then, the sacred is to be preferred because it frees us from making gods the object of religion. But this would seem to substitute a broader necessity for a narrower one.

Second, Fitzgerald (1996: 216) remarks that it is „unclear ... whether Byrne is advocating a use for the word religion, or merely drawing our attention to how it is in fact used." That observation touches on a crucial problem: how to go from an understanding of the way people actually use many words and concepts to the scholarly prescription of an analytical category.

Byrne recognizes common uses of the term religion. He goes on to draw a distinction between operational and essentialist definitions, a distinction that Fitzgerald finds unconvincing. In an effort to formulate an operational definition, Byrne proffers a definition by genus and differentiae. He describes religion as an „institution" with four dimensions: the theoretical, the practical, the sociological, the experiential. These conjunctively establish it as a genus, albeit he notes that „a religion need not show all four dimensions in developed form" (Byrne 1988: 8–9). The institution, moreover, „may be further distinguished by three types of differentiae which qualify the dimensions making up its genus." These are the *object* of the complex („gods or sacred things"), *goals* („salvation or ultimate good"), and *functions* („giving an overall meaning to life or providing the identity or cohesion of a social group") (Byrne 1988: 7). This neat and cerebral exercise, if not actually a case of essentialist recidivism, strikes me as coming uncomfortably close to being such.

Byrne, nevertheless, verges on a solution that could be true to the spirit of family resemblance. He notes that ordinary usage of the term religion points to Christianity, Judaism, Islam, Hinduism and Buddhism as religions, but that we get „no clear guidance from ordinary usage as to whether Confucianism" is to be included as a religion or as an ethical system. And in various places in his essay he talks of „central examples of religion" (e.g., Byrne 1988: 9, 20). Unfortunately, however, Byrne does not enlarge productively on these insights. He might have done so had he invoked some arresting findings and powerful theorizing in the cognitive sciences.

In any case, Byrne's self-defeating maneuvers to solve the definitional problem by invoking family resemblance indirectly support what I regard as an important point: namely, that a family resemblance approach by itself is inadequate to the task of formulating a prescriptive analytical category. Something else is also required.

We can begin to solve the definitional problem by first considering family resemblance and then going beyond it in directions taken by prototype theory. These directions are suggested to some extent by certain of Wittgenstein's insights, such as his recognition of the centrality or paradigmatic status of natural numbers for the conceptualization of other kinds of numbers (Wittgenstein I.67; see also Kenney 1973: 224). But prototype theory goes further.

Family Resemblance

Wittgenstein's application of family resemblance, as Richard Chaney (1978: 139) points out, has „to do with how we use our words and concepts." When, for instance, we apply a general word such as „game" to a diversity of different games, it is not because all games share some one feature or some specific conjunction of features in common. „Don't say:," Wittgenstein advises, „There *must* be something common, or they would not be called 'games' – but *look and see* whether there is anything common to all." And when you look, you do not find some specific commonality. Rather, you see „a complicated network of similarities overlapping and criss-crossing: sometimes overall similarities, sometimes similarities of detail" (Wittgenstein I.66–67: see also Kenney 1973: 224).

Wittgenstein does not claim that members of groups never share something in common. Rather, he holds that the same general term can be applied to diverse phenomena even when they do not share any one feature or specific conjunction of features in common. Indeed, in some cases some things to which the same general term is applied share no discrete features in common. In such cases, however, they typically overlap in features with still other things called by the same general term, those others serving as intermediaries that link together those that share no features, just as the intermediary links in a chain connect the peripheral links on either end.

The philosopher J. Renford Bambrough (1960), in explicating Wittgenstein's concept of family resemblance, compares and contrasts Wittgenstein to nominalists and realists. The nominalist, Bambrough says, is right to insist that the instances of a general term need not share some one feature in common; but the nominalist is wrong to suppose that the application of such a term lacks objective justification. And the realist is right to maintain that there is some objective justification for the application of a general term; but the realist is wrong to insist that the instances of a general term must share some common feature in addition to being instances.

Wittgenstein, says Bambrough, is in accord with what is supportable in the respective positions of nominalists and realists while avoiding their respective mistakes. „He asserts at one and the same time," says Bambrough, „the realist's claim that there is an objective justification for the application of the word 'game' to games and the nominalist's claim that there is no element that is common to all games" (Bambrough 1960: 218). That objective justification is the linkages, the apperceived overlapping similarities, that support the practice of applying the same general term to those diverse phenomena that we call „games."

The same, I think, can be said of our application of the term „religion." We – both as scholars and as participants in other discourses – use the term „religion" in various ways. I advocate that for scholarly purposes we build on this, and that we formally conceive of religion in terms of a pool of elements that more or less co-occur in what scholars generally regard as the clearest or least problematical examples of what they call religion. Those elements – we could conceive of them as a set of predicates – collectively define our conceptual model. The instantiations of that model are what we call religions, and they differentially participate in the pool. The instantiations are linked by family resemblances; they need not all share some one element or some specific subset of elements. Further, the category facilitated by our model is unbounded in that there is no sure or stable border where religion ends and non-religion begins. Rather, we have some very clear cases of what we mean by religion, and then increasingly peripheral cases. Whether or not to admit peripheral cases (e.g., Canonical Theravada Buddhism, Confucianism, Taoism, Communism) is a matter for scholarly argument relative to our defining pool of features and their linkages rather than a matter to be settled by definitional fiat.

The elements that we predicate of our general model of religion are what Jackendoff calls typicality features (Jackendoff 1983: 139). That is, they can be said to be typical of religion, although they may sometimes be discerned in the instantiations of other categories. All of them pertain to our conceptual model of religion, and many of them are found in our clearest exemplars of the category. Less clear cases are less clear because, typically, they manifest fewer of the typicality features of our model; moreover, they typically show less elaboration and emphases of those features.

Attempting to use an analytical category that is organized by family resemblances does pose various problems. Analytical categories are likely to engender problems in application regardless of how they are organized. But there are special difficulties that attach to family resemblance categories. Fitzgerald voices the most commonly heard complaint when he warns (wrongly, I believe) that if religion has no „essential characteristic, ... then the family of religion becomes so large as to be practically meaningless and analytically useless" (Fitzgerald 1996: 216). He misses what I regard as the paramount difficulty. That is, if we once accept and try to use „religion" as an analytical category organized by family resemblances, our commitment to the very idea of family resemblance may well lead us to recognize a terrible (but not a fatal) truth: that it is family resemblances all the way down! I illustrate what I mean at two different analytical levels.

First, denominated religions, such as Judaism, Christianity, Islam, Hinduism, Buddhism and so forth, are not unitary phenomena. They constitute families of religions, and each of those families is organized by resemblances. Thus, for instance, Christianity is a congeries of many Christianities linked by overlapping similarities but divided by differences. Elements that unite some Christianities separate off still others. Take, for example, the doctrine of the dual nature of Christ, a doctrine specifically predicable of the Christian family of religions but not predicable of all Christianities. Monophysite churches reject the doctrine.

And so, too, do various persons who consider themselves Christians but hold that Christ is human and not divine. Some other Christians, who claim that Christ is both human and divine, reject as Christians those who do not profess belief in the divinity of Christ. And some persons who deem themselves Christians repudiate the Monophysites as well, on the ground that a „true" Christian regards Christ as fully human as well as fully divine. In either case, of course, the rejecters essentialize Christianity since they stipulate a necessary condition for being Christian.

What is the scholar to do? Take sides and say that some people who call themselves Christian are not really such? Or treat them all as Christians, though of different kinds? The latter alternative, in my opinion, is the responsible and productive one.

Second, the elements that we predicate of our general model of religion – theism, belief in souls, ritual, sacrifice, sacred canon, eschatology, pilgrimage, etc. – are themselves family resemblance categories. While many anthropologists may not quite realize that is so, numbers of them recognize that conventional, essentialist definitions of category terms do not suffice for cross-cultural purposes in any precise fashion. Thus, for example, Maurice Bloch writes:

> Anthropologists are increasingly familiar with the idea that such terms as „sacrifice," „possession" and „initiation" have a very limited validity in religious anthropology. Such definitions are always rooted in a specific cultural tradition, whether that of the author or of the people he writes about, and are therefore inadequate for cross-cultural analyses. They may be used provisionally, as convenient pointers, but if their application is stretched beyond that they become arbitrary. If general theoretical interpretations are to be attempted at all, they cannot be confined within these sorts of boundaries. (Bloch 1992: 2)

And, again,

> Like a number of recent writers ... I believe it is right to stress the great variety that exists among the various examples of „sacrifice" as they have been described in the anthropological literature .... The phenomena which have been called by names such as totemism or sacrifice are not so varied as to make the words useless as general indicators of linked manifestations. On the other hand these manifestations are so loosely connected that it would be totally pointless to look for an explanation of sacrifice as such ... (Bloch 1992: 25)

Prototype Theory

While there may be no necessary core element, no common essence, to all of the phenomena that scholars treat as examples of „sacrifice" in religions, two observations can be entered by way of suggesting that there is some systematicity to such treatments.

First, scholars tend to identify occurrences in non-Western cultures as instances of „sacrifice" by positing analogies to what they elsewhere call sacrifices. Analogies are ways of discerning similarities in things that otherwise differ. Analogous things are not identical. Grouping by analogy is common, both in ordinary life and in scholarship, and things grouped together are typically assigned the same general term. Thus, for instance, the Western scholar identifies „religion" in non-Western societies that have no name for, or concept of, „religion" by finding analogies to what that scholar regards as instances of religion elsewhere. This, of course, raises a very important question: analogy to what?

Second, phenomena that serve as springboards for drawing analogies are usually things that we take to be fairly clear examples of their categories. With respect to „sacrifice," for instance, scholars may have in mind ancient Greek sacrifices (which were varied), Jewish sacrifices at the Temple in Jerusalem (which arose out of earlier forms of sacrifice), and Christian ideas about the sacrifice of Christ (where in most accounts the sacrificer sacrifices himself). None fully matches in form, content, meaning or social significance the sacrifices performed by the Dinka of the Sudan as described and analyzed by Lienhardt (1961) and discussed by Bloch (1992). It would be foolish to impose, say, Christian ideas about Christ's sacrifice in an effort to achieve an understanding of Dinka practices. But if we suppose, as Bloch maintains, that there is no common essence to all sacrifices, our clearest examples of sacrifice can nevertheless prove useful. They can provide the wherewithal for drawing analogies and foregrounding similarities and differences.

Our clearest examples, indeed, can prove useful for purposes of illustration, reference and comparison. But they themselves do not disclose the structure of their category. We may call these clearest examples „prototypes," or the most prototypical exemplars of their category, following the psychologist Eleanor Rosch, who writes: „By prototypes of categories we have generally meant the clearest cases of category membership defined operationally by peoples' judgments of goodness of membership in the category" (Rosch 1978: 36). And this serves to introduce the subject of prototype theory.

Prototype theory can be narrowly characterized as systematic efforts to account for prototype effects. Prototype effects are asymmetries in judgments people render respecting how well examples or instantiations of categories exemplify their categories. Thus, for example, some people judge apples and oranges to be clearer examples of fruit than olives, and some people judge robins and sparrows to be clearer examples of birds than penguins.

Research indicates that prototype effects are virtually ubiquitous for natural language categories of all sorts, including not only those organized by family resemblance but essentialist categories as well (Armstrong et al 1983). Prototype effects, for instance, are registered for ungraded bounded categories such as „bird" as well as for graded categories such as „tall person."

These finding cannot be accounted for by the classical or essentialist Western theory of categorization. That theory holds that all members of a category must meet the same necessary conditions for inclusion, and that those that do are equally members of the group comprehended by the category. The classical view constitutes a bivalent (or, metaphorically speaking, a „digital") approach to categorizing whereby everything in the world is either a member or not a member of any denominated category. What, then, gives rise to prototype effects? Prototype theorists propose various answers for different sorts of categories, and they suggest that for some (but not necessarily all) categories a multivalent (or, metaphorically speaking, an „analog") approach is realistic. Instead of category membership always being a matter of „yes or no," it is sometimes a matter of „more or less," as, I argue, is the case for the category religion (Saler 1993).

The discovery that prototype effects are virtually ubiquitous for all sorts of natural language categories, and the recognition that the classical theory of categorization is inadequate because it cannot account for that finding, have momentous implications for the scholarly enterprise. Our attentions to the world, and our understandings, depend on categorization. And now we have evidence that our classical theory of categorization – the theory entertained (and positively cathected) by many (probably most) of the readers of these lines – needs to be discarded and to be replaced by a new theory – one that will take adequate account of the appreciable complexity in the developments, structures, and uses of categories. The linguist George Lakoff affirms – and he should be taken seriously – that, „To change the very concept of a category is to change not only our concept of the mind, but also our understanding of the world" (Lakoff 1987: 9).

Prototype theory complements and in certain ways incorporates Wittgenstein's family resemblance construct. Indeed, it celebrates various of his ideas, including, as Eleanor Rosch phrases it, the important „insight that we can judge how clear a case something is and deal with categories on the basis of clear cases in the total absence of information about boundaries" (Rosch 1978: 36).

Prototype theory goes beyond family resemblance. While Wittgenstein's construct is a handy, colloquially derived, way of freeing us from certain „bewitchments" in our thinking about the ways we use terms and concepts, prototype theory seeks to comprehend and explain the structures of different sorts of categories (e.g., graded categories, radial categories, and others). In one promising line of investigation, for example, efforts are made to posit different sorts of „idealized cognitive models" that could account for those different structures (Lakoff 1987). It also has much of value to say about tropes and their important place in human life.

My recommendation, given in greater detail elsewhere, is that we view religion as a graded category the instantiations of which are linked by family resemblances (see Saler 1993). Graded categories are exemplified by such familiar categories as „tall person" and „rich person." There are no universally accepted standards for drawing a sharp line between the tall and the not tall and the rich and the not rich, although public and private agencies sometimes offer guidelines. And these categories are graded because some tall persons are taller than others and some rich persons are richer than others. Religion, of course, is a far more complex matter than these homey examples, since it rests on a large set of elements or predicates and, moreover, we need to take account of their elaborations and complexities. But it otherwise resembles the examples cited. Some religions are characterized by more of the typicality features that we associate with religion than others. In a manner of speaking, some religions (e.g., Judaism, Christianity, Islam, Hinduism, Buddhism) are more religious than what some (but not all) scholars regard as other religions (e.g., Taoism, Confucianism, Communism).

Where, you may ask, does the category give out? There is no sharp cutoff point, nor do we need one. Rather, we have some clear cases of religion and then increasingly less clear ones. As I suggested earlier, scholars must make recommendations about inclusion or exclusion relative to their interests, and they must support those recommendations with analysis and argument, not definitional fiat. While the category is in this sense unbounded, this does not mean, as Fitzgerald (1996: 216) charges, that „the family of religion becomes so large as to be practically meaningless and analytically useless." As our typicality features increasingly diminish, there will be fewer reasons to label increasingly peripheral candidates „religion." Our category is distinguished by central tendencies, not necessary features, and centrality implies periphery rather than fixed borders.

Perhaps I can render this strategy more understandable by using illustrations drawn from recommendations about defining religion proposed by my fellow panelists at the 1997 Annual Meeting of the Society for the Scientiflc Study of Religion, Stewart Guthrie and Brian K. Smith.

Smith (1987) proposes to define religion in terms of canonical reflexivity. Using this as a distinguishing feature, he is compelled by the logic of his position to include „Marxism" and „Freudianism" under the rubric of religion. I deem Smith's discussion of canonical reflexivity to be a valuable contribution to the study of religions. But I regard canonical reflexivity to be typical of religions and not, by itself, definitive of them. The fact, then, that it can be predicated of both Marxism and Freudianism does not, ipso facto, identify them as religions.

Guthrie's (1993) discussion of the significance of anthropomorphism in human life is the most wide-ranging by far of any that I have seen, and I find his account of why anthropomorphism is so widely distributed to be cogent and persuasive. His characterization of religion in terms of what he calls „systematic" anthropomorphism, moreover, seems agreeably analog, for systematicity cannot be fixed in any precise or exhaustive way. I regard anthropomorphism to be typical of religions. But, as Guthrie demonstrates, it is also found in many other things. I do not deem systematic anthropomorphism in itself to be definitive of religion. Religion, like love, is „a many-splendored thing," and I prefer to conceptualize it as such.

Religion as a Causal Factor

Based on my conceptualization of religion, I can suggest a partial answer to the question posed by Luther Martin and his fellow panelists at the 1996 Annual Meeting of the Society for the Scientific Study of Religion. If we invoke religion as a causal factor in explanatory chains, to what are we attributing causality? My answer, very briefly, is that while we may use „religion" as a term of convenience, we need to identify in each instance those specific aspects or elements of religion to which we might ascribe causal powers. Other features of religion may well support those aspects or elements, and so might be said to have causal value also, but less intensely or less directly in whatever may be the case at hand. In most instances, I think, it will be specific aspects of religions, as variously localized in time and place, that deserve emphasis in causal posits.

Substituting Categories

Finally, I want to enter a brief caveat respecting calls to do away with popular analytical categories – and perhaps the disciplines with which they are associated – because they are problem-plagued. Fitzgerald, it may be recalled, urges scholars of religion to abandon „religion" in favor of „cultural studies," the „analysis and interpretation of the values institutionalized by different societies" (Fitzgerald 1996: 232).

I think it very likely that if we substitute one category for another, let alone one discipline for another, we will find that we have substituted one set of problems for some other. The term „value," for example, has a number of senses. It is not easy to define in a way that elicits consensus among scholars, and values are sometimes difficult to establish in any clear way (see, for example, Albert 1956; Ayoub 1968; F. Kluckhohn and Strodbeck 1961). And „ideology," which is currently very fashionable, is difficult to discuss without waxing ideological.

Terms such as „religion," „sacrifice," „value" and so forth are conveniences. They allow us to talk about things that interest us in more or less intelligible fashion. And we can do so even though the terms themselves are polysemous and the categories to which they pertain are organized by family resemblances. We need to be cognizant of their complexities and subtleties, however, if we are to avoid using them in rigid and otherwise nonproductive ways. And we need also to have some sense of their connotations. That is an especially vexing source of problems in the human sciences for, as John Dewey notes:

> Such words as „mind," „subject," „self," „person," „the individual," to say nothing of „value," are more than tinged in their current usage . . . with significations they absorbed from beliefs of an extranatural character. There

is almost no word employed in psychological or societal analysis and description that does not reflect this influence (Dewey 1944: 2).

If substitution of categories or disciplines will not save us from problems, how, then, might scholars avoid them? We could attempt to emulate that paragon of philosophers, Cratylus, who eventually judged language to be so deceitful that he retired into silence, wagging a finger now and then to communicate. He, it must be admitted, adopted a solution that was consistent with his analysis. But I suspect that most of you will join me in rejecting it. And by rejecting it, we go on talking in a scholarly vein: which is to say, problematically.

Conceptualizing Religion: The Matter of Boundaries[2]

Abstract: This essay enriches the argument for conceptualizing religion made in the preceding essay. It does so particularly with respect to the question of bounding religion. It draws a distinction between bounded and unbounded categories, and assigns religion to the latter type. It suggests, moreover, that we may expect to find elements that we sometimes think of as „religious" elements outside of complexes that we readily label religions. By systematically studying such elements, we may hope to extend our understandings of a religious dimension in human life while transcending the category religion.

1

I have been requested to speak about my approach to conceptualizing religion, an approach set out in a book entitled *Conceptualizing Religion* (Saler 1993). I am pleased to comply with that request, all the more so because it gives me an opportunity to clarify certain matters.

The subtitle of the book is *Immanent Anthropologists, Transcendent Natives, and Unbounded Categories*. Reviewers and commentators seem to have little or no difficulty understanding my uses of „immanent" and „transcendent", and they do not appear to take umbrage at those uses. But that is not the case for "unbounded categories". It is particularly not the case when I advocate that religion be conceptualized as an unbounded category. That recommendation troubled some commentators at the recent International Congress for the History of Religions in Mexico City, and I imagine that it may trouble some of you.

If we conceptualize religion as an unbounded category, some wondered, would that not in effect render almost everything religious and gather together a huge and bewildering diversity of things under the rubric „religion"? No, not really, I can reply in good faith. It would

---

2 „Conceptualizing Religion: The Matter of Boundaries." In Hans-Joachim Klimkeit (ed.), *Vergleichen und Verstehen in der Religionswissenschaft*, 27–35. Wiesbaden: Harrassowitz Verlag, 1997.

enlarge our field of scholarship, however, by facilitating the transcendence of religion in our attentions to the religious dimension in human life, a matter that I return to later in this lecture. And to the closely related complaint, „How could we do responsible, systematic scholarly work if our central organizing category is unbounded?", I answer that attempting to work with an unbounded category is worth the experiment. All the more so, I add, because all efforts to bound the category of which I have knowledge strike me as failures, even though the arguments given in support of those efforts sometimes extend our knowledge and understandings.

But let me first sketch my approach before further discussing these criticisms and my replies to them.

I begin with an observation that I think that all of you would accept: Western scholars who study religions develop some understanding of what is meant by religion in their society long before they become scholars. This observation is so unremarkable, so obvious and seemingly trite, that I would be embarrassed to voice it were it not important. But it is important. Long before European scholars of religion become scholars of religion, they have fairly well developed ideas of what to look for in searching the world for religions. In large measure, indeed, their scholarly efforts to define or characterize religion are efforts to refine and deepen the folk category that they began to use as children, and to foreground what they deem most salient or important about religion.

Both of these scholarly interests – refining and deepening the folk category, and, at the same time, pointing out what is held to be most salient or important – are well illustrated by the anthropologist Melford Spiro's attempt to define religion. Since „religion", he writes,

> is a term with historically rooted meanings, a definition must satisfy not only the criterion of cross-cultural applicability but also the criterion of intra-cultural intuitivity; at the least, it should not be counter-intuitive. For me, therefore, any definition of „religion" which does not include, as a key variable, the belief in superhuman – I won't muddy the metaphysical waters with „supernatural" – beings who have power to help or harm man is counter-intuitive. Indeed, if anthropological consensus were to exclude such beliefs from the set of variables which is necessarily designated by „religion", an explanation for these beliefs would surely continue to elicit our research energies (Spiro 1996: 91).

Spiro then goes on to offer us what he terms a „substantive" definition of religion. He defines it as „an institution consisting of culturally patterned interaction with culturally postulated superhuman beings" (Spiro 1996: 96). This definition can also be described as „monothetic." That is, it stipulates a conjunction of features that are jointly necessary and sufficient for identifying religion wherever it may occur. Spiro furnishes us with two features: culturally postulated superhuman beings and culturally patterned interaction with them. These two distinctive features jointly describe what Spiro regards as the essence of religion, which, presumably, all religions share. And his definition, I think you will agree, is not counter-intuitive for Westerners. It fits the religions that most of us have known from childhood.

Now, in proffering this definition of religion, Spiro is willing, „for the sake of brevity," he says, to refer to „superhuman beings" as „gods" (Spiro 1996: 92). Spiro acknowledges, moreover, that Durkheim rejected a theistic definition of religion based on his understanding of Buddhism. But Durkheim, he opines, was wrong to do so. „If gods," Spiro writes,

> are important for their believers because – as I would insist is the case – they possess power greater than man's, including the power to assist man in, or prevent him from, attaining mundane and/or supermundane goals, even Theravada Buddhism – Mahayana is clearly not at issue here – most certainly contains such beliefs. With respect to supermundane goals, the Buddha is certainly a superhuman being. Unlike ordinary humans, he himself acquired the power to attain Enlightenment and, hence [sic!] Buddhahood. Moreover, he showed others the means for its attainment. Without his teachings, natural man could not, unassisted, have discovered the way to Enlightenment and to final Release (Spiro 1996: 92).

In a later work based on his fieldwork in Burma, Spiro cogently argues that Theravada Buddhism in Burma does not constitute a monolithic religion but is actually a family of religions (Spiro 1982). Most Burmese Buddhists, he tells us, are what he calls „Kammatic" Buddhists. Rather than attempting to end the accumulation of karma, they desire to obtain good karma so that they may improve their worldly positions in future rebirths. At the same time, however, they express admiration for what Spiro calls „Nibbanic" Buddhism, the Buddhism of the Pali Canon. Those who practice Kammatic Buddhism generally maintain that they are too worldly and weak to follow strictly the teachings of the Buddha, though they greatly value those teachings. In any case, Spiro's depiction of the Buddha as godlike in his 1966 essay presumably applies to both Nibbanic and Kammatic forms of Theravada Buddhism, and also to what Spiro calls Apotropaic and Esoteric Buddhism.

Martin Southwold, a British social anthropologist who studied Buddhist villagers in Sri Lanka, rejects Spiro's interpretation of the Buddha. Spiro's claim, Southwold maintains, is „sheer equivocation, exploiting the vagueness of the word 'superhuman'." For even if it could be argued that the Buddha was „superhuman" in some respect, Southwold states, he is „quite definitely ... not ... godlike in the sense required by the theistic conception" of religion (Southwold 1978: 365). Southwold supplies some reasons, based on his study of Buddhists in Sri Lanka, for faulting not only Spiro's analysis of the significance of the Buddha in Buddhism but also a parallel yet quite distinct analysis put forth by Richard Gombrich.

Without rehearsing here the details of Southwold's analysis of Buddhism, suffice it to summarize certain of his conclusions. Since, he points out, it is a formal requirement of the kind of definitional approach used by Spiro that all instantiations of religion must share the same distinctive features, „even one exception is sufficient to refute the definition" (Southwold 1978: 367). Southwold claims to have supplied us with such an exception because, he writes, „We have in Buddhism (which in fact is not wholly unique) a well-authenticated instance of a system of religious behavior without a central concern with godlike beings" (Southwold 1978: 367). He concludes that theism is a contingent but not a necessary feature of religion. And he advocates an approach to conceptualizing religion based on so-called „polythetic classification." I criticize his notion of „polythetic classification" at some length in my 1993 book. I opine, nevertheless, that Southwold is heading in the right direction.

Now, while I deem Southwold to be heading in the right direction, and while I think that Spiro's general approach is about as practical as an essentialist approach can be, both Spiro and Southwold strike me as over-generalizing when it comes to Buddhism. Spiro, despite his own impressive work on variations within the family of religions that we call „Buddhism," seems to imply that the Buddha is superhuman in all Buddhisms. He allows that this is not the case for some Buddhist philosophical schools, but these, he asserts, are not to be confused with religions (Spiro 1966: 93). Hence, for Spiro, Buddhism as a religion is theistic. And Southwold, who studied only a small population of Sinhalese Buddhists, generalizes his conclusion about the absence of a central concern with theism from that population to Theravada Buddhists at large.

When it comes to Buddhism, I much prefer the approach of the philosopher W. D. Hudson. Hudson applies Wittgenstein's version of the idea of family resemblances to the question of whether or not Buddhism is theistic. Spiro and Southwold mutually treat that question as entailing response within a binary frame, Spiro answering „yes" and Southwold answering „no." Hudson does not feel obliged to resolve the matter bivalently. He allows that there may be some Buddhisms that are „atheistic," as Durkheim and others supposed. Yet there are other branches of Buddhism that are clearly theistic. Hence, Hudson maintains, theism is among the family resemblances of Buddhism, and it can be predicated of Buddhism in general even if it cannot be predicated of all forms of Buddhism (Hudson 1977: 238).

2

This matter of family resemblances can be taken as suggesting the complexity of religion. Yet although Western academic students of religion are generally equipped by experience to have some appreciation of such complexity, when they write papers purporting to set forth the essence of religion, they tend to strip religion down in the effort to capture and describe its most fundamental and universal features. In doing so, they may well say some interesting things. But definitional exercises that narrow religion down to one or a few features potentially deflect our attention away from other elements that deserve consideration. They invite us, moreover, to so interpret phenomena that we intuit to be religions as to make them conform to the definition, thus legitimating and formalizing our intuitions, but perhaps at the cost of distorting our understanding of the phenomena in question.

My proposals for conceptualizing religion, in comparison, take better account of the complexity of religions and religion, and they are less likely to turn our intuitions into springboards for distortion. I argue that in transforming the Western folk category „religion" into an analytical category suitable for cross-cultural studies, we can productively conceptualize it in terms of a pool of elements. I have in mind such elements as theism, extra-human justifications of a moral code, rituals with eschatological, soteriological, and extra-human referents, and various other features that scholars discern in religion. All of these elements are predicable of our analytical category, but not all of them will apply to the different instantiations of that category. Those instantiations, which we call religions, will overlap, but they will not necessarily share any one element, or any specific conjunction of elements, that we predicate of our analytical model. Rather, they will be linked together by their overlaps, by their sharing of family likenesses but not complete identity. They have no single essence.

This logic applies also to families of religion. I referred earlier to Hudson's argument that theism is among the family resemblance predicates of Buddhism although it may not be predicable of all forms of Buddhism. Another example that I give in the 1993 book is the doctrine of the dual nature of Christ. That doctrine is predicable of the Christian family of religions even though monophysite Christians reject it in one way while some other Christians reject it in another.

Within a discernible religious tradition, I might add, elements that pertain to our general model are likely to be weighted differently. Some, that is, will be privileged over others, perhaps by receiving greater elaboration or other forms of attention. Furthermore, the relative weightings may change over time. Thus, for example, while the crucifixion and resurrection are important elements in mainstream Christianity, at different times and in different places one may receive more emphasis than the other in sermons, religious paintings, and the like.

3.

Now, while a family resemblance approach to conceptualizing religion has been suggested by others, I enlarge that approach by incorporating certain elements of prototype theory.

Prototype theory, conservatively characterized, attempts to analyze and account for prototype effects. Prototype effects are asymmetries in the judgments that people make about how well examples of a category exemplify that category. In Massachusetts, for instance, robins are generally deemed clearer or better examples of the category „bird" than penguins.

Prototype effects are important, all the more so since they are virtually ubiquitous. They themselves, however, do not disclose the structures of their categories. Indeed, in attempting to account for prototype effects, it is necessary to theorize about the structures of categories and what may produce them. All natural language categories do not have the same structure.

The linguist George Lakoff (1987) trys to explain prototype effects in terms of what he calls „idealized cognitive models," and in doing so he suggests a fair amount of complexity in the structure of human thought. For my purposes, however, it is unnecessary to probe that complexity in any profundity. Rather, it will suffice to point to two broadly conceived sorts of categories.

One sort we will call bounded. Such categories can be defined by necessary and sufficient conditions. Many of these categories, nevertheless, are associated with prototype effects. This is even true, for example, of that seemingly simple, clearly bounded category known as „odd number." The category label refers to all integers that cannot be divided by 2. The category is not graded or „fuzzy" because all integers indivisible by 2 are equally and fully members of the group comprehended by it. Yet the psychologists Armstrong et al (1983) find that experimental subjects deemed 7 a better exemplar of the category than 23. Among other things, subjects are quicker in recognizing the former as an example than the latter.

The other sort of broadly conceived category we will call unbounded. Depending on perspective and circumstances, such categories might also be called „graded," „scalar," or „fuzzy." They lack sure or firm boundaries, although persons may sometimes attempt to stipulate them. An example is the category „tall man." Membership in that category is graded, for some tall men are taller than others. The line between tall men and not-tall men, moreover, is fuzzy, although in some societies tailors, basketball coaches, dating services, and others may set their own standards.

Clear examples of either sort of category, bounded or unbounded, can be used as cognitive reference points in thinking about the categories to which they relate and in making inferences about newly encountered phenomena that may fit those categories, if only peripherally. Prototype theorists call the clearest or best examples of a category „prototypes." Prototypes are determined operationally from the judgments that people make about which examples of a category best exemplify that category.

Now, whatever the folk status of religion may be in different places, I advocate that it be conceptualized for scholarly purposes as an unbounded analytical category. I suggest, moreover, that for Western scholars, the most prototypical examples of religion are those families of religion that we term „Judaism", „Christianity", and „Islam".

This does not mean that the Western monotheisms directly and immediately yield the structure of our analytical category. Nor does it mean that they suffice for the representation of what we mean by religion, nor for a sophisticated understanding of religion and why we have it. Our general model and understanding of religion must be deliberately formulated on the basis of our accumulated knowledge of what we have thus far deemed religions in different areas of the world, Western and non-Western.

The elements that we assign to our general analytical model are formally predicated of that model. The Western monotheisms are among our clearest examples of that model. Not only do they express phenomenally most of the elements of the model, but they elaborate and integrate those elements in meaningful ways, ways that resonate with our experientially derived intuitions about religion. As the most prototypical exemplars, the Western monotheisms are useful for purposes of reference, illustration, and· comparison. They do not, however, define our model. Our analytical model is a formal model,

Not all exemplars of the model will share the same elements or identical structures and functions. Those that exhibit both the greatest number of elements and the highest degrees of elaboration and integration of those elements are likely to be among the most prototypical. And prototypicality will diminish as we extend our purview to cases that are increasingly peripheral to the model.

Where does the analytical category based on the model give out? Where, that is, is the line between religion and non-religion? This is a matter that troubled some commentators in Mexico City, and it may trouble some of you. Yet as Wittgenstein realized, we can deal with categories in the absence of information about boundaries. As a practical matter, moreover, the community of scholars has done so in the past and can continue to do so.

There is, I think, no line that we could all agree on. Nor do we need some sharp cut-off point. Scholars will disagree – as they always have – about what might be included under the rubric religion. Now, however, they will be obliged to justify explicitly their decisions to include or exclude specific candidates by referring to a complex formal model and, if useful for purposes of explication, a set of cognitive reference points that are commonly accepted by the community of scholars. Intelligibility within the scholarly community should be enhanced in consequence, and our conceptual tools for dealing with a world of complex variations and multiple shadings should be greatly improved.

Insofar as its instantiations are concerned, our analytical category is unbounded. It is a graded category, and some of its instantiations are more religious than others, just as some tall men are taller than others.

Scholars working with essentialist conceptions of religion have long recognized so-called borderline cases of religion, cases that resemble commonly accepted religions in some respects but not in others. But borderline cases, it is well to remember, are created by borders. The matter of borders, moreover, may be important to some of us because of our metaphysical leanings and associated desires for a neat and tidy world. Imposing sharp boundaries on a fuzzy world, however, is distorting. And we can get along quite well without doing so.

Those religions now commonly recognized to be religions will remain such. The inclusion or exclusion of more peripheral cases will be a matter for scholarly debate rather than definitional fiat. And by systematically exploring elements that we associate with religion among relatively lesser, or less clear, exemplars of religiosity – among what some now call „quasi-religions," or „secular religions," or „semi-religions," – as well as among the instantiations of other categories, we expand our opportunity to study elements that we ascribe to our model of religion in a rich diversity of settings. Our attentions to the complexities and subtleties that attach to such elements in variegated and differently-nuanced contexts should enhance our appreciation of religious longings and expressions, even as they may occur outside of a complex that we unhesitatingly identify as a „religion." In short, we may hope to transcend religion while coming to understand more about the religious dimension in human life.

Comparison: Some Suggestions for Improving the Inevitable[3]

Abstract: Some of the intellectual processes of the human mind-brain are crucially comparative. Comparison, indeed, is ineluctable in monitoring the world and in coming to understand newly encountered events. Perhaps, then, we may consciously improve on what is cognitively inevitable. This possibility is discussed with reference to some classical posits of cultural universals, certain complementary problems of language in the work of cross-cultural comparativists and cross-species comparativists, and a distinction drawn by the philosopher H. H. Price between what he calls „The Philosophy of Universals" and „The Philosophy of Resemblances."

1

In an essay published in 1863, the poet Charles Baudelaire identified „modernity" in art with the transient, the fleeting, and the contingent, in contrastive tension with the eternal and the immutable. Relative to that tension, later essayists emphasized a tension between the particular and the general as another of the discernable hallmarks of modernity or modernism, those terms now being variously applied to more than we conventionally associate with art.

Postmodernism, in comparison, would reduce tension by celebrating and otherwise privileging the particular. In celebrating the particular, it also accepts, as David Harvey (1989: 44) puts it, „the ephemerality, fragmentation, discontinuity, and the chaotic that formed the one half of Baudelaire's conception of modernity." Hence the postmodernist's avowed rejection (if not always a rejection in other respects) of „meta-narratives" and „totalizing" theories. But in endorsing only one-half of what produces the distinctive tension of modernity/modernism, and in recommending that we eschew the general, some postmodernists urge us to do what we cannot. For the general is inti-

---

3 „Comparison: Some Suggestions for Improving the Inevitable." *Numen* 48 (3): 267–275, 2001.

mately associated with the comparative, and the comparative cannot be eschewed.

Comparison is vital in certain of the activities of the mind-brain. We regularly monitor the world, and in doing so we creatively and selectively compare newly encountered phenomena to established representational structures. Comparative processes are thus of crucial importance in cognition.

The representational structures to which I refer are sometimes called „schemas." They are, in George Mandler's words, „abstract representations of environmental regularities," and our comprehension of newly encountered events is often triggered by the more-or-less matching schemas that they activate (Mandler 1984: 56). Schemas are thus processors as well as representations. As Roy D'Andrade puts it, from a certain perspective they „are a kind of mental recognition 'device' which *creates* a complex interpretation from minimal inputs," and as such they are more than just „pictures" in the mind (D'Andrade 1995: 136) This is also the case for what cognitive scientists mean by „prototypes." Prototypes can be thought of as highly typical instantiations of schemas. As such, they consist of relatively specified expectations, in comparison to the more „schematic" or open-slotted constitution of schemas in general (for an application of prototype theory to religion, see Saler 2000a [1993]). To quote D'Andrade once more, „The filling in of the slots of a schema with an individual's standard default values creates a *prototype*" (1995: 124).

While schema theory has undergone important developments in the last several decades, and has become increasingly assimilated to models of parallel distributed processing or „connectionist" networks (Norman 1986; D'Andrade 1995: 138–143), it has always supported the understanding that certain of the most important activities of the mind-brain are crucially comparative. It helps us to appreciate more profoundly than we otherwise might that our scholarly efforts at studying some denominated or otherwise identified religious complex are in significant ways motivated, figured, and constrained by our understandings (and misunderstandings) of other religious complexes and their larger cultural and situational contexts. What we are sometimes pleased to call our discoveries or fresh understandings ineluctably occur within comparative frameworks, regardless of whether or not we explicitly acknowledge that that is so. Inasmuch as comparison is inescapable in our intellectual engagements, then perhaps raising and attempting to answer significant questions about it could help us to improve the inevitable.

In the remainder of this paper I touch on two sets of topics respecting comparative structures and processes that I deem especially interesting to students of the human condition. First, I discuss the matter of generalizations as expressed in efforts to posit so-called „cultural universals" or „human universals." Second, I suggest that juxtaposing cross-cultural comparativists to phylogenetic comparativists helps illumine certain problems of language that bedevil efforts at explicit comparisons.

2

Landmarks within cultural anthropology in the specification of cultural or human universals include Clark Wissler's discussion of „The Universal Pattern" in a 1923 book, George Peter Murdock's 1945 essay „The Common Denominator of Cultures," Clyde Kluckhohn's 1953 paper „Universal Categories of Culture," and Donald E. Brown's 1991 book, *Human Universals*. Each, I think, broaches some interesting considerations.

Thus, for example, Murdock identifies cultural universals with commonalities in form rather than in content. He opines, for instance, that while funeral rites throughout the world vary greatly in content, they can be viewed as formally similar in terms of analytical sub-universals, such as institutionalized means of disposing of corpses, expressing grief and solacing mourners, and addressing potential rends in the fabric of social relations occasioned by the demise of social actors. And Donald Brown, who agreeably (for me at least) relates his discussion to developments in evolutionary psychology, offers some sophisticated caveats, insights, and perspectives. Thus, for example, he appreciates the fact that the positing of human universals typically rests on limited cases (1991: 51). That is, the supposition that certain things are universal in human life is not supported by exhaustive studies of all humankind but only by the cases actually known and reasonable inferences or hypotheses related to those cases. Further, seemingly negative cases, if such are encountered, are to be discounted if good reasons can be adduced for doing so.

Now, despite Brown's sophistication and general good sense, I am uncomfortable with the notion of human universals. I will now briefly sketch some reasons for my discomfort, as preparation for proposing that instead of talking about human universals we speak about natural resemblances, and that instead of attempting to identify cultural universals we look for cultural resemblances.

To begin, discussions such as Brown's should be related to what others have proposed. Putting aside for the moment arguments among philosophers regarding what they call „the problem of universals," arguments that Brown and his predecessors largely ignore, we find an almost bewildering variety of stipulated sorts of „universals" to consider. Brown lists, and to varying extents describes, the following: substantive universals, formal universals, near universals, absolute universals, statistical universals, implicational or conditional universals, unrestricted or non-conditional universals, innate universals, manifest universals, experiential universals, universals of content, universals of classification, another (albeit unlabeled) conception of universals embodied in universal models or universal frameworks, emic universals, etic universals, universals stated in the negative (for example, „no society is a matriarchy"), and then some as yet unused or underused universals that Brown deems potentially useful, namely universals of essence and universals of accident and new universals and former universals (Brown 1991: 39–53).

These universals are not arranged into any sort of discernable, overall classificatory scheme, nor are they all of comparable type. Some of them, moreover, may be combined with others, as, for example, in the case of implicational and statistical universals. In any case, this profusion – and, I fear, confusion – of universals is enough to cross a medieval schoolman's eyes.

While Donald Brown serves as our initial guide for defining or characterizing the listed kinds of universals, there is another question about definition or characterization that is more troublesome and not as well handled. That is, how are we to recognize or justify possible examples of various posited universals? Or, to rephrase it with greater substantive focus, how are we to recognize or justify purported examples of human or cultural universals? If, for instance, we suppose that funeral rites are a cultural universal, how are we to identify funeral rites not only within some culturally-organized population but also among different culturally-organized populations?

This question touches on what philosophers call „the problem of universals," although social scientists, insofar as I am aware, generally pay little attention to the literature in philosophy addressed to that topic.

A weak excuse for neglecting it could rest on the fact that what philosophers traditionally mean by the term „universal" is not the same thing as what social scientists usually mean by „universal" when they posit cultural or human universals. But while there is a genuine difference, the philosophical problem relates significantly to invocations of the term „universal" in the social sciences.

„The problem of universals" in philosophy is actually a congeries of problems. There is, however, a central motivating concern that is captured in this question: *How do we justify applying the same general term to a diversity of particulars?* Classical attempts to answer that question include the Platonic *universalia ante rem*, the Aristotelian *universalia in rebus*, and various permutations or refinements of these. In the twentieth century, however, a new set of answers has been proposed, a set of answers subsumable under the rubric of „resemblance theory," and I recommend that we embrace resemblance theory in our efforts to make and sustain explicit comparisons and generalizations.

In resemblance theory, objects are apperceived as resembling one another in different respects and in different degrees (Price 1971: 45). As the philosopher A. D. Woozley puts it,

> Red objects are to be called red simply because they resemble each other in a way in which they do not resemble blue objects or hard objects ... There is a similarity between the red of one and the red of the other, and the similarity might be anything from being virtually exact ... to being only approximate and generic. (1967: 204)

The philosopher H. H. Price distinguishes between what he calls the Philosophy of Universals and the Philosophy of Resemblances. Proponents of both philosophies generally agree that there can be a class of red objects. But, Price writes,

> The question is, what sort of a structure does a class have? That is where the two philosophies differ. According to the Philosophy of Universals, a class is so to speak a promiscuous or equalitarian assemblage. All its members have, as it were, the same status in it. All of them are instances of the same universal ... But in the Philosophy of Resemblances a class has a more complex structure than this ... Every class has, as it were, a nucleus, an inner ring of key members, consisting of a small group of standard objects or exemplars ... [and] every other member of the class should resemble the class exemplars as closely as they resemble one another. (1971: 46–47)

My suggestion for improving the comparative enterprise is that we refrain from positing universals in favor of rendering explicit judgments about resemblances. Instead, that is, of asking, „What might be human universals?," it would be better to ask, „What might be significant natural resemblances among humans?" (e.g., Needham 1972). My reasons for making this suggestion include the conviction that „The Philosophy of Resemblances" receives greater support from the theorizing and findings of the contemporary cognitive sciences than does „The Philosophy of Universals". That is so not only with respect to increasing recognition of the widespread distribution of „prototype effects" (popular judgments that some instantiations of natural language categories are better exemplars of their categories than others; see, for example, Lakoff 1987), but in much else as well, including connectionist theory, which imputes to cognizing subjects connection networks and weightings while not necessarily imputing rules (D'Andrade 1995: 143–146). Further, while the term „universal" may connote something „out there" that is independent of cognitive mediation, „resemblance" suggests a judgment that *someone* makes, and makes within a mediating framework (Saler 2000a [1993]).

3

Finally, by way of concluding, I touch very briefly on another problem that has been viewed as bedeviling cross-cultural comparisons: the problem of *ethnocentric* language. That problem, interestingly enough, is paralleled by a problem faced by phylogenetic comparativists, the problem of *anthropocentric* language. Both are problems in finding appropriate language to be used across conceptualized boundaries, in one case cultural boundaries, in the other case species boundaries. As it happens, however, the boundaries of the former are often shifted in keeping with the methodology of the latter, thus reminding us of the strategic and tactical flexibility that we actually enjoy in pursuing our intellectual interests.

In phylogenetic perspective, *inter*-cultural differences among human beings are to all intents and purposes collapsed into *intra*-cultural differences. That is, in comparing human beings to other animals, differences between cultures of the sort that otherwise interest anthropologists are effectively ignored or treated as if they were merely varied expressions of human universals. By so doing we envision a human situation that admits to some extent of internal cultural heterogeneity but that is otherwise treated as if it were phenomenally homogeneous for purposes of phylogenetic comparisons. The desire of the cross-cultural comparativist to identify pan-human regularities or recurrences is thus realized to a certain extent in the comparative operations of his colleague or other self, the phylogenetic comparativist.

Despite, however, such strategic and tactical maneuvers in serving the purposes of phylogenetic comparativists, the problem of finding appropriate language has not really been solved when we look at cross-cultural comparisons through a closer lens. It is here, I think, that the Philosophy of Resemblances offers us advantages in achieving comparisons. It inspires us to select and order apperceived resemblances in things that we explicitly recognize to differ rather than translate similarities into identities and so eclipse differences. Under its aegis, and with heightened sensitivity to the powerful roles of analogy in human cognizing, our comparisons will change in the direction of greater complexity and subtlety. They will take greater account of variations and differential weightings of elements and their associations than is mandated by the traditional Philosophy of Universals and the perspectives on categories and comparisons that it supports. In short, our comparisons are likely to become more realistic, both existentially and cognitively.

Biology and Religion: On Establishing a Problematic[4]

Abstract: Scholars opt for different ways of relating biology and religion, depending on their interests and the problem-sets that concern them. Much of this essay is addressed to the classicist Walter Burkert's efforts to establish a problematic by positing a „biological landscape" for religion. Several criticisms are made of those efforts, particularly with respect to Burkert's attempts to relate human pars pro toto (part for the whole) rituals to the escape behaviors of various nonhuman animals. Thus, for instance, Burkert is criticized for ignoring the different cultural meanings to different populations of one of his chief human examples, the intentional cutting off of a finger or a finger joint. And, as a general criticism of his approach, Burkert is faulted for appearing to do what Tooby, Cosmides, and Barkow warn us against: „leapfrogging" the psychological in applying evolutionary biology directly to human social life.

1

In an article on Steven Pinker's *How the Mind Works*, Steve Jones opines that for most scientists, „philosophy is to science as pornography is to sex: it is cheaper, easier, and some people seem, bafflingly, to prefer it" (1997: 13–14). The sort of philosophy to which Jones refers is the interpretation of nature „in metaphysical terms" (Jones 1997: 13), an enterprise warned against in the motto of the Royal Society of London, *Nullius in verba*, trust not in words (Jones 1997: 13). But while we might incline to the Royal Society's aversion to metaphysical conjectures, we would do well not to conflate such conjectures with philosophical concerns and reflections of an epistemological and analytical sort.

Philosophical concerns of an epistemological and analytical sort are of importance for establishing a problematic in the study of biology and religion. Such concerns can be expressed in the form of questions such as these: What do we want to know? Why do we want to know those things? And what sorts of constraints might affect our understandings?

---

4 „Biology and Religion: On Establishing a Problematic." *Method and Theory in the Study of Religion* 11 (4): 386–394, 1999. A shorter version of this paper was read at the 96th annual meeting of the American Anthropological Association, Washington, D.C., November 23, 1997.

The study of biology and religion implicates at least two interests: an interest in religion and, more broadly, an interest in the human condition, particularly as that condition may be illuminated by theorizing about evolutionary developments and human nature. But while establishing a problematic embraces both interests, different scholars are guided by different agendas and emphases. In some cases, primary emphasis is directed to religion as explanandum, the thing to be explained or to be better understood. In other cases, consideration of religion is largely instrumental or illustrative.

Gravitating toward one interest rather than the other will have consequences. That is so not only respecting treatment of the interest that receives relatively less emphasis, but also for the sorts of criticisms likely to be raised by other scholars.

An example of what I mean can be drawn from a two-part essay in the *New York Review of Books* by Stephen Jay Gould (1997a; 1997b). That essay is followed by Gould's responses to some criticisms of the essay by Steven Pinker (Gould 1997c). Gould suggests that religion is a „spandrel." Spandrel is a term that Gould and Richard Lewontin (1979) borrow from architecture and incorporate into evolutionary biology. They use it to mean a non-adaptive evolutionary development. That is, it is an architectural byproduct of other evolutionary changes. Although not originally adaptive, it may eventually take on functional significance. Gould relates that he and Lewontin borrowed the term spandrel to make „a crucial distinction between nonadaptive *origin* and possible later utility." They did so, indeed, „in order to expose one of the great fallacies so commonly made in evolutionary argument: the misuse of a current utility to infer an adaptive origin" (Gould 1997c: 57; emphasis in original).

Now, in treating religion as a spandrel, Gould is not primarily interested in religion in the essay and responses cited above. His emphasis there is on criticizing what he calls „Darwinian fundamentalists" (i.e., adaptationists who treat natural selection as if it were the sole mechanism in evolution). Gould, in contrast to that species of „fundamentalists," advocates a pluralistic view of evolution. He maintains that natural selection is the *primus inter pares* of evolutionary principles, and he argues that we ought to take account of other evolutionary laws or mechanisms in addition to natural selection. He contends, moreover, that we should also make allowance for historical contingencies (1997b: 47).

Gould's invocations of religion and of Sigmund Freud's theorizing about religion are given in this passage in the essay:

> Even such an eminently functional and universal institution as religion arose largely as a spandrel if we accept Freud's old and sensible argument that humans invented religious belief largely to accommodate the most terrifying fact that our large brains forced us to acknowledge: the inevitability of personal mortality. We can scarcely argue that the brain got large so that we would know we must die! (1997b: 52)

The above statement forms a very minor part of Gould's overall argument. Students of religion, nevertheless, may regret it as simplistic, both with respect to religion, a multi-faceted and variable phenomenon, and with respect to Freud's theorizing about religion, which strikes out on multiple tacks in such richly varied works as *Totem and Taboo*, *Moses and Monotheism*, and *The Future of an Illusion*. Gould's treatment of religion and Freud's theorizing exemplifies what is sometimes the case in presenting complex arguments: a lavishing of care and effort on the central thesis, accompanied by an almost casual handling of peripheral elements. Focus on a center does not logically entail or otherwise mandate oversimplification of the mainly illustrative or peripheral, but oversimplification does sometimes occur. A partial prophylactic against such occurrence in construing a problematic is sensitivity to its possibility.

2

Gould's essay provides us with a minimal example of one way of relating biology and religion: that is, referring to religion to illustrate some biological point or set of points (in Gould's case, the utility of the idea of spandrels in resisting or correcting the fallacy of conflating contemporary functional utilities with adaptive origins). Another way of relating biology and religion is to render religion or some attribute of religion the thing to be explained or explicated by biological references. A major strategy employed in attempting to do so is sometimes termed „reverse engineering." As Steven Pinker (1997: 21) characterizes it, „In forward-engineering, one designs a machine to do something; in reverse-engineering one figures out what a machine was designed to do." This strategy is widely utilized in sociobiology and evolutionary psychology, and, indeed, in historical disciplines generally.

A still different strategy, one that at first blush might seem to be a perspectival variant of reverse engineering, can be called „the continued program." Putative examples of it are given by the classicist Walter Burkert in his book, *The Creation of the Sacred* (1996). For reasons soon to be given, however, I regard Burkert's examples as actually representing what might better be termed „an analogous program." In any case, while one cannot say that Burkert's work clearly marks a significant „biological turn" in the humanities, his efforts to discern biological substrates underlying various religious phenomena are noteworthy, all the more so because of the scholarly eminence of their author.

Both Burkert's scholarly eminence and his efforts to relate biology and religion are recognized and appreciated by the contributors to a review symposium on his book that was published in this journal (10/11 [1998]: 84–132). Willi Braun (1998) wrote the Introduction, and his informed and well considered remarks are matched by the thoughtful statements of his fellow reviewers, Pascal Boyer (1998), C. Robert Phillips III (1998), Tomoko Masuzawa (1998), and Daniel C. Dennett (1998). Burkert (1998) responded to the reviews in a graceful and forward-looking fashion.

While I cannot rehearse here the many valuable points made in the Symposium, three salient aspects of the reviews can be usefully summarized. First, the majority of the reviewers think it worthwhile to attempt to relate biology and religion. Second, most evince some sympathy for Burkert's efforts to do so (all the more so, perhaps, because many of his fellow humanists avoid and/or oppose such attempts). And third, despite his good intentions, great erudition, and stimulating suggestions, the various contributors, in their respective ways, suggest that Burkert falls short of achieving a cogent, persuasive, and powerful theory that relates biology and religion. Thus, for instance, Boyer (1998: 89) opines that two of what he identifies as three general assumptions underlying Burkert's argument are „misguided," and that „Burkert's intuition of links between evolution and religious representations can be in fact pushed further than he suggests." And Dennett, who relatively early in his essay credits Burkert with „the rudiments of a theory" (1998: 119), later hardens his position and states that Burkert's strength „is more as the alert and imaginative guide to the available resources" on religion accumulated by anthropologists and historians „than as a theorist" (1998: 127).

Burkert, Dennett (1998: 122) remarks, „has whetted my appetite beyond what he can satisfy with his feast of good suggestions." That is also my view. I endorse Burkert's goal of relating biology and religion, and I am intellectually enriched by his treatments of various examples of religiosity. At the same time, however, I think that there are serious shortcomings in his book. He is vague about how we might productively conceptualize a problematic for relating biology and religion. He is reticent, moreover, when it comes to hypothesizing specific mechanisms that might have explanatory worth respecting the origin(s) and/or persistence of religion. And in substitution for the clear specification of a problematic and the adumbration of mechanisms, Burkert offers us an analogous program approach that is mistakenly presented as if it were a continued program approach for relating biology and religion. I turn to that approach below, and then go on to conclude that we need to explore what Burkert does not if we are to develop a productive problematic in the effort to relate biology and religion.

3

Burkert's basic strategy is to find similarities between widely-distributed, patterned religious behaviors and the patterned behaviors of a variety of non-human animals. The latter, he suggests, point to what he calls the „biological landscape" underlying the former and human experience in general.

One of Burkert's examples is resemblances between certain escape behaviors of various non-human animals and human pars pro toto or 'part for the whole' rituals. The leg of a spider breaks off and continues moving for a while, thus distracting predators; a lizard's tail detaches in the mouth of a pursuer, allowing the rest of the lizard to escape; a bird experiences „terror molting," leaving an attacker with a mouth full of feathers but little else; and a fox caught in a trap gnaws off its paw to escape. Similarly, says Burkert, humans will engage in sacrificial mutilations, sacrificing a part of the body – a finger or part of a finger, for example –„accepting the small loss in order to save the whole" (Burkert 1996: 51).

Burkert does not claim that such human sacrificial rituals represent „a definite inherited program of behavior, encoded genetically and passed on" (Burkert 1996: 41). On the other hand, he remarks, their widely distributed recurrences in time and space render it difficult to suppose that they owe their „whole existence to some form of intracultural learning, to observation or empathy, or to sheer creative fantasy" (Burkert 1996: 42). Rather, he opines, they point to a „biological landscape" underlying human experience.

„The human makeup," Burkert (1996: 42) states, „includes biological programs dealing with anxiety and flight that are older than the human species, and these comprise or engender at least the rudiments of the ritual pattern, correlating threat, alarm, pursuit, flight, and the trick of abandoning what can be spared." And he maintains that the pars pro toto examples he gives illustrate a point made by Lumsden and Wilson (1983: 20), who, in conceptualizing the co-evolution of genes and culture, assign criterial importance to „memoirs most easily recalled, emotions they are most likely to evoke."

While genes do not prescribe culture, Burkert writes,

> it could be said that they give recommendations that become manifest in the repetition of like patterns .... The biological makeup forms preconditions or „attractors" to produce phenomena in consistent fashion, even if these patterns are created and recreated afresh in each case. Scientific proof of such connections by means of statistics or experiment will remain impossible; what can be shown is the near-universality and persistence of patterns through time and place, and the existence of certain analogies or even homologies in structure and function in animal behavior. This suggests that details and sequences in rituals, tales, works of art, and fantasies hark back to more original processes in the evolution of life; they become understandable not in isolation nor within their different cultural contexts, but in relation to this background.(Burkert 1996: 22)

4

While Burkert's suggestions are arresting, certain considerations mitigate against incorporating them unmodified into a problematic that could productively guide research.

First, while Burkert has pointed to some interesting resemblances between religious behaviors and phylogenetically distributed behaviors among non-human animals, all that he can effectively demonstrate are analogies, not homologies. He intimates that the wide distribution of pars pro toto human rituals and their analogs among other animals suggest a connection between such human rituals and a biological landscape. But the suggested connection strikes me as tenuous.

It is all the more so when we take a wider view of his human examples – for instance, the removal of all or a part of a finger. Burkert cites some instances from the ancient Mediterranean basin, where individuals apparently sacrificed a finger in order to be cured of sickness or otherwise to propitiate, invoke, or thank a deity. But there are other cases where cutting off a finger or a finger joint has a different significance. Among the Blackfeet of the U.S. Plains (Ewers 1958: 108) and the Dugum Dani of New Guinea (Gardner and Heider 1968: 95–96), by way of two examples, it constitutes an institutionalized way of expressing grief at the death of a close relative (I am indebted to George N. Appell for these examples). In a case that may overlap on occasion with Burkert's cases, members of certain criminal gangs in Japan sometimes accept amputation of a finger or finger joint as a token of fealty to a leader; in some instances they do so because they have committed a delict against their leader, which could lead us to interpret the amputation in such cases as having, in part, a pars pro toto significance (I am indebted to Thomas Shulich for discussion of the Japanese example).

Consideration of different understandings and presumed motives that attach to the same overt physical act in different societies – cutting off a finger, say, to signal grief over the passing of a relative, or cutting off a finger to save one's own life by detaching a part of one's being – brings us to the matter of cultural contexts. Burkert claims that „details and sequences in rituals, tales, works of art, and fantasies hark back to more original processes in the evolution of life" and do not become understandable „within their different cultural contexts, but in relation to this background." That is a claim that runs counter to much received anthropological wisdom. It suggests, moreover, that a more profound or elemental understanding and perhaps a deeper appreciation of rituals, tales, works of art, and fantasies are to be gained by relating them to „more original processes in the evolution of life."

I think, however, that three sets of considerations argue against that claim and suggestion, at least in the forms in which Burkert presents them.

First, cultural context is important in several ways. Some understanding of the meanings of actions to actors is necessary in sorting out human behaviors and rendering them meaningful for ourselves. While the significance of a fox gnawing off its paw when trapped is painfully obvious to us, that is not the case for removal of a finger or finger joint. Removal occurs for different reasons among some peoples, and it occurs not at all, or it occurs with no cultural support, among others. Further, where severing a finger does constitute a pars pro toto sacrifice, our understanding of it would be enriched by viewing it within larger cultural and social contexts. Do people who sacrifice fingers to the gods regularly deal with humans of superior status by offering gifts, particularly of a personal nature? If so, might we explain finger sacrifices and similar acts as an extension into the other-than-human realm of modalities that have been established within the human sphere for relating persons of different social positions?

Second, Burkert's attempt to understand religious expressions against a biological landscape strikes me as no less contextually based and no less hermeneutical than attempting to understand them within their cultural contexts. The context in Burkert's case is a set of phylogenetically-referenced observations. And the operant hermeneutical task is to relate these to selected cultural expressions in order to effect an understanding bordering on explanation. But there is something missing in Burkert's recommendations, which brings me to my third point.

Third, I find Burkert's vague remarks about the genes giving „recommendations that become manifest in the repetition of like patterns" to be unsatisfying. There is too much missing in his efforts to relate biology and religion. In my opinion, Burkert's efforts suffer from a malaise and a lack of remedy succinctly described in general terms by Cosmides, Tooby, and Barkow (1992: 3). „[T]o understand the relationship between biology and culture," they write, „one must first understand the architecture of our evolved psychology.... Past attempts to leapfrog the psychological – to apply evolutionary biology directly to human social life – have for this reason not always been successful. „

And that, I think, is an important cautionary consideration that ought to inform our efforts to establish a problematic for relating biology and religion.

Toward a Realistic and Relevant „Science of Religion"[5]

Abstract: This essay sets forth the author's opinions about how we may best work toward achieving a science of religion that is both relevant to the findings and methodologies of established sciences that deal with the human condition and realistic about what we may hope to achieve in view of the lack of full transparency in language, the deficiencies of „The Standard Social Science Model," and other matters. It describes and endorses some contemporary efforts to advance our understandings of religion by drawing on the cognitive and evolutionary sciences. And it relates those efforts to the author's preferences, discussed in some of the preceding essays, for conceptualizing religion. While it repeats to some extent certain points made in those preceding essays, it introduces some new material, and it works toward a larger perspective for studying and understanding religion.

1. Introduction

In approaching the country that some call „the science of religion," I feel obliged to identify myself as a sympathetic alien. In light of certain of my research interests, moreover, I hasten to add that I am fully terrestrial. But my passport is from an anthropology department rather than from a department of religion.

While anthropologists sometimes use the expression „science of religion," it is my impression that we more commonly talk about „the anthropology of religion." In doing so, some of us identify ourselves as anthropologists with special interests in religion, just as other anthropologists have special interests in nutrition, law, economics, and so forth.

---

5   „Towards a Realistic and Relevant 'Science of Religion'." *Method and Theory in the Study of Religion* 16 (3): 205–233, 2004. This essay is a revised version of a lecture presented at a conference sponsored by the Universities of Turku and Åbo in April, 2000. I am grateful to Professor Veikko Anttonen and his colleagues at both universities for inviting me to Finland.

In addition to resembling members of departments of religion by virtue of mutual interests in scholarly explorations of religion, anthropologists of religion overlap with them in another way. That is, members of both sorts of departments in the modern, secular academy recognize an obligation to bracket judgments about the truth-values of magico-religious claims (Wiebe 1988, 1990).[6] In practice, however, scholars in both groups sometimes resist or reject bracketing. Thus, for example, Evans-Pritchard relates much of his analysis in *Witchcraft, Oracles and Magic among the Azande* (1937) to his explicitly declared assumption that magic as such is false. And in his famous work, *The Meaning and End of Religion* (1962), Wilfred Cantwell Smith emphasizes what he calls the „impingement" of the Transcendent in human life, doubtlessly aware that for many of his readers impingement implies an impinger.

In any case, members of departments of religion and members of anthropology departments have engaged in lively debates in recent years about the nature, limitations, and possibilities of the scholarly study of religion. Both, indeed, have argued about whether or not their respective scholarly pursuits can be „science" in any acceptable, substantive sense of that term.

In the past (and even to some extent today) such debates sometimes touched on considerations of „autonomy." But when they did, they tended to do so with this difference: numbers of anthropologists argued about whether or not *culture* may be said to be autonomous, while members of departments of religion raised a parallel argument about *religion*. A parallel argument, but, of course, a different argument. Among themselves, anthropologists did not usually engage in debates about the possible „autonomy" of religion because many of them deemed religion to be a sort of department or subdivision of culture.

---

6   Some students of religion have gone well beyond minimalist commitments in that regard. Some have argued that magico-religious beliefs can only be properly understood within the context of the form of life that includes them, and were we to judge them true or false without such an understanding, we would be judging our own misunderstandings. Others have taken such a perspective even further. Maintaining that there are no transcendental, rational canons for truth and falsehood that apply universally, they hold that truth and falsehood are authorized by discourses. Since there are no universal standards, and since discourses differ, it would be meretricious, they suggest, to assert unequivocal, public judgments respecting the truth values of other people's magico-religious beliefs.

But some members of departments of religion, at least in Canada and the United States, explicitly raised the issue of the autonomy of religion. And, typically, advocates of a science of religion argued *against* the idea of autonomy. They sometimes did so in open opposition to those of their own academic colleagues who maintained that religion pivots on something that is irreducibly religious.

While agreeing with those scholars in departments of religion who argue against the idea that religion is autonomous or „*sui generis*," and while sympathetic to their desire to develop and sustain a science of religion, I have some reservations about the accomplishments of some (but not all) of them to date. My reservations also apply to the publications of many (but not all) anthropologists who study religion.

First, in my opinion, the outputs of both sorts of scholars of religion have not been as *relevant* to the findings of the sciences as they might have been (albeit I see signs of genuine – indeed, major – improvement in recent years). Second, and closely related to the matter of relevance, numbers of scholars of religion, both anthropologists and others, have not always been as *realistic* as they might have been. I turn now to considerations of what I mean by being realistic and relevant.

2. Being Relevant

I begin with relevance. At the very outset of my remarks about it, I acknowledge the clear relevance of the academic study of religion to both the goals and much of the substance of liberal arts curricula in European and North American universities. Religion has played a diversity of significant roles in much of human history. And, despite the predictions of the secularization hypothesis of some decades ago, religion continues to flourish. For these reasons, historical and comparative studies of religion are important not only for humanist scholars within the academy, but also for people outside of it who reflect seriously on the human condition. It is fitting, therefore, that the academy should recognize the significance of religion in human life by sheltering the study of it. But I am talking about the traditional locus of such study in the humanities. What of the call for a „science of religion"?

It seems to me that Donald Wiebe and numbers of others among our contemporaries express relatively modest views when they champion a „science of religion." Basically, they advocate four things.

First, they demand that the study of religion in secular universities be emancipated from theological advocacies or other insinuations of positive religious biases. Some go further in that they require that the scientific study of religion be unencumbered by social and political concerns and involvements. As Wiebe put it at the 1997 Åbo Symposium on Methodology in the Study of Religions:

> the task of the scientific student of religion as a scientist is not a moral or social one; it is merely to describe and explain as comprehensively as possible the phenomenon of religious behavior. If we are to avoid the decomposition of the academic study of religion into a pseudo-science we must leave broader Religious Studies – with its political and social agendas – to the humanists and religious devotees concerned with their place as public intellectuals in the life of society. (Wiebe 1999: 260–261)

Second, proponents of the scientific study of religion advocate that some of the perspectives of scientists and philosophers of science, and certain of their standards or recommendations for doing scientific research, be adopted as guidelines by scholars of religion.

Third, they incline to the view that the science of religion can seek in some sense to explain religious phenomena as distinct from „interpreting" such phenomena.

Finally, and in consonance with the first three points, some proponents of a science of religion recommend that the scientific study of religion be deemed a social science. As a social science, it will have its own subject matter, but it will invoke relevant psychological and sociological theories and constructs whenever it seems productive to do so.

While I think that those ambitions constitute steps in the right direction, I judge them to be inadequate. I do so because in social sciences such as cultural anthropology and sociology the dominant traditional model guiding research is defective.[7] Among other things, it does not emphatically and consistently encourage students of religion to connect their findings and theorizing to the findings and theorizing of other sciences, particularly the biological and cognitive sciences.

---

7   Some anthropologists and sociologists reject the idea that members of their disciplines should aspire to science. Instead of attempting to explain cultural phenomena, they hold, we should furnish „thick descriptions" and cogent interpretations. Others, however, call for theorizing that incorporates or emphasizes causality. I am concerned here with the dominant model that traditionally has guided the latter set of social scientists.

Here and there, to be sure, we encounter statements such as one offered by Wiebe at Åbo: that, as he puts it, „We need ... to establish more appropriate relations between our research and that of other established scientific fields ..." (1999: 267). Wiebe, moreover, concludes his paper with what I deem a welcome suggestion: that „we need to reconsider the value of a return to evolutionary theory to re-establish a unifying framework for the study of religion" (1999: 269). Yet although I agree with his remarks, I wonder about their context. Wiebe and like-minded others seem to be advocating the creation of yet another discipline within the framework of the existing social sciences. They remind me to some extent of those of the elders of Israel who demanded of the prophet Samuel, „make us a king to judge us like all the nations" (*First Samuel* 8). The „nations" that Wiebe and his cohort would join, however, have recently been subjected to some adverse judgments.

I refer to criticisms made of the social sciences in general by John Tooby, an anthropologist, and Leda Cosmides, a psychologist, in a jointly authored, long essay entitled „The Psychological Foundations of Culture" (1992). I deem those criticisms to be cogent and arresting. I think, moreover, that they apply to what seems to be envisioned by some proponents – and *de facto* practitioners – of a science of religion (as well as applying to legions of anthropologists engaged in the anthropology of religion). They do not apply, however, to the theorizing of those students of religion who affiliate themselves with the contemporary cognitive and evolutionary sciences. Some of these, in my opinion, have already taken important steps in the creation of a truly exciting science of religion (I shall say more about this later).

Tooby and Cosmides are judicious in their examination of what they call „The Standard Social Science Model." They find elements of truth in it. They acknowledge, moreover, that that model would not have become as influential as it is if it didn't impress many persons as being plausible and anchored in reality (1992: 33). At the same time, however, they think that it suffers from some major defects. In consequence of those defects, they argue, the Standard Social Science Model seems to make the social sciences autonomous from the rest of science (1992: 33). Such apparent isolation, they opine, is regrettable, and emancipation from the traditional model would be a positive good. They recommend efforts to replace the Standard Social Science Model with what they and Jerome Barkow call „integrated theory." An integrated theory, as they and Barkow describe it, is „one framed so that it is compatible with data and theory from other relevant fields" (Cosmides, Tooby, and Barkow 1992: 4).

The Standard Social Science Model

What is „The Standard Social Science Model?" As Tooby and Cosmides characterize it, it is founded on, and seeks to deal with, observations of cultural and behavioral similarities *within* human groups and observations of cultural and behavioral differences *between* human groups. Contemporary social scientists correctly maintain that neither cultural similarities nor cultural differences can be explained by discrete and variable racial or genetic factors in human populations. All normal human infants everywhere enjoy much the same biological endowment, an endowment that makes possible a human level of existence. And biological factors as such do not determine which particular language people will speak or which particular culture they participate in.

Unfortunately, Tooby and Cosmides aver, while social scientists correctly maintain that the common biological endowment of normal human infants is everywhere much the same, many of them impose erroneous suppositions on that understanding. They hold that „human nature" is a constant, and a constant cannot explain a variable, the observed diversity of cultures. As the young of the human species develop, social scientists generally suppose, they must acquire what leads to differences among them, and they must acquire it from sources outside of themselves. They must acquire it, that is, from extra-genetic, extra-somatic sources: from socio-cultural, not biological, sources. In the Standard Social Science Model, socio-cultural factors in effect create the individual and largely determine adult mental organization, with little or no input from biological variables.

The social scientists who argue this way usually acknowledge that „human nature" – which Tooby and Cosmides identify as „the evolved architecture of the human mind" (1992: 28) – is a necessary condition for the cultural organization of human life. But they otherwise deny significant causal powers to it in accounting for cultural diversity. Many agree with Emile Durkheim's assertion that human nature is „merely the indeterminate material that the social factor molds and transforms" (quoted by Tooby and Cosmides 1992: 28). Or, adopting a more contemporary idiom, they suppose, as does Clifford Geertz (1973: 35), that the human mind is a sort of general purpose computer that requires the downloading of cultural programs if it is to operate in a discernibly human way. And, in something of a parallel to Mircea Eliade, the anthropologist Robert Lowie stoutly proclaims that „Culture is a thing *sui generis* which can be explained only in terms of itself ... *Omnis cultura ex cultura*" (quoted in Tooby and Cosmides 1992: 28).

The Standard Social Science Model, Tooby and Cosmides (1992: 28) point out, „removes from the concept of human nature all substantive content, and relegates the architecture of the human mind to the delimited role of embodying 'the capacity for culture'." Even emotions such as sexual jealousy or paternal love, they note, are accounted to be cultural products. This viewpoint has nurtured all sorts of ancillary ideas, including, among others, both assumptions and problematics relating to the specifics of culture and the ways in which it is transmitted from generation to generation. It nurtures, for example, the assignment of importance to learning theory in psychology (with a concomitant relative neglect of other topical concerns in that discipline), the notion that the mind-brain is a general purpose processor (rather than an assemblage of domain specific modules), and the prepossessing idea that the evolution of our capacity for culture has endowed our species with an enormous potentiality for behavioral flexibility, a flexibility that is ultimately constrained by culture itself.

Tooby and Cosmides call our attention to some specific defects in the Standard Social Science Model. For one thing, they write, its central logic

> rests on naïve and erroneous concepts drawn from outmoded theories of development. For example, the fact that some aspect of adult mental organization is absent at birth has no bearing on whether it is part of our evolved architecture. Just as teeth or breasts are absent at birth, and yet appear through maturation, evolved psychological mechanisms or modules (complex structures that are functionally organized for processing) could develop at any point in the life cycle. For this reason, the many features of adult mental organization absent at birth need not be attributed to exposure to transmitted culture, but may come about through a large number of causal avenues not considered in traditional analyses. (1992: 33)

For another thing, Tooby and Cosmides maintain, the Standard Social Science Model „rests on a faulty analysis of nature-nurture issues, stemming from a failure to appreciate the role that the evolutionary process plays in organizing the relationship between our species-universal genetic endowment, our evolved developmental processes, and the recurring features of developmental environments" (1992: 33).

They go on to say that the critique of the standard model „that has been emerging from the cognitive and evolutionary communities" is not simply the charge that proponents of that model have underestimated the importance of biological factors in human life. Rather, the target of criticism „is the whole framework that assumes that 'biological factors' and 'environmental factors' refer to mutually exclusive sets of causes that exist in some kind of explanatory zero-sum relationship ..." (1992: 33).

Perhaps an even more devastating criticism is this: „The Standard Social Science Model," Tooby and Cosmides write,

> requires an *impossible* psychology. Results out of cognitive psychology, evolutionary biology, artificial intelligence, developmental psychology, linguistics, and philosophy converge on the same conclusion: A psychological architecture that consisted of nothing but equipotential, general-purpose, or content-free mechanisms *could not successfully perform* the tasks the human mind is known to perform or solve ... from seeing, to learning a language, to recognizing an emotional expression, to selecting a mate, to the many disparate activities aggregated under the term „learning culture" ... *It cannot account for the behavior observed, and* [in light of our understandings of the *ad hoc*, opportunistic nature of natural selection] *it is not a type of design that could have evolved.* (1992: 34, emphases added)

Without going any further into the particulars of the criticisms voiced by Tooby and Cosmides, suffice it to say that there is enough wrong with the Standard Social Science Model as to render it a dubious model for the science of religion. Its celebration of the imputed autonomy and power of culture nurtures close-ended hermeneutical and/or functionalist studies that have little or no cumulative payoff. As a paradigm for research and theorizing, moreover, the Standard Social Science Model serves to isolate many social scientists from exciting developments in contemporary philosophy, the cognitive sciences and linguistics, the neural sciences, evolutionary biology, and developmental and evolutionary psychology. Indeed, the business-as-usual and almost exclusive emphasis on culture, ironically enough, works to inhibit the emergence of balanced and warrantable understandings of culture. As the anthropologist Roy D'Andrade (1995: 216) puts it,

> Many anthropologists believe culture does just about everything ... But culture does not really do *everything*. The effect of culture is greatly exaggerated by many anthropologists. So far as we know, no cultural particulars are needed for humans everywhere to do *modus ponens*, or remember the color of apples, or perceive that a hawk is different than a handsaw.

A major, promising alternative view to that championed by the Standard Social Science Model is characterized in these words by Tooby and Cosmides (1992: 34):

> human psychological architecture contains many evolved mechanisms that are specialized for solving evolutionarily long-enduring adaptive problems and ... these mechanisms have content-specialized representational formats, procedures, cues, and so on. These richly content-sensitive evolved mechanisms tend to impose certain types of content and conceptual organization on human mental life and, hence, strongly shape the nature of human social life and what is transmitted across generations

Towards Relevance

How may the science of religion position itself with respect to the promises of that alternative view? How, indeed, may it render its research and theorizing *compatible with,* and *complementary to,* the research and theorizing of other sciences concerned with the human condition, and by so doing make itself more *relevant* to those sciences? I think that there are a number of things that it can and should do. I limit myself here to advocating three of them.

First, the science of religion ought to be clear about the phenomenal subjects of its research. Those subjects, in my opinion, are not religions or cultures. Rather, they are human beings. Religion and culture are constructs that we associate with human beings. The emerging science of religion already views religion as a human creation, and we need to expand our knowledge of human beings if we are to expand our knowledge of why and how they go about creating religions. To borrow an insight from theologians, a global perspective on creatures requires some understanding of their creator.

Second, the science of religion ought to address the most interesting and important questions that we can ask about religion. Namely: What should we mean by „religion?" Why are there religions? How are they organized and transmitted? In what ways do religions resemble one another and in what ways do they differ? And why do many people continue to invest themselves in religion whereas others distance themselves from it or actively attempt to debunk it?

Third, and in consonance with the above recommendations, the science of religion should be explicitly affiliated with the cognitive and evolutionary sciences. This does not mean that it would exclude descriptive or experimental studies that are outside of self-consciously cognitive and/or evolutionary frames. Descriptions, however, are observations that have been selected, organized, and re-worked, and as such they are inevitably theory-laden. As Popper (1962) cogently argues, observations are perceptions that have been prepared by biases or, broadly put, by theories. Experiments, moreover, are normally organized to test hypotheses, and they are thus exercises in the service of theories. What I advocate, therefore, is that the dominant questions that frame the science of religion, and the methodological and theoretical weightings that identify it, be relevant to, informed by, and contributory to, work in the contemporary cognitive and evolutionary sciences.

The Cognitive Approach

Eschewing „superorganic" cultures, disembodied „social facts," and suprapersonal „structures" of appropriateness, contemporary cognitive studies take human beings as their phenomenal subjects, especially as they credit those subjects with mind-brains. Religion, in a manner of speaking, bubbles up from the mind-brain.

Many (perhaps most) contemporary students of religion who espouse cognitive approaches endorse what has come to be known as the modular theory of mind (Hirschfeld and Gelman 1994). That is, the mind-brain is envisioned as including a number of different „modules" or „intelligences." These are evolved and varied mental structures that are sensitive, respectively, to different sorts of inputs that stem from our perceptual machinery and/or the outputs of other modules. They are disposed, moreover, to process information in determinate ways. It is hypothesized, for example, that while some module(s) may be engaged mainly with language disposition and acquisition, others are primarily involved with mathematical skills, or agent detection, or hazard avoidance, and so on.

Our conceptual and inferential systems, in this view, are modularly funded, and as such not everything goes. The mind-brain is not content free, and our concepts and inferences are disposed in certain ways, regardless of our culture. The mind-brain, moreover, is not unconstrained, and neither are our concepts and inferences. Since religion relates to our conceptual and inferential propensities, we do not find in actuality certain imaginable kinds of religion (Boyer 1994, 2001), just as language users do not normally make certain imaginable kinds of syntactical errors.

We humans, cognitive students of religion maintain, enjoy a number of capacities, dispositions, and processing capabilities that originally had, and that still have, adaptive significance. Thus, by way of three examples: we have agent-detection sensitivities (useful not only in social relations with conspecifics but also in monitoring the world for real and imagined opportunities and dangers); we can imagine virtual realities (which allows us both to envision future what-if scenarios and to account in one way or another for the past); and we have metarepresentational abilities that we employ in attempting to understand and predict the behavior of others.

Such capacities, propensities, and processual capabilities, as Boyer (2004) argues, would be with us regardless of whether or not we have religion. They underwrite multiple domains of human life and religion is among their derivatives. Thus, by way of a very brief (and simplified) effort at illustration, our agent-detector sensitivities, coupled with our capacities and dispositions to imagine virtual realities, may lead us to infer and conceptualize non-existent beings of the sort that students of religion call gods. And our metarepresentational capacities and propensities may support the attribution of will, desire, and purpose to those imagined gods by persons who deem them real.

Acknowledgment of the derivative nature of religion raises problems for the explanation of religion. It cannot suffice either to rely on religious people for sufficient leads or to rely on the constructs of armchair theorists. Cogent and persuasive explanations of religion must depend on bringing to light the mental structures that underwrite religion and much else in human life, and it is unlikely that questioning religious people or closely reading the classical literature will do that adequately. That is why numbers of cognitive students of religion have designed and executed various experiments, as well as accessing the already established experimental literature in psychology. Not all experimenters, by the way, are psychologists. Anthropologists such as Scott Atran and Pascal Boyer, and humanists-turned-scientists such as Ilkka Pyysiäinen, have resorted to experiments in order to test hypotheses and so better understand why we have religion. This does not mean that future fieldwork, or survey research, or textual analysis, or many other traditional avenues of scholarship are to be ruled out. It does mean, however, that a truly scientific study of religion is unashamedly reductive (Boyer 2004), and that it will make sense of the fruits of other research by relating them to cognitive (and perhaps eventually neural) processes.

Evolution

Our descriptive and experimental studies could benefit by relating to evolutionary theory for at least two reasons. First, since religions are human creations, our understanding of them (as I suggested earlier) will be advanced by a greater knowledge of their creators, and a global understanding and appreciation of the human condition requires a phylogenetic perspective (Hallowell 1960a). Second, Darwinian (or, if you prefer, Neo-Darwinian) theory is supported by a great deal of empirical evidence, it is underwritten by sound logic, and it is powerful in that it is used to explain much.

Now, evolutionary interests were in evidence among some 19th century students of religion. Their ways of addressing and expressing those interests, however, eventually displeased later students of religion. Evans-Pritchard (1965), for example, dismissed Edward Burnett Tylor's intellectualist and evolutionary theorizing as summing to a „Just-So" story.

Today, however, we are in a better position to support an evolutionary perspective and shelter the science of religion under it. We benefit from a much more sophisticated understanding of evolution than that enjoyed by our 19th century predecessors. This better understanding rests on a host of developments. They include (but are not limited to): the creation of new disciplines such as genetics and molecular biology and the flourishing of organic chemistry, paleontology, and evolutionary biology; advances in the cognitive and neural sciences; the development of increasingly sophisticated mathematical and statistical techniques (as in population genetics and in numbers of other fields); the use of electronic computers for handling large amounts of data; new discoveries in paleoanthropology and the rise and promise of cognitive archeology; and, after some mixed reviews for sociobiology, the florescence of evolutionary psychology.

Perhaps the most important evolutionary question a student of religion may ask is this: Did religion evolve? No, Scott Atran (2002) answers, because there neither is nor was an „it" to have evolved. Religion, as I (Saler 1994, 1997, 1999, 2000a [1993], 2000b) argue in a non-essentialist vein, is a variable congeries of different elements and not some specific this or that. The elements that we associate with religion did not all evolve together; rather, they arose as spandrels in the evolution of certain capacities and dispositions that offered adaptive advantages. Religion, Boyer (2001, 2004) points out, is parasitic on different evolved adaptive capacities and propensities that, quite apart from religion, play important roles in sustaining human life.

Given the understandings outlined above, it follows that the evolutionary studies that are most immediately relevant to the science of religion are those that illumine, and that seek in some sense to account for, the emergence of the cognitive capacities and dispositions that support religion. But, as claimed above, such capacities and dispositions support much else, and they did not originally emerge because of their importance to religion. These views are fundamental to an important book published by the archeologist Steven Mithen (1996) and appropriately entitled *The Prehistory of the Mind*. The encompassing nature of that study, already affirmed by the title, is reinforced by the subtitle: *The cognitive origins of art, religion and science*.[8]

Mithen incorporates some of his findings into a later and more particularized paper entitled „Symbolism and the Supernatural" (1999), and it is worth citing here some of what he says in that essay by way of further supporting the recommendation that the science of religion incorporate an evolutionary dimension.

„Symbolism and the Supernatural"

Mithen holds that ideas about the supernatural can be anchored in the mind with the help of material artifacts, and that without such anchorage religious institutions and thought about the supernatural would be severely constrained (1999: 148). Archeologists, of course, are professionally motivated and trained to unearth and analyze material artifacts, and so, among other things, to look for material symbols that might promote religious conceptualizations (1999: 50).

In surveying the archeological record both in the 1996 book and in the later paper, Mithen comes to conclusions that some may regard as surprising. Contrary to the supposition that religious thought is ancient

---

8   That subtitle is given on the title page of the paperback edition in my possession. The cover of that edition, however, does not include religion in the subtitle.

in our *genus,* Mithen claims that „the archeological evidence suggests that religious ideas and ritual activities appeared relatively recently in human prehistory" (1999: 151). While archaic members of the *genus* Homo appeared in the fossil record 2.5 million years ago, our first unambiguous (albeit slight) evidence for religious rituals is not more than 100,000 years old (1999: 151). That evidence comes from burials where animal remains were interred with human dead. But evidence of *manufactured or artificially made symbols* suggests that religion is no earlier than perhaps 30,000 years ago (1999: 151).

Mithen thinks it likely that religious beliefs arose as „mental spandrels," that is, as originally non-adaptive by-products of other, adaptive cognitive developments (1999: 157). He hypothesizes a „proto-symbolism" among our ancestors in the Upper Paleolithic (1999: 153–154). Prior to some 60,000 to 30,000 years ago, he conjectures, early human ancestors had at least three specialized cognitive domains, to whit, intelligences concerned with material objects, with living entities, and with the human social world. While each of these domains may have facilitated discrete or specialized complexities (such as Neanderthal skills in producing levallois flakes and points) (1999: 158), early humans did not connect skills facilitated by one domain with skills facilitated by other domains (1999: 159). Mithen thinks it likely that that was because „their thoughts about the social, natural, and technical worlds were quite isolated from each other" (1999: 159).

Eventually, however, Mithen suggests, there was a transition to what he calls „cognitive fluidity" (1999: 159), where the different domains penetrated and supported one another. That transition was of immense evolutionary significance. The integration of the three kinds of intelligence facilitated not only the design of new hunting weapons, but also the production of artifacts such as beads and necklaces that conveyed social messages (1999: 159). Mithen supposes *Homo sapiens sapiens* to have attained greater „cognitive fluidity" than Neanderthals, and that that achievement was a major factor in accounting for the replacement of the latter by the former.

Mithen applies these claims to the development of religious ideas and their expression and anchorage in material artifacts. Drawing on Pascal Boyer's (1994) emphasis on the distinction between intuitive and counter-intuitive ontologies, and Stewart Guthrie's (1993) treatment of anthropomorphism, Mithen suggests that cognitive fluidity makes possible the combining of the intuitive and the counter-intuitive and the anthropomorphizing of animals by attributing to them human-like intelligence, will, and purpose. Such combinations and attributions, he argues, need not have any adaptive value. Indeed, these and other religious ideas can be non-adaptive or even mal-adaptive. But whatever their possible cost, that cost is „more than compensated for by the benefits of cognitive fluidity gained from other types of thinking" (1999: 160).

Now, Mithen's thesis has a certain plausibility to it. And, when evaluated against the artifactual evidence for it, it is a brilliant demonstration of how archeologists can sometimes make much out of relatively little. While decidedly speculative, it does, however, have three things in its favor. First, it takes account of the actual material evidence available. That evidence clearly confronts us with puzzles. Artifacts thus far unearthed indicate that for hundreds of thousands of years our early tool-making ancestors were decidedly „conservative," turning out much the same crude tools year after year. Then, rather suddenly, there was a florescence of new types of tools and, necessarily, new techniques for producing them. Why? Mithen supposes that something in the nature of a cognitive revolution must have occurred. Second, Mithen takes account of a large and diverse literature on the nature of the mind, and he selectively and adroitly applies that literature to solving some archeological puzzles. Third, he attempts to account for the emergence of religion by relating it both to the material evidence in hand and to some powerful theories of religion offered by contemporary cognitive students of religion. In my opinion, Mithen deserves our admiration on all three counts, even if he does not fully persuade us.

Now, at first glance, Mithen's approach may seem to clash with that of one of my teachers, Anthony F. C. Wallace. I think, however, that those approaches can be productively related to one another and that both should be taken into account by the science of religion.

Anthony F. C. Wallace

Wallace was fond of telling his students that if they were to seek the origins of religion, they should look not to the Paleolithic but to their daily newspapers. That is because, he continued, religion originates again and again in human history. Because it does, he held, it becomes possible through ethnographic, historical, and comparative research to identify the typical conditions under which religions emerge. We can hope, indeed, to develop a model of religion's usual patterns of emergence and development, and to hypothesize relevant explanatory mechanisms that might account for components of the model. In consonance with those convictions, as some of you may know, Wallace (1956b) offers us his model of „revitalization movements." Drawing, moreover, on Pavlov's work on ultraparadoxical reactions, on Selye's work on stress and „The General Adaptation Syndrome", and on much else, he adumbrates the mechanism of „mazeway resynthesis." Wallace's major paper on mazeway resynthesis (1956a), be it noted, is subtitled „A Biocultural Theory of Religious Inspiration."

Wallace more or less assumes the existence of the cognitive capacities and propensities the emergence of which Mithen seeks to trace in the archeological record. That is why I think that the different approaches of these two scholars are sequentially compatible. There is, moreover, a larger lesson to be drawn from that compatibility. Part of the work of the science of religion, in tandem with other sciences, is to understand the emergence and nature of the cognitive capacities that underwrite religion. And in illuminating the possibilities and limitations of those capacities, we provide other scholars with powerful tools for better understanding the careers of religions mentioned in their daily newspapers.

3. Being Realistic

I have devoted much of this essay to sketching some of my views on the matter of relevance. Now I turn to the related challenge of rendering the science of religion more realistic. I do not employ „realistic" in any formal philosophical sense. Rather, I use it in its common and idealized acceptations: that is, as having to do with accommodations to facts and to good arguments, and a corresponding disinclination to accept the fanciful and the illogical.

The place to start, I think, is with our understandings of language. More particularly, we may start with a realistic appreciation of language's limitations. The most important of those limitations as they relate to the study of religion is language's lack of full transparency in communicating thought and in representing the world. There are several reasons for why that is the case. Thus, for instance, structural requirements internal to any system of signs constrain the arbitrariness of expressive vehicles if meaning combinations are to be predictable from sign combinations; language, in consequence, cannot be internally cohesive as well as fully transparent to the meanings it expresses (Parmentier 1985: 372). For another thing, we humans are prone to expand our understandings analogically, and analogical expansions motivate tropes. We must reckon with the fact that our uses render many of the terms that we employ polysemous (i.e., a given term takes on different meanings, though those meanings are systematically related to one another)[9]. Terms, moreover, are likely to be loaded with connotations, and sensitivities (or insensitivities) to connotations may vary among members of a speech community. For these and other reasons, the goal of a tidy and strictly neutral scientific language would seem to be unrealistic, especially when it comes to the study of human affairs. The conceit that students of the human condition can systematically and consensually employ one term for one thing is not supportable, either historically or in principle.

What are we to do? We can endorse some realistic suggestions offered by the philosopher Karl Popper (1962). We should strive not for utter or exhaustive precision in specifying what may be meant by our analytical terms but for serviceable clarity in explicating how they are used.

In attempting to implement Popper's suggestion, some plain talk about categories and concepts can be useful. „Categorization," the psychologist Douglas Medin writes,

> involves treating two or more distinct entities as in some way equivalent in the service of accessing knowledge and making predictions ... a *concept* is an idea that includes all that is characteristically associated with it. A *category* is a partitioning or class to which some assertion or set of assertions might apply (Medin 1989: 1469, emphases in original).

Categories, in brief, are classificatory devices. As such, they relate to other categories, other classificatory devices, in larger classificatory structures. Categories, moreover, express, and may be motivated by, knowledge and theories about the world, including knowledge and theories about what counts as meaningful resemblances. Altering what we may mean by some category – religion, say – is therefore not as easy or as unconstrained as some may suppose although, of course, history teaches us that categories and larger classificatory structures do change.

Apposite to the subject matter of this essay is the category religion. Numbers of students of religion have remarked on the contested nature

---

9   If the different meanings were not systematically related to one another, we would encounter homonomy, not polysemy.

of the category. Because some of them deem definitional issues to be crucial for marking out an area of study, I will center the rest of this essay on that subject. A realistic „science of religion," many will agree, requires a realistic explication of „religion."

A Few Examples of Approaches to the Definitional Problem

Many persons have sought to define religion by specifying putative „distinctive features,"[10] features represented to be both necessary and sufficient for identifying instances of the category (see Saler 2000a [1993]: 87–157 for criticisms of a diversity of examples). A smaller number of authors have advocated an anti-essentialist „family resemblance" approach to defining religion, but some of them have subverted their own recommendations in ways that suggest essentialist recidivism (e. g., Peter Byrne 1988: 7, 9; see Fitzgerald 1996: 227 and Saler 1999: 393–394 for some criticisms of Byrne).

Other scholars have advocated, for one reason or another, that we jettison the category and category label. W. C. Smith (1962), for example, recommends that we substitute „cumulative traditions" and „faith" for „religion." Timothy Fitzgerald (1996, 1997, 2000), penning an even more radical set of suggestions, would have us do away not only with the category but also with departments of religion or religious studies as presently constituted; he advocates that such departments be converted into departments of cultural studies dedicated to the exploration of values and power realities.

A concern with „power" also animates much of Talal Asad's 1983 essay, „Anthropological Conceptions of Religion: Reflections on Geertz," an essay well received by numbers of anthropologists. Asad does not advocate that we do away with the term and category religion. But because of an unfortunate incoherence in his argument, he in effect turns the category into one that might more appropriately be labeled „je ne sais quoi." Asad maintains the following: (1) Clifford Geertz's famous 1966 characterization of religion, one that emphasizes meaning and

---

10 I prefer the expression „distinguishing features" to the more commonly employed „distinctive features." The latter is more likely than the former to suggest characteristics or qualities that are independent of human judgments. „To distinguish," in contrast, implies the interposition of human agency in simultaneous acts of identifying and classifying.

general order, is a privatized, „Christian" conception of religion and is unsuitable as a cross-cultural analytical category. (2) Many anthropologists have operated with similar conceptions of religion, and they would do well to purge themselves of such conceptions in light of the criticisms made of Geertz. (3) Instead of addressing the questions about meaning that Geertz favored in 1966, students of religion should address this question: how does power create religion? Asad, however, fails to bridge a rather daunting gap between his first two points and the third. That is, if we truly purged our minds of Geertz-like conceptions of religion, conceptions that (allegedly) have hitherto guided us, don't we need some new conception if we are going to study how „power" creates „religion?" Asad, alas, fails to supply anything in the way of a substitute. And so, in the end, he in effect recommends that we study how power creates je ne sais quoi (or something equivalently vacuous).

In that we have touched on considerations of „power," it seems relevant to consider an assertion that, if accepted at face value, would greatly empower scholars. I refer to a statement made by Jonathan Z. Smith: „'Religion' is not a native term; it is a term created by scholars for their intellectual purposes and therefore is theirs to define" (1998: 281). While I do not accept that statement as it stands, it can be reduced to the making of a sustainable point: that scholars have some options in defining religion.

Scholars, however, are not the only people who talk about religion. Nor are they the only ones who sometimes raise questions about the meaning of the term. To restrict our purview to contemporary American society, there are, for example, the courts that interpret and generalize constitutional restrictions on the Congress respecting the establishment and prohibition of religion. And then there are various federal, state, and local agencies that require standard conceptions of religion for some of their routine work (e. g., in granting tax exemptions, adhering to zoning rules, and so forth). And, for that matter, there are also radio and television „talking heads," barbers and pastry chefs, mafia dons and copy editors, priests, ministers, rabbis, and imams, and all the other millions and millions of native or naturalized Americans who use the word „religion" and who occasionally venture explications of it. In actuality, while scholars have options when it comes to talking about religion, they are also constrained if they would communicate with one another and with a larger audience. And that's where being realistic could improve matters.

Some Realistic Considerations

Religion, the anthropologist Melford E. Spiro notes, „is a term with historically rooted meanings" (1966: 91). Because of that, Spiro opines, „a definition must satisfy not only the criterion of cross-cultural applicability but also the criterion of intra-cultural intuitivity; at the least, it should not be counter-intuitive" (1966: 91).

Religion is indeed a term with „historically rooted meanings." And its history is decidedly complex. Furthermore, as numbers of scholars have noted, many non-Western populations lack traditional terms and categories that approximate to terms and categories for „religion" in the contemporary West. Euro-Americans, however, have exported — in some cases imposed — conceptions of religion, and vocabularies for talking about it, throughout the globe.

The emergence of modern Western conceptions of religion is related in multiplex ways to the Reformation and accompanying wars and persecutions, the influx of information from the New World and the desires of Europeans to classify and assimilate that information, the Enlightenment and the rise of deism, the developments of capitalism and colonialism, the florescence of secular scholarly studies, and still more.

Today, „religion" is a widely diffused popular term and category in Euro-American societies. Scholars have appropriated both, and numbers of them have sought to refine, reform, or reinvent the category (only a minority, insofar as I am aware, express themselves in favor of doing away with it). Efforts at scholarly refinement, reform, or reinvention often involve some distancing from popular uses, but largely in attempts to foreground what, in the variegated opinions of scholars, may be most noteworthy, salient, or important about religion. Scholarly interests in religion, nevertheless, relate in great measure to the fact that religion has been, and remains, a matter of interest and concern in Euro-American societies.

However distanced scholarly applications of the term religion may become from popular applications, it is unlikely that they will break entirely with them. Maintaining universes of discourse is important not only within scholarly communities but also between such communities and the larger societies that support them. And here is where one of the major problems in religious studies lies.

Prototypical Exemplars

As I suggest elsewhere (Saler 2000a [1993]), for many Euro-Americans, those large families of religion that are popularly denominated „Judaism" and „Christianity" constitute *the most prototypical exemplars* of religion. I employ „prototype" in the sense described by the psychologist Eleanor Rosch (1978: 36): „By prototypes of categories, we have generally meant the clearest cases of category membership defined operationally by people's judgments of goodness of membership in the category."[11] The judgment that „Judaism" and „Christianity" are prototypical poses a serious but not insurmountable problem for the prescription of a scholarly analytical category.

„Judaism" and „Christianity" constitute peculiar developments when compared, say, to traditional religions in highland New Guinea or lowland South America. They have published canons, articulated creeds, and accreted theological literatures, for example, and these were facilitated by a host of distinct economic, organizational, and technological developments. Many contributors to the developing theologies of those religions, moreover, found stimulation, positive and negative, in intellectual traditions originating outside of distinctly Jewish or Christian religious frames (e. g., in the panoplies of classical Greek and Hellenistic thought).

Coming to understand religion on the basis of cases that many Euro-Americans deem the most prototypical exemplars of the category can have – and has had – some unfortunate consequences (I furnish an example from lowland South America in Saler n.d.). As Pascal Boyer puts it,

> The focus on what we are familiar with – those highly doctrinal phenomena people call „world religions" – is the source of many a confused view about religion. For instance, it is in my experience exceedingly difficult to convince most people ... that most religion is not about the creation of the world, that it is rarely about God, that it is very seldom about the salvation of the soul. More important and more difficult to impress upon most people: most religion has no doctrine, no set catalogue of beliefs that most

---

11 A great deal of research has demonstrated that people often judge some instantiations of a category to be „clearer" or „better" exemplars than others. Thus, for example, some English speakers judge robins to be clearer exemplars of the category „bird" than penguins, and chair to be a better exemplar of „furniture" than radio. Disparities in judgments rendered have been called „prototype effects" (see, for example, Lakoff 1987).

members should adhere to, no overall and integrated statements about supernatural agents. Most religion is piecemeal, mostly implicit, often less than perfectly consistent and, most importantly, *focused on concrete circumstances*. (Boyer 2004: 28, emphasis in original)

„Doctrinal" or so-called „world" or „organized" religions, Boyer (2004: 29) argues, do not *displace* non-doctrinal religions but *supplement* them. They manifest an „additional growth." As such, they constitute „a secondary, derivative development of a much more general and deeply human tendency to imagine important supernatural agents and to entertain precise descriptions of their powers" (2004: 28). One must understand this „general mental disposition," Boyer maintains, in order to understand much about „the special case" of religion as exemplified by so-called world religions (2004: 28). Yet many students of religion, Boyer notes, have used doctrinal religions as a starting point in the attempt „to climb all the way up to a general understanding of religion in human kind," and doing so „was not always very successful" (2004: 28).

I agree with much of what Boyer says in the citations given above. I wish, however, that he had expressed himself differently when he suggests that because the foregoing is the case,

> ... the dull business of demarcating what is „religion" from what is not is better left to lexicographers; it should not unduly trouble scholars. Whether accounts of religion are of interest depends, not on where they place its boundaries but on how they account for the observed behavior they purport to explain. (Boyer 2004: 27)

Boyer is clearly operating with a concept of religion. Elsewhere, indeed, he tells us much about it (e.g., Boyer 2001). In the passage quoted, however, he appears to slight interest in specifying (and justifying) that concept in favor of emphasizing the importance of good explanation.

Inasmuch as this essay is concerned with developing a science of religion, I will outline what I prefer to mean by „religion." Before doing so, however, it may prove useful to take another look at „doctrinal" religion as a starting place for coming to understand religion. Such a starting place, it should be noted, can be problematic not only for understanding „traditional" religions, but also for understanding what occurs among the adherents of doctrinal religions. Many Christians, for example, are not very knowledgeable about Christian doctrines as described in textbooks or theological tracts. Or, even when knowledgeable, some reject various doctrines. Numbers of them, indeed, evince ideas, norms, and behaviors that are given little or no public endorsement by „mainstream" Christian theologians and church leaders.

Many field anthropologists, nevertheless, identify what they take to be religion in non-Western societies by finding analogies to what they deem to be „religion" at home. Given our intellectual propensities to assimilate new information, at least initially, by relating it to established representations and theories, that is hardly surprising. While this can sometimes conduce to errors, I do not think that it always does. Intelligence and hard work – and enough time in the field to maximize their possibilities – have often overcome initial bias. We can now, moreover, enhance prospects for realistic descriptions of religions by instituting safeguards derived from cognitive approaches. One very important safeguard is the recognition that „doctrinal" religions do not displace or obviate more general and widespread religious proclivities, even among declared adherents of „doctrinal" religions. Another is the understanding that because „doctrinal" religions show us what may become of more general religion under certain circumstances, they have to be selectively discounted as templates in the study of other religions.

Categories and Categorization

A science of religion, in my opinion, needs to consider what psychologists, philosophers, linguists, and others have learned and proposed about categories and categorization. That is, we need to consider such matters as they may apply to us as analysts, in addition to considering what they may purport for the people we study. One might, for example, expand on what Coleman and Kay (1981: 27) describe as „ ... the obvious pretheoretical intuition that semantic categories frequently have blurry edges and allow degrees of membership." And one might also explore Wittgenstein's insight: that, as Rosch (1978: 36) describes it, „we can judge how clear a case something is and deal with categories on the basis of clear cases in the total absence of information about boundaries."

In an old and idealized approach to categorization, the members of a group comprehended by a category – the instantiations of the category – are viewed as fully and equally members by virtue of sharing in common one or more „distinctive features." Those features define the category and serve as standards for admission. This understanding works in the case of some categories (e.g., „triangle"). It is unsatisfactory, however, where some of the instances labeled by a term appear to have little or nothing in common with some of the other instances labeled by that same term. In the case of „game," for instance, what distinctive features does solitaire share with baseball? In this case, the philosopher Wittgenstein advises,

> Don't say: „There *must* be something common, or they would not be called 'games'" – but *look and see* whether there is anything common to all. – For if you look at them you will not see something that is common to all, but similarities, relationships, and a whole series of them at that. (*Philosophical Investigations* I.66, emphasis in original)

Games, Wittgenstein says, „form a family" *(Philosophical Investigations* I.67), and they are linked together by „a complicated network of similarities overlapping and criss-crossing: sometimes overall similarities, sometimes similarities of detail" *(Philosophical Investigations* I.66). Wittgenstein adds that he „can think of no better expression to characterize these similarities than 'family resemblances'" (I.67). (Wittgenstein, by the way, did not invent the expression „family resemblances." It or similar expressions have long been in use in English, German, and other languages.)

„Game" constitutes a fairly extreme illustration because of the great diversity of games. In the particular examples that I have supplied, solitaire and baseball, there are no obvious similarities. Those examples, however, are linked together by networks of other games that resemble one or both. Thus bridge resembles solitaire in being a card game, and partnerships in bridge resemble to some extent the division into teams that we find in baseball.

Wittgenstein maintains that *it is not necessary* for all the instantiations of a category to share features in common in order for them to be labeled by the same category term. He allows, however, that sometimes the instantiations of a category do share elements in common, albeit that sharing may not be of primary importance for understanding meaning.

Something of a parallel claim has been entered in an approach to summarizing the distribution of recognized features in a classification. I refer to „numerical phenetics" in biological systematics and its emphasis on so-called „polythetic classification." The anthropologist Richard Chaney (1978: 139–140) points out that while Wittgenstein's employment of the expression „family resemblance" has to do with „how we use our words and concepts," „polythetic classification," in contrast, is „actuarial data summary."

Both Wittgenstein and numerical pheneticists attempt, in their different ways and for different purposes, to comprehend phenomena in multi-factorial fashion. Wittgenstein, as noted earlier, allows that in some cases all of the instantiations of a category may share one or more features in common, but that even if they do that fact by itself may not disclose what is most significant about the category. Numerical pheneticists, for their part, allow that the members of a biological taxon are likely to share one or more „character states" in common (Sokal and Sneath 1963: 14). But even though „natural taxa are usually not fully polythetic," for operational purposes pheneticists proceed as if they were (Sneath and Sokal 1973: 21–22). Polythetic taxa, indeed, may revolve around monothetic cores.

Without going any further into technicalities,[12] suffice it to say that the two quite different intellectual engagements referred to above mutually support an important point. Briefly put, in anything as complex as biological systematics or the exploration of how we use terms and concepts in everyday life, we need to maximize the diversity of relevant variables and values taken into account. This is so even if we can identify one or more common features. In applying that insight to our interest in concepts and categories, it can be argued that we ought to consider a wealth of possibilities. That would include possible theories or „idealized cognitive models" that may help explain the structures of categories, the relevance of contexts for affecting conceptual strategies and tactics, variable weightings of features, and constraints on what people may be prepared to recognize (Lakoff 1987, Medin 1989). Rather than pursue this line of thought abstractly, however, I turn now to a limited discussion of a particular case: that of „supernatural agents" as we find them not only in what we unhesitatingly regard as „religion" but elsewhere as well.

Supernatural Agents

Boyer makes the postulation of supernatural agents central to his conceptualization of religion. Such agents conform for the most part to intuitive ontologies and expectations about persons as agents while departing from those ontologies and expectations in a relatively small

---

12 More substantial descriptions and comparisons of polythesis and family resemblance can be found in Saler 2000a [1993]: Chapter 5.

number of arresting particulars (Boyer 1994, 2001). Supernatural agents, Boyer writes, are „defined as violations of intuitions about agents" (2004: 31).[13] But as Boyer acknowledges on the same page, in addition to occurring in religion, „supernatural characters" are also „found in folktales and other minor cultural domains." I would go further. In our society, certainly, references to supernatural agents are widely encountered, if only as rhetorical ploys. Many such references are not usually taken as assertions of the reality of such agents (except, perhaps, as tropes). There are, however, references that do appear to implicate ontological commitments.

Supernatural agents are encountered in what we are likely to regard as the most prototypical (the adjudged „clearest") cases of religion. And they can be absent in some instances of what certain authors call „secular religions" or „quasi-religions," assemblages of elements that resemble more prototypical exemplars of religion, but not sufficiently enough to escape qualification. To complicate matters further, they are sometimes encountered in cases that many classify without explicit qualification as „religion" while deeming them somewhat ambiguous instances of that category. The canon of Canonical Theravada Buddhism, for example, recognizes gods but does not assign them salvific functions (salvation is realized only by following the teachings of the Buddha). Largely because it does not, both Durkheim (1965 [1912]) and Southwold (1978) deny that theism is crucial to the definition of religion (Southwold argues that gods are contingent elements in religion, not necessary ones). But, as Spiro (1982 [1970]) points out, many Theravada Buddhists, despite what is inscribed in the canon, seek to invoke, propitiate, or avoid a variety of beings that he terms „superhuman." Spiro (1966) also argues that the Buddha is himself a „superhuman" being and therefore godlike, an argument that Southwold (1978) rejects as vague and unpersuasive.

Putting aside arguments about the Buddha, suffice it to suggest that the resolution of arguments about the status of gods and other supernatural agents in Theravada Buddhism ought to involve some functional considerations. Because the canon stresses salvation and accords no crucial or central importance to gods or other supernatural agents for obtaining it, we can argue that it does not render them religious objects. Many Theravada Buddhists, however, in invoking or propitiating

---

13 Defining *supernatural* agents as counter-intuitive could go a long way toward resolving old arguments about the probity and utility of the term „supernatural." See Pyysiäinen 2001.

godlike beings in the hope of relieving sickness or enhancing prospects for success in various undertakings do treat them in a way that can induce us to classify them as religious objects.

Functional considerations also apply to other cases where (according to Boyer's characterization) we find supernatural agents but it would be stretching things to call them religious objects. Our allowance that this is so conduces, in my opinion, to at least three conclusions.

First, references to supernatural agents do not by themselves establish the existence of religion. While such references are *typical* of religion, they are certainly not *sufficient* for applying the category label. People, in my opinion, must deem supernatural agents to offer prospects of making significant differences in their lives if we are to account those agents religious objects. While postulations of supernatural agents can be numbered among religion-constituting elements, it is only when they are supported by other religion-constituting elements in appropriate contexts that we have religion.

Second, if we deem admission to a group comprehended by the category religion to be a matter of „more or less" rather than a matter of „yes or no," then an argument can be made for admitting „secular religions" and „quasi-religions" as peripheral members. Some of these peripheral cases, as indicated earlier, do not accord functional significance to supernatural agents or even call attention to them, unlike more central (more prototypical) exemplars of religion. If this be accepted, we could go on to argue that supernatural agents, though clearly typical of religion, are not *necessary* elements for recognizing religion.

Third, the wide occurrence of supernatural agents outside of what we unhesitatingly call religion is a matter of considerable interest. Boyer explains cogently *why* supernatural agents occur. But, despite some interesting things that he says in Boyer 2001, he does not broadly assess *the consequences* of their occurrences in diverse areas of human life. The developing science of religion may profitably do so. Indeed, by tracing the significance of elements that we deem typical of religion as they occur outside of the clear purview of what we conventionally call religion, we transcend religion. To the extent, that is, that we study elements that we regard as especially typical of religion in less typical settings, we attend to a *religious dimension* in human life that reaches out beyond religion.

Toward a Scholarly Model of Religion

A scholarly model of religion, as I conceive it, should consist of a pool of elements that scholars associate with religions. Not all will be found in all religions. Some will be more typical of what we mean by religion than others, both in terms of distributions and weightings. And many will be found outside of the purview of what scholars conventionally designate as religions. None by themselves are necessary for identifying religion, and none by themselves are sufficient for doing so.

The approach outlined above emphasizes central tendencies rather than essences, fuzzy peripheries rather than sharp boundaries, resemblances rather than identities, and typical features rather than distinctive ones. Grounded in informed accommodations to the realities of language and categorization rather than in quixotic requirements for transparency and precision, and with relevance to the cognitive and evolutionary sciences, it encourages us both to explore religion and to transcend it. While religion and a religious dimension in human life are neither *sui generis* nor autonomous, and so not immune to reductive explanation, they are facets of the human condition, and it makes analytical as well as existential sense to conceptualize them as such.

References Cited

Aaron, Richard I. *The Theory of Universals*, 2nd ed. Oxford: The Clarendon Press., 1967.
Aberle, David F. et al. "The Functional Prerequisites of a Society." *Ethics* 60, 100–111, 1950.
Albert, Ethel M. "The Classification of Values." *American Anthropologist* 58, 221–248, 1956.
Appell, George N. Personal communication, 1999.
Aquinas, Thomas. *Summa contra gentiles*, Book IV, trans Charles O'Neil. Notre Dame, IN: University of Notre Dame Press, 1975.
Arieti, Sylvano. *Interpretation of Schizophrenia*, 2nd ed. New York: Basic Books, 1941.
Aristoteles. *The Basic Works of Aristotle*, trans Richard McKeon. New York: Random House, 1941.
Armstrong, Sharon Lee, Lila R. Gleitman, and Henry Gleitman. "On What Some Concepts Might Not Be." *Cognition* 13, 263–308, 1983.
Asad, Talal. "Anthropological Conceptions of Religion: Reflections on Geertz." *Man* 18 (2): 237–259, 1983.
Athanasius of Alexandria. *The Orations Against the Arians*. London: Griffith Farrar, 1912.
Atran, Scott. *In Gods We Trust: The Evolutionary Landscape of Religion*. Oxford: Oxford University Press, 2002.
Ayoub, Victor. "The Study of Values." In Clifton, James A., ed, *Introduction to Cultural Anthropology*, 244–272. Boston, 1968.
Bailey, Cyril. *Phases in the Religion of Ancient Rome*. Berkeley: University of California Press, 1932.
Bambrough, J. Renford. "Universals and Family Resemblances." *Proceedings of the Aristotelian Society* 61, 207–221, 1960/61.
Barkow, Jerome H., Leda Cosmides, and John Tooby, eds. *The Adapted Mind: Evolutionary Psychology and the Generation of Culture*. New York: Oxford University Press, 1992.
Barnes, B., and D. Bloor. "Relativism, Rationalism and the Sociology of Knowledge." In Hollis, M. and S. Lukes, eds, *Rationality and Relativism*, 21–47. Oxford: Blackwell, 1982.
Barrett, Justin L. *Why Would Anyone Believe in God?* Walnut Creek, CA: Altamira Press, 2004.
Baudelaire, Charles. *Selected Writings on Art and Artists*. Harmonsworth: Penguin, 1972.
Bell, Catherine. *Ritual Theory, Ritual Practice*. New York: Oxford University Press, 1992.
Benveniste, Emile. *Problems in General Linguistics*, trans Mary Elizabeth Meek. Coral Gables: University of Florida Press, 1971 [1966].

— *Le Vocabulaire des Institutions Indo-Européennes*, Vol. 2. Paris. Éditions de Minuit, 1969.
Bigger, Charles P. *Participation: A Platonic Inquiry*. Baton Rouge: Louisiana State University Press, 1968.
Bloch, Maurice. *Prey Into Hunter: The Politics of Religious Experience*. Cambridge: Cambridge University Press, 1992.
Bloom, Harold. *The American Religion: The Emergence of the Post-Christian Nation*. New York: Simon & Schuster, 1992.
Boas, Franz. "The Limitations of the Comparative Method in Anthropology." In Boas, Franz, *Race, Language, and Culture*, 270–280. New York: Macmillan, 1940 [1896].
Boyer, Pascal. *The Naturalness of Religious Ideas: A Cognitive Theory of Religion*. Berkeley: The University of California Press, 1994.
— "Creation of the Sacred: A cognitivist view." *Method & Theory in the Study of Religion* 10 (1): 88–92, 1998.
— *Religion Explained: The Evolutionary Origins of Religious Thought*. New York: Basic Books, 2001.
— "Out of Africa: Lessons From a By-product of Evolution." In Light, Timothy and Brian C. Wilson, eds, *Religion as Human Capacity: A Festschrift in Honor of E. Thomas Lawson*, 27–43. Leiden and Boston: Brill, 2004.
Braun, Willi. "Introduction." *Method & Theory in the Study of Religion* 10 (1): 84–88, 1998.
Brookesmith, Peter. *Alien Abductions*. New York: Barnes and Noble, 1998.
Brown, Donald E. *Human Universals*. New York: Mc Graw Hill, 1991.
Bryan, Courtland D. *Close Encounters of the Fourth Kind: Alien Abductions, UFOs and the Conference at MIT*. New York: Alfred Knopf, 1995.
Bullard, Thomas. *UFO Abductions: The Measure of a Mystery*. Mt, Ranier, MD: Fund for UFO Research, 1987.
— "UFOs: Lost in the Myths." In Jacobs, David, ed, *UFOs and Abductions: Challenging the Borders of Knowledge*, 141–191. Lawrence: University Press of Kansas, 2000a.
— Proposal for "A Mote to Trouble the Mind's Eye." Unpublished book Proposal, 2000b.
Burkert, Walter. *Creation of the Sacred: Tracks of Biology in Early Religions*. Cambridge, MA and London: Harvard University Press, 1996.
— "Response: Exploring Religion in a Biological Landscape." *Method & Theory in the Study of Religion* 10 (1): 129–132, 1998.
Byrne, Peter. "Religion and the Religions." In Sutherland, S. R. et al, eds., *The World's Religions*, 3–28. London: Routledge, 1988.
— *Natural Religion and the Nature of Religion: The Legacy of Deism*. London, Routledge 1989.
Campbell, Keith. "Family Resemblance Predicates." *American Philosophical Quarterly* 2, 238–244, 1965.
Caudmont, Juan. "Cuentos y leyendas de la Guajira." *Revista Colombiana de Folklore*, segunda época 2: 167–174, 1953.
Cazeneuve, Jean. *Lucien Lévy-Bruhl*, trans Peter Rivière. New York: Harper and Row, 1972 [1963].

Chaney, Richard Paul. "Polythematic Expansion: Remarks on Needham's Polythetic Classification." *Current Anthropology* 19 (1): 139–143, 1978.

Chaves, Miliciades. "Mitos, leyendas y cuentos de La Guajira." *Boletín de Arqueología (Bogotá):* 2(4): 305–331, 1946.

— "La Guajira: una región y una cultura de Colombia." *Revista Colombiana de Antropología* 1 (1): 123–195, 1953.

Chomsky, Noam. "Review of B. F. Skinner's Verbal Behavior." *Language* 35, 26–58, 1956.

Coleman, Linda and Paul Kay. "Prototype Semantics: The English Word Lie." *Language* 57: 26–44, 1981.

Cooper, David E. "Alternative Logic in Primitive Thought." *Man* 10, 238–256, 1975.

Cosmides, Leda, John Tooby, and Jerome H. Barkow. "Introduction: Evolutionary Psychology and Conceptual Integration." In Barkow, Jerome H. Leda Cosmides, and John Tooby, eds, *The Adapted Mind: Evolutionary Psychology and the Generation of Culture*, 3–15. New York and Oxford: Oxford University Press, 1992.

D'Andrade, Roy. *The Development of Cognitive Anthropology*. Cambridge: Cambridge University Press, 1995.

Darwin, Charles. *The Expression of the Emotions in Man and Animals*. London: Murray, 1872.

Davidson, D. *Mind and Language: Wolfson College Lectures, 1974*. Oxford: Clarendon Press, 1975.

Dawkins, Richard. *The God Delusion*. London: Bantam, 2006.

Dennett, D. C. *Kinds of Minds: Toward an Understanding of Consciousness*. New York: Basic Books, 1996.

— *Brainchildren: Essays on Designing Minds*. Cambridge, MA: MIT Press (Bradford Books), 1998.

— "The Evolution of Religious Memes: Who – or What – Benefits?" *Method & Theory in the Study of Religion* 10 (1): 115–128, 1998.

Denzler, Brenda. *The Lure of the Edge: Scientific Passions, Religious Beliefs, and the Pursuit of UFO's*. Berkeley: University of California Press, 2001.

Dewey, John. "Antinaturalism in Extremis." In Krikorian, Yervant H., ed, *Naturalism and the Human Spirit*, 1–16. New York: Colombia University Press, 1944.

Disch, Thomas M. *The Dreams Our Stuff is Made Of: How Science Fiction Conquered The World*. New York: The Free Press, 1998.

Dodds, E. R. *Pagan and Christian in an Age of Anxiety*. Cambridge: Cambridge University Press, 1965.

Domarus, Ernst von. "The Specific Laws of Logic in Schizophrenia." In Kasanin, J. S., ed, *Language in Thought and Schizophrenia*, 101–14. Berkeley: University of California Press, 1954.

Durant, Robert J. "Evolution of Public Opinion on UFOs." *International UFO Reporter*, November/December, 9–23, 1993.

Durkheim, Emile. *The Elementary Forms of the Religious Life*, trans. Joseph Ward Swain. New York: The Free Press, 1965 [1912].

Evans-Pritchard, Edward E. *Witchcraft, Oracles and Magic Among the Azande.* Oxford: Clarendon, 1937.
— *Nuer Religion.* Oxford: Oxford University Press, 1956.
— *Theories of Primitive Religion.* Oxford: Oxford University Press, 1965.
Ewers, John C. *The Blackfeet: Raiders on the Northwestern Plains.* Norman: University of Oklahoma Press, 1958.
Fitzgerald, Timothy. "Religion, Philosophy and Family Resemblance." *Religion* 26: 215–236, 1996.
— "A Critique of 'Religion' as a Cross-Cultural Category." *Method and Theory in the Study of Religion* 9: 91–110, 1997.
— *The Ideology of Religious Studies.* New York: Oxford University Press, 2000.
Fowler, Raymond. *The Andreasson Affair.* Englewood Cliffs, NJ: Prentice Hall, 1979.
— *The Andreasson Affair, Phase 2.* Engelwood Cliffs, NJ: Prentice Hall, 1982.
— *The Watchers.* New York: Bantam Books, 1990.
— *The Allagash Abductions.* Tigard, OR: Wild Flower Press, 1993
— "The UFO Abduction Controversy in the United States." In David M. Jacobs, ed., *UFOs and Abductions: Challenging the Borders of Knowledge*, 192–214. Lawrence: University Press of Kansas, 2000.
Fowler, W. Warde. "The Latin History of the Word 'Religio.'" *Transactions of The Third International Congress for the History of Religions* 2: 169–175, 1908.
Frazier, K. "UFOs as ET Spacecraft." *Skeptical Inquirer* 16 (4), 346, 1992.
Fuller, John. *The Interrupted Journey.* New York: Berkeley Publishing Co, 1966.
Gallup, G. and F. Newport 1991. "Belief in Paranormal Phenomena Among Adult Americans." *Skeptical Inquirer* 15 (2), 137–146, 1991.
Gardner, Robert and Karl G. Heider. *Gardens of War: Life and Death in the New Guinea Stone Age.* New York: Random House, 1968.
Geertz, Clifford. "Religion as a Cultural System." In Banton, Michael, ed, *Anthropological Approaches To the Study of Religion*, 1–16. London: Tavistock, 1966.
— *The Interpretation of Cultures.* New York: Basic Books, 1973.
Goodenough, Ward. H. *Cooperation in Change.* New York: Russell Sage Foundation, 1963.
Gould, Stephen Jay. "Darwinian Fundamentalism." *The New York Review of Books* (June 12), 34–37, 1997a.
— "Evolution: The Pleasures of Pluralism." *The New York Review of Books* (June 26), 47–52, 1997 b.
— "Replies." *The New York Review of Books* (October 9), 56–58, 1997 c.
Gould, Stephen Jay and Richard C. Lewontin (1979). "The spandrels of San Marcos and the Panglossian Paradigm." *Proceedings of the Royal Society of London, 1979.*
Goulet, Jean-Guy A. *El Universo Social y Religioso Guajiro.* Caracas: Biblioteca Corpazulia y UCAB, 1980.
Guthrie, Stewart Elliott. *Faces in the Clouds: A New Theory of Religion.* Oxford: Oxford University Press, 1993.

Hahn, Robert A. "Understanding Beliefs: An Essay on the Methodology of the Statement and Analysis of Belief Systems." *Current Anthropology* 14 (3), 207–229, 1973.
Hallowell, A. Irving. "Some Empirical Aspects of Northern Saulteaux Religion." *American Anthropologist* 36, 389–404, 1934.
— "Myth, Culture, and Personality." *American Anthropologist* 49, 544–556, 1947.
— "Personality Structure and the Evolution of Man." *American Anthropologist* 52, 159–173, 1950.
— "The Self and Its Behavioral Environment." In Hallowell, A. Irving, *Culture and Experience*, Philadelphia: The University of Pennsylvania Press, 75–110, 1955.
— "Self, Society, and Culture in Phylogenetic Perspective." In Tax, Sol, ed, *Evolution after Darwin*, Vol. II, Chicago: The University of Chicago Press, 309–371, 1960a.
— "Ojibwa Ontology, Behavior, and World View." In Diamond, Stanley, ed, *Culture in History: Essays in Honor of Paul Radin*, 19–52. New York: Columbia University Press, 1960b.
Hallpike, C. R. *The Foundations of Primitive Thought*. Oxford: Oxford University Press, 1979.
Harris, Marvin. *The Rise of Anthropological Theory*. New York: Crowell, 1968, 1975.
Harvey, David. *The Condition of Postmodernity: An Enquiry into the Origins of Cultural Change*. Oxford: Basil Blackwell, 1989.
Hirschfeld, Lawrence A. and Susan Gelman, eds, *Mapping the Mind: Domain Specificity in Cognition and Culture*. New York: Cambridge University Press, 1994.
Holden, Katharine J. and Christopher C. French. "Alien Abduction Experiences: Some Clues From Neuropsychology and Neuropsychiatry." *Cognitive Neuropsychiatry* 7 (3): 163–178, 2002.
Hollis, Martin and Steven Lukes, eds. *Rationality and Relativism*. Oxford: Blackwell, 1982.
Hopkins, Budd. *Missing Time*. New York: Ballantine Books, 1981.
— *Intruders: The Incredible Visitations at Copley Woods*. New York: Bantam, 1987.
Horgan, T. and J. Tienson. *Connectionism and the Philosophy of Psychology*. Cambridge, MA: MIT Press (Bradford Books), 1996.
Horton, Robin. "A Definition of Religion, and Its Uses." *Journal of the Royal Anthropological Institute* 90, 201–226, 1960.
— "Lévy-Bruhl, Durkheim and the Scientific Revolution." In Horton, Robin and Ruth Finnegan, eds, *Modes of Thought: Essays on Thinking In Western and Non-Western Societies*, 249–305. London: Faber, 1973.
Horton, Robin and Ruth Finnegan, eds. *Modes of Thought: Essays on Thinking in Western and Non-Western Societies*. London: Faber, 1973.
Hudson, W. D. "What Makes Religious Beliefs Religious?" *Religious Studies* 13, 221–242, 1977.

Hufford, David J. *The Terror that Comes in the Night: An Experience-Centered Study of Supernatural Assault Traditions*. Philadelphia: University of Pennsylvania Press, 1982.
Hume, David. *A Treatise of Human Nature*. Oxford: Clarendon Press, 1896 [1739].
Hultkrantz, Åke. "The Concept of the Supernatural in Primal Religion." *History of Religions* 22 (3), 231–253, 1983.
Jackendoff, Ray. *Semantics and Cognition*. Cambridge, MA: The MIT Press, 1983.
Jacobs, David M. *Secret Life: Firsthand Accounts of UFO Abductions*. New York; Simon and Schuster, 1992.
— *The Threat—The Secret Agenda: What the Aliens Really Want and How They Plan to Get It*. New York: Simon and Schuster, 1998.
Jones, Steve. "The Set Within the Skull." *The New York Review of Books* (November 6): 3–16, 1997.
Jones, Todd. *Translation and Belief Ascription: Fundamental Barriers*. Paper presented at the Wenner-Gren Conference on Translation in Anthropology, Barnard College, Nov. 10–12, 1998.
Jung, Carl G. *Flying Saucers: A Modern Myth of Things Seen in the Sky*. New York: Harcourt Brace, 1959.
Justin the Martyr. *Dialogue with Trypho, a Jew*. London: Lutterworth Press, 1963.
Kenny, Anthony. *Wittgenstein*. Cambridge, MA: Harvard University Press, 1973.
Kenny, Michael G. "Alternative Logic in 'Primitive Thought'." *Man* 11 (1): 116, 1976.
Kluckhohn, Clyde. "Universal Categories of Culture." In Kroeber, Alfred L., ed, *Anthropology Today*, 507–523. New York: Columbia University Press, 1953.
Kluckhohn, Florence and Fred L, Strodbeck, et al. *Variations in Value Orientations*. Evanston, Il.: University of Illinois Press, 1961.
Kolp, Alan Lee. *Participation: A Unifying Concept in the Theology of Athanasius*. Unpublished Ph.D. dissertation, Harvard University, 1975.
Kroeber, Alfred A. and Clyde Kluckhohn. *Culture: A Critical Review of Concepts and Definitions*. Cambridge, MA: The Peabody Museum, 1952.
Lakoff, George. *Women, Fire, and Dangerous Things: What Categories Reveal About the Mind*. Chicago: The University of Chicago Press, 1997.
Leach, Edmund. R. Virgin Birth. *Proceedings of the Royal Anthropological Institute* 1966, 39–49, 1967.
Leenhardt, Maurice. "Preface." In Lévy-Bruhl, Lucien, *The Notebooks on Primitive Mentality*, xi–xxiv, trans Peter Rivière. New York: Harper and Row, 1975 [1949].
Lévy-Bruhl, Lucien. *L'Ame primitive*. Paris: Alcan, 1927.
— *Le Surnaturel et la nature dans la mentalité primitive*. Paris: Alcan 1931.
— *La Mythologie primitive*. Paris: Alcan, 1935.
— *L'Expérience mystique et les symbols chez les primitives*. Paris: Alcan, 1938.

— *The Notebooks on Primitive Mentality*, trans Peter Rivière. New York: Harper and Row, 1975 [1949].
— *How Natives Think*, trans Lilian A. Clare. Princeton: Princeton University Press, 1985 [1910].
Lienhardt, Godfrey. *Divinity and Experience: The Religion of the Dinka*. Oxford: Clarendon Press, 1961.
Lloyd, G. E. R. *Demystifying Mentalities*. Cambridge: Cambridge University Press, 1990.
Locke, John. *An Essay Concerning Human Understanding*. New York: Dover, 1959 [1689].
Lorenzen, Carol. "The Disappearance of Rivalino Mafra da Silva: Kidnapped by a UFO?" *Fate* 16 (6), 26–33, 1963.
— *The Shadow of the Unknown*. New York: New American Library, 1970.
Lorenzen, Carol and Jim. *Abducted*. New York: Berkeley Publishing Co, 1977.
Lowie, Robert H. *Primitive Religion*. New York: Liveright Publishing Corp, 1948 [1924].
Lubac, Henri de. "Remarques sur l'histoire du mot 'Surnaturel.'" *Nouvelle Revue Théologique* 61, 225–249, 1934.
— *Le surnaturel: études historiques*, Paris: Aubier, 1946.
Lukasiewicz, Jan. *Elements of Mathematical Logic*, 2nd ed., trans Olgierd Wojtasiewicz. New York: Macmillan, 1964.
— *Selected Works*, L. Borkowski, ed., trans Olgierd Wojtasiewicz. Amsterdam: North-Holland, 1974.
Lumsden, C. J. and E. O. Wilson. *Genes, Mind, and Culture: The Coevolutionary Process*. Cambridge, MA: Harvard University Press, 1981.
Lutz, Catherine A. *Unnatural Emotions: Everyday Sentiments on a Micronesian Atoll And Their Challenge to Western Theory*. Chicago: University of Chicago Press, 1988.
Mack, John. *Abduction*. New York: Charles Scribner's Sons, 1994.
Mandler, George. *Mind and Body: The Psychology of Emotion and Stress*. New York: Norton, 1984.
Malinowski, Bronislaw. *Argonauts of the Western Pacific*. New York: E. P. Dutton, 1961 [1922].
Masuzawa, Tomoko. "In Nature's Trail." *Method & Theory in the Study of Religion* 10 (1): 106–114, 1998.
Matheson, Terry. *Alien Abductions: Creating a Modern Phenomenon*. Amherst, NY: Prometheus Books, 1998.
Matos Romero, Manuel. *Juitatay juyá. La Guajira. Su importancia*. Caracas: Imprenta El Cojo, 1971.
McNally, Richard J., et al. "Psychophysiological Responding During Script-Driven Imagery In People Reporting Abduction by Space Aliens." *Psychological Science* 15 (7): 493–497, 2004.
Medin, Douglas L. "Concepts and Conceptual Structure." *American Psychologist* 44: 1469–1481, 1989.
Mithen, Steven. *The Prehistory of the Mind: The Cognitive Origins of Art, Religion and Science*. London: Thames and Hudson, 1996.

— "Symbolism and the Supernatural." In Dunbar, Robin, Chris Knight, and Camilla Power, eds, *The Evolution of Culture: An Interdisciplinary View*, 147–169. New Brunswick, NJ: Rutgers University Press, 1999.
Moore, Wilbert E. and Melvin Tumin. "Some Social Functions of Ignorance." *American Sociological Review* 14 (6), 787–795, 1949.
Murdock, George Peter. "The Common Denominator of Culture." In Linton, Ralph, ed, *The Science of Man in the World Crisis*, 123–141. New York: Columbia University Press, 1945.
Nash, Dennison. "Hallowell in American Anthropology." *Ethos* 5 (1), 3–12, 1977.
Needham, Rodney. *Belief, Language, and Experience*. Chicago and Oxford: University of Chicago Press and Basil Blackwell and Mott, 1972.
Newman, John. H. *An Essay in Aid of a Grammar of Assent*. London: Longmans, Green & Co, 1913 [1870]
Norman, Donald A. "Reflections on Cognition and Parallel Distributed Processing." In McClelland, J. L., D. E. Rumelhart, and the PDP Research Group, eds, *Parallel Distributed Processing (Vol. II)*, Cambridge, MA: MIT Press, 1986.
Parmentier, Richard J. "Semiotic Mediation: Ancestral Genealogy and Final Interpretant." In Mertz, Elizabeth and Richards J. Parmentier, eds, *Semiotic Mediation: Sociocultural and Psychological Perspectives*, 359–385. Orlando, FL: Academic Press, 1985.
Paz Ipuana, Ramón. *Mitos, leyendas y cuentos Guajiros*. Caracas: Instituto Agrario, 1972.
Peebles, Curtis.. *Watch the Skies: A Chronicle of the Flying Saucer Myth*. Washington: The Smithsonian Institution Press, 1994.
Perrin, Michel. *The Way of the Dead Indians: Guajiro Myths and Symbols*, trans. Michael Fineberg. Austin: University of Texas Press, 1987 [1976].
Phillips, C. Robert III. "Walter Burkert In Partibus Infidelium: A Classicist Appraisal of Creation of the Sacred." *Method & Theory in the Study of Religion* 10 (1): 92–105, 1998.
Piaget, Jean. *The Child's Conception of the World*. London: Routledge, 1929.
— *The Principles of Genetic Epistemology*, trans Wolfe Mays. New York: Basic Books, 1972.
— *The Essential Piaget*, ed Howard F. Gruber and J. Jacques Voneche. New York: Basic Books, 1977.
Pineda Giraldo, Roberto. "La chama, un mito Guajiro." *Revista del Instituto Etnológico Nacional (Bogotá)* 2: 113–126, 1947.
— "Aspectos de la magica en La Guajira." *Revista del Instituto Etnológica Nacional (Bogotá)* III (1): 1–163, 1950.
Pinker, S. *How the Mind Works*. New York and London: W. W. Norton and Co, 1997.
Placher, William C. *A History of Christian Theology: An Introduction*. Philadelphia: Westminster Press, 1983.
Pouillon, J. "Remarks on the Verb 'To Believe.'" In Izard, M. and P. Smith, eds, *Between Belief and Transgression: Structuralist Essays in Religion, History,*

and Myth, trans J. Leavitt, 1–8. Chicago: University of Chicago Press, 1982 [1979].
Popper, Karl R. *Conjectures and Refutations: The Growth of Scientific Knowledge.* New York: Basic Books, 1962.
Preus, J. Samuel. *Explaining Religion: Criticism and Theory from Bodin to Freud.* New Haven: Yale University Press, 1987.
Price, H. H. *Belief.* London: Allen and Unwin, 1969.
— *Thinking and Experience,* 2nd ed, London, 1969.
— "Universals and Resemblances." In Landesman, Charles, ed, *The Problem of Universals,* 36–55. New York: Basic Books, 1971.
Pyysiäinen, Ilkka. *How Religion Works: Towards a New Cognitive Science of Religion.* Leiden: E. J. Brill, 2001.
— "Intuitive and Explicit in Religious Thought." *Journal of Cognition and Culture* 4 (1), 123–150, 2004.
Randle, Kevin D., Russ Estes, and William P. Cone. *The Abduction Enigma.* New York: Forge, 1999.
Randles, Jenny. *Abduction: Over 200 Documented UFO Kidnappings Investigated.* London: Robert Hale, 1988.
Rogo, D. Scott, ed. *UFO Abductions: True Cases of Kidnappings.* New York: Signet, 1980.
Rosch, Eleanor. "Principles of Categorization." In Rosch, Eleanor and Barbara B. Lloyd, eds, *Cognition and Categorization,* 27–48. Hillsdale, NJ: Lawrence Erlbaum Associates, 1978.
Runciman, W. G. "The Sociological Explanation of 'Religious' Beliefs.'" *Archives Européennes de Sociologie* 10, 149–191, 1969.
Saler, Benson. "Supernatural as a Western Category." *Ethos* 5 (1), 31–53, 1977.
— "Principios de compensación y el valor de las personas en la sociedad Guajira." *Montalban* 17: 53–65, 1986.
— *"Religio* and the Definition of Religion." *Cultural Anthropology* 2(3): 395–399, 1987.
— "Los Wayú (Guajiro)." In Coppens, Walter, Bernarda Escalante, and Jacques Lizot, eds, *Los aborígenes de Venezuela,* Vol. III, 25–145. Caracas: Fundación La Salle de Ciencias Naturales/Monte Avila Editores 1988.
— "Cultural Anthropology and the Definition of Religion." In Bianchi, Ugo, ed, *"The Notion of 'Religion' in Comparative Research,"* Selected Proceedings of the XVIth Congress of the International Association for the History of Religion, Rome, 1990, 831–836. Rome: L'Erma di Bretschneider, 1994.
— "Conceptualizing Religion: The Matter of Boundaries." In Klimkeit, Hans-Joachim, ed, *Vergleichen und Verstehen in der Religionswissenschaft,* 27–35. Wiesbaden: Harrassowitz Verlag, 1997.
— "Family Resemblance and the Definition of Religion." *Historical Reflections/ Réflexions Historiques* 25 (3): 391–404, 1999.
— *Conceptualizing Religion: Immanent Anthropologists, Transcendent Natives, and Unbounded Categories,* with a Preface for the Paperback Edition. New York and Oxford: Berghahn Books, 2000a [1993].
— "Responses." *Method and Theory in the Study of Religion* 12 (1/2): 323–338, 2000b. Also in Geertz, Armin and Russell T. McCutcheon, eds, *Perspectives*

on *Method and Theory in the Study of Religion: Adjunct Proceedings of the XVIIth Congress of the International Association for the History of Religions, Mexico City, 1995,* 323–338. Leiden: E. J. Brill, 2000b.
— "On What We May Believe About Beliefs." In Andresen, Jensine, ed, *Cognitive Perspectives on Religious Belief, Ritual, and Experience,* 47–69. Cambridge: Cambridge University Press, 2001.
— "Finding Wayú Religion." *Historical Reflections/Réflexions Historiques 31 (2), 255–270, 2005.*
Saler, Benson, Charles. A. Ziegler, and Charles. B. Moore. *UFO Crash at Roswell: The Genesis of a Modern Myth.* Washington: The Smithsonian Institution Press, 1997.
Saler, Benson and Charles A. Ziegler. "Atheism and the Apotheosis of Agency." *Temenos* 42 (2), 7–41, 2006.
Schatzki, Theodore R. "Objectivity and Rationality." In Natter, Wolfgang et al, eds, *Objectivity and Its Other,* 137–78. New York: The Guilford Press, 1995.
Scheffler, Israel. *Conditions of Knowledge.* Glenview, IL: Scott, Foresman and Company, 1965.
Searle, John R. *Intentionality: An Essay in the Philosophy of Mind.* Cambridge: Cambridge University Press, 1983.
Shulich, Thomas. *Personal Communication,* 1997.
Shweder, Richard A. "Likeness and Likelihood in Everyday Thought: Magical Thinking in Judgments about Personality." *Current Anthropology* 18 (4) 637–58, 1977.
— "Rationality 'Goes Without Saying.'" *Culture, Medicine and Psychiatry* 5 (4) 348–58, 1981.
— "On Savages and Other Children." *American Anthropologist* 84, 354–66, 1982.
Skorupski, John. *Symbol and Theory: A Philosophical Study of Theories of Religion in Social Anthropology.* Cambridge: Cambridge University Press, 1976.
Slone, D. Jason. *Theological Incorrectness: Why Religious People Believe What They Shouldn't.* Oxford: Oxford University Press, 2004.
Smart, Ninian. *The Science of Religion and the Sociology of Knowledge.* Princeton, 1973.
Smith, Brian K. "Exorcising the Transcendent: Strategies for Defining Hinduism and Religion." *History of Religions* 27 (1), 32–55, 1987.
Smith, Jonathan Z. "Religion, Religions, Religious." In Taylor, Mark C., ed, *Critical Terms for Religious Studies,* 269–284. Chicago: University of Chicago Press 1998.
Smith, Wilfred Cantwell. *The Meaning and End of Religion.* New York: The Macmillan Company, 1962.
Sneath, Peter H. A. and Robert A. Sokal. *Numerical Taxonomy: The Principles And Practices of Numerical Classification.* San Francisco: W. H. Freeman, 1973.
Sokal, Robert A. and Peter H. A. Sneath. *Principles of Numerical Taxonomy.* San Francisco: W. H. Freeman, 1963.

Southwold, Martin. "Buddhism and the Definition of Religion." *Man* 13: 362–379, 1978.
Sperber, Dan. "Apparently Irrational Beliefs." In Hollis, M. and S. Lukes, eds, *Rationality and Relativism,* 149–180. Cambridge, MA: MIT Press, 1982.
Spiro, Melford E. "Religion: Problems of Definition and Explanation." In Banton, Michael, ed, *Anthropological Approaches to the Study of Religion,* 85–126. London: Tavistock, 1966.
— "Virgin Birth, Parthenogenesis and Physiological Paternity: An Essay in Cultural Interpretation." *Man* n.s. 3, 242–261, 1968.
— *Buddhism and Society: A Great Tradition in Its Burmese Vicissitudes.* Berkeley: University of California Press, 1982 [1970].
— "Some Reflections on Cultural Determinism and Relativism with Special Reference to Emotion and Reason." In Shweder, Richard A. and Robert A. LeVine, eds, *Culture Theory: Essays on Mind, Self, and Emotion,* 323–346. Cambridge: Cambridge University Press, 1984.
Stich, Stephen. P. *From Folk Psychology to Cognitive Science: The Case Against Belief.* Cambridge, MA: MIT Press (Bradford Book), 1983.
— *Deconstructing the Mind.* Oxford: Oxford University Press, 1996.
Stocking, George W., Jr. *Victorian Anthropology.* New York: The Free Press, 1987.
Streiber, Whitley. *Communion: A True Story.* New York: Morrow, 1987.
— *Transformation: The Breakthrough.* New York: Avon, 1989.
Tooby, John and Leda Cosmides. "The Psychological Foundations of Culture." In Barkow, Jerome H., Leda Cosmides, and John Tooby, eds, *The Adapted Mind: Evolutionary Psychology and the Generation of Culture,* 19–136. New York and Oxford: Oxford University Press, 1992.
Tylor, Edward B. *The Origins of Culture* and *Religion in Primitive Culture,* Vols. 1 and 2 of the 1873 edition of *Primitive Culture.* New York: Harper Bros, 1958 [1873, 1871].
Vega, Garcilaso de la. *Royal Commentaries of the Incas and General History of Peru,* Part Two, trans Harold V. Livermore. Austin: University of Texas Press, 1966.
Wallace, Anthony F. C. "Dreams and Wishes of the Soul: A Type of Psychoanalytic Theory among the Seventeenth Century Iroquois." *American Anthropologist* 60, 234–248, 1958.
— "Mazeway Resynthesis: A Biocultural Theory of Religious Inspiration." *Transactions of the New York Academy of Sciences* XVIII: 626–638, 1956a.
— "Revitalization Movements: Some Theoretical Considerations for Their Comparative Study." *American Anthropologist* LVIII: 264–281, 1956b.
— "The Psychic Unity of Human Groups." In Kaplan, Bert, ed, *Studying Personality Cross-Culturally,* 129–63. Evanston, IL: Row, Peterson and Co, 1961.
Wallace, Anthony. F. C., and John Atkins. "The Meaning of Kinship Terms." *American Anthropologist* 62, 58–80, 1960.
Walton, Travis: *The Walton Experience.* New York: Berkeley, 1978.
Whitehead, Alfred N. *Symbolism: Its Meaning and Effect.* New York, 1959 [1927].

Whitehouse, Harvey. *Arguments and Icons: Divergent Modes of Religiosity.* Oxford: Oxford University Press, 2000.
Wiebe, Donald. "Postulations for Safeguarding Preconceptions: The Case of the Scientific Religionist." *Religion* 18: 11–19, 1988.
— "Disciplinary Axioms, Boundary Conditions and the Academic Study of Religion: On Pals and Dawson." *Religion* 20: 17–29, 1990.
— "Appropriating Religion: Understanding Religion as an Object of Science." In Ahlbäck, Tor, ed, *Approaching Religion*, Part I, 253–272. Åbo: The Donner Institute for Research in Religious and Cultural History (Distributed by Almqvist & Wiksell, Stockholm), 1999.
Wikan, Unni. *Managing Turbulent Hearts: A Balinese Formula for Living.* Chicago: The University of Chicago Press, 1990.
Wilbert, Johannes. "Literatura oral y creencias de los indios Guajiros." *Memoria de la Sociedad de Ciencias Naturales La Salle* XXII (62): 103–115, 1962.
Wilson, David Sloan. *Darwin's Cathedral: Evolution, Religion, and the Nature of Society.* Chicago: University of Chicago Press, 2002.
Wissler, Clark. *Man and Culture.* New York: Thomas Crowell, 1923.
Wittgenstein, Ludwig. *Philosophical Investigations*, Third Edition, trans. G. E. M. Anscombe. New York: Macmillan, 1958.
Woodfield, Andrew. "Foreward." In Woodfield, Andrew, ed, *Thought and Object: Essays on Intentionality*, v-xi. Oxford: Clarendon Press, 1982.
Woozley, A. D. "Universals." In Edwards, Paul, ed, *The Encyclopedia of Philosophy*, 194–206. New York, Collier-Macmillan, 1967.
Young, Allan. "When Rational Men Fall Sick: An Inquiry into Some Assumptions Made by Medical Anthropologists." *Culture, Medicine and Psychiatry* 5 (4): 317–35, 1981.
Ziegler, Charles A. *A Proposed Theoretical Framework for the Examination of Witchcraft, Satanic Ritual Abuse, and Alien Abduction.* Manuscript, n.d.

Source Acknowledgments

"The Ethnographer as Pontifex" is reprinted here with permission of A&C Black Publishers Ltd, of which Berg Publishing is now an imprint.

"E.B. Tylor and the Anthropology of Religion" was first published in *The Marburg Journal of Religion*, which grants authors republishing rights without solicitation.

"Lévy-Bruhl, Participation, and Rationality" is reprinted here with permission of Aarhus University Press.

"On What We May Believe About Beliefs" is reprinted here with permission of Cambridge University Press.

"Finding Wayú Religion" and "Family Resemblance and the Definition of Religion" are reprinted here with permission of *Historical Reflections/Réflexions Historiques*. The present publisher of that journal, Berghahn Books, does not require an author of a journal article to solicit permission to reprint his or her own work.

The following four essays, "On Credulity," "Comparison: Some Suggestions for Improving the Inevitable," "Biology and Religion: On Establishing a Problematic," and "Towards a Realistic and Relevant 'Science of Religion'" are reprinted here with permission of Koninklijke Brill NV (Brill Academic Publishers).

"Secondary Beliefs and the Alien Abduction Phenomenon" is reprinted here with permission of Syracuse University Press.

"Conceptualizing Religion: The Matter of Boundaries" is reprinted here with permission of Harrassowitz Verlag.

The author takes this opportunity to express his gratitude to the above publishers both for originally publishing his essays and for facilitating their re-publication in this collection.

Index

Aaron, Richard I, 160
Abductees, see Experiencers
Abductive Thinking, 112
Aberle, David F, 138; Aberle et al, 138
Abreactive Therapy, 155
Affectivity in Thought, 11, 27, 28, 55, 63, 67-71, 72-73, 75
Agent Detection, 205, 206
Agents, Supernatural, 18, 23, 217, 220-222; see also Supernatural
Ain (Heart, Soul, Essence of a Person) among Wayú, 128
Albert, Ethel M, 170
Alexander, Bishop at Council of Nicea, 65
Alien Abductions, 20, 111, 112, 147-156
Analogy, 31, 46, 55, 166, 187, 218
Animism, 9, 52, 53-54, 56
Anthropocentric Language, 186
Anthropomorphism, 28, 169, 209
Anttonen, Veikko, 196
Appell, George N, 194
Aquinas, Thomas, 36, 100
Arieti, Sylvano, 72, 76-77
Aristotle, 76, 77, 98
Arius, 34, 35, 65
Armstrong, Sharon Lee, Lila R. Gleitman, and Henry Gleitman, 167, 178
Arunta, 10, 66
Asad, Talal, 120, 213-214
Assent, 101, 102
Atahuallpa, 31, 39, 43
Athanasius of Alexandria, 34, 35, 65
Atheism, 9-10
Atran, Scott, 10, 28, 206, 207
Augustine of Hippo, 34, 100, 136

Autonomy of Religion, 197-198, 223; Autonomy of Social Sciences, 200
Ayer, A.J., 160
Aymará, 77
Ayoub, Victor, 170
Azande, 78, 116-118, 120, 144, 197

Bailey, Cyril, 46
Balinese, 68
Bambrough, J. Renford, 160, 163
Baptism among the Wayú, 124
Barkow, Jerome H., Leda Cosmides, and John Tooby, 145, 200
Barnes, B., and D. Bloor, 70, 99
Barrett, Justin L., 10, 16, 17
Baudelaire, Charles, 181
Behavioral Environment, Culturally Constituted, 83, 85, 87-88, 90, 91
Behavioral Flexibility, 202
Behaviorism, 103-104
Belief:
- De Re and De Dicto, 37
- Intuitive/Counter-Intuitive Beliefs, Ideas, Ontologies, and Expectations, 14, 19, 33, 39-42, 44, 111, 136, 137, 173, 209, 220-221, 221 n.23
- Intuitive (Non-Reflective) and Reflective, 16-18, 19
- Knowledge distinguished from, 98-99, 100, 101
- Pragmatics, 20
- Primary and Secondary, 20, 147, 152-154, 155
- Real and Notional, 37
- Simulated and Suspension of Disbelief, 21-22

238   Index

- Systems/Systematicity of, 15, 16, 116-120, 121, 128, 130
- Theologically Incorrect, 17
- Theories of (Cognitivist, 95, 97, 104-107, 114, 115; Disposition, 95, 97, 101, 102-104, 115; Mental State or Occurrence Theory, 95, 97, 101-102, 103, 104, 105, 115)
- Unnatural, 14, 42
- Variety of, 14-15
Belief-Desire Psychology, 102, 112
Believers, Skeptics, and Debunkers (respecting UFOs and Alien Abductions), 147, 151, 153, 154, 155, 156
Bell, Catherine, 59
Benavides, Gustavo, vii
Benedict, Ruth, 84
Benveniste, Emile, 45, 120
Bigfoot, 21-22
Bigger, Charles P., 64
Biological Systematics, 220
Blackfeet, 193
Bloch, Maurice, 165, 166
Bloom, Harold, 51, 55-56
Boas, Franz, 7-8, 10, 84
Bororo, 10, 66
Boyer, Pascal, 10, 14, 17, 18, 19, 24, 28, 39, 40-42, 47, 95, 111-115, 117, 127, 130, 136, 137, 144, 191, 205, 206, 208, 209, 216, 217, 220-221, 222
Braun, Willi, 191
Brooksmith, Peter, 149
Brown, Donald E., 183, 184
Bryan, Courtland D., 149
Buddha, The, 174-175, 221
Buddhism, see Theravada Buddhism
Bullard, Thomas, 149, 150
Burkert, Walter, 29-30, 188, 191-195
Byrne, Peter, 160-162, 213

Campbell, Keith, 160
Canonical Reflexivity, 33, 169

Cappadocian Fathers (Basil the Great, Gregory of Nyssa, and Gregory of Nazianzus), 35
Categories and Categorization
- Characterizations of, 23, 26, 164, 167-169, 172-173, 178-180, 212, 218-220
- Realities of, 223
Caudmont, Juan, 129
Cazeneuve, Jean, 63, 67
Central Tendencies, 169
Chaney, Richard Paul, 162, 219
Chaves, Miliciades, 129
Chomsky, Noam, 103
Churchland, Paul, 104-105
Cognitive Contrasted with Epistemic in Boyer, 95, 113-115, 128, 130
Cognitive Fluidity/Cognitive Revolution, 209-210
Cognitive Non-Uniformity as Functional Desideratum, 139-140
Cognitive Sciences and Religion, 9, 10, 16, 90, 196, 200, 204, 205-206, 218, 222, 223
Cohen, Albert K, 138
Coleman, Linda and Paul Kay, 218
Collective Representations, 66, 67, 70
Communicatio Idiomatum, 66
Comparative Method in Anthropology, 7
- Boas's criticisms of, 7-8
- Diffusion and Evolutionary Stages, 7
- Tylor's Application of, 54
Comparison, 26-27, 181-182, 183
Connectionism/Connectionist Networks, 182, 186
Contactees, 150
Contemporary Ancestors, 7
Cooper, David E, 72, 77-79
Cosmides, Leda, John Tooby, and Jerome H. Barkow, 30, 195, 200
Council of Nicea, 34, 35, 65
Cratylus, 171
Credulity, Stipulative Definition of, 132-133, 145, 147-148, 153
- and Faith, 134, 136-137

– and Trust, 134-136
Criminal Gangs in Japan, Certain of Them, 194
Criticism, Religious, 55-56
Cross-Cultural Comparativists, 181, 183, 186-187
Cross-Species Comparativists, 181, 183, 186-187
Cultural Studies, 159, 170, 213
Culture: Anthroplogical Concept, 6
– As Construct, 204
– Importance of Cultural Context, 194-195
– Imputed Autonomy of, 197, 203
– In Hallowell, 90-91
– In Wallace as Contract and Policy, 140
– Sui Generis, 201-202
– Universals, Cultural: see Universals
Culture and Personality Movement, 83, 84
Cyril of Alexandria, 66

D'Andrade, Roy, 182, 186, 203
Darwin, Charles/Darwinian, 9, 68, 207
– Darwinian Fundamentalists, 189
– "Darwin's Rottweiler," 9
Davidson, Donald, 105
Davis, Arthur K, 138
Dawkins, Richard, 9
Deconstructionists, 59
Definitions, 3, 22-24, 25, 26, 74, 98, 103, 121, 132-133, 147, 159, 160, 161, 162, 164, 165, 169, 173, 174, 175, 176, 180, 184, 212-213, 215, 221
Degenerationist Theories of Religion, 52
Delphic Imperative, 48
Dennett, Daniel. C, 29, 104-105, 191
Denzler, Brenda, 149
Dependency, Cognitive or Informational, 133-134
Dewey, John, 170
Diffusion, 7
Dinka, 116, 118-120, 166

Disch, Thomas M, 40
Distinctive Features, 25, 26, 213, 218-219
– Distinguishing Features, 213 n.20, 223
Dodds, E. R, 100
Domarus, Ernst von, 72, 76-77
Doxastic Neighborhoods, 15, 16, 114, 115, 116, 118, 130
Dugum Dani, 194
Durant, Robert J, 95-96
Durkheim, Emile, 10, 13, 14, 55, 64, 161, 176, 201, 221

Eliade, Mircia, 51, 56, 202
Eliminativism, 104
Emic/Etic, 16, 95, 114-115
Equivalence Structures, 138-140; see Wallace, Anthony F.C.
Escape Behaviors of Non-Human Animals, 188, 192
Essentialism/Essentialist/Essence, 24, 112, 150, 159, 161, 164, 165, 167, 174, 175, 176, 177, 180, 213, 223
Ethnocentric Language, 186
Ethnography of Sincerity, 156
Ethnohistory, 83-84
Ethno-Epistemology, 144
Ethnopsychology, 67, 68
Evans-Pritchard, Edward E, 6, 12, 43-44, 55, 60, 116-118, 144, 197, 207
Evolutionary Biology, 5, 188, 195, 203
Evolutionary Psychology, 5, 30, 183, 190, 203, 207
Evolutionary Sciences and Religion, 27-30, 82, 196, 200, 204, 205, 223
Ewers, John C., 193
Experiencers (Abductees, Primary Believers), 147, 150, 151, 152, 155, see also Alien Abductions

Faith, 98, 100, 101; see also Credulity

Family Resemblances (Family Likenesses), 25-26, 41, 47, 112, 144, 159, 160-161, 162, 163, 164-165, 168, 170, 176, 177, 213, 219-220, 220 n.22
Felipe of Puna, 31, 32, 42
Fitzgerald, Timothy, 23, 159-161, 164, 169, 170, 213
Forms/Ideas, 64, 98
Fowler, Raymond, 149
Fowler, W. Warde, 120
Frazier, K, 95
Freud, Sigmund/Freudian, 77, 83, 169, 189
Friedman, Stanton T, 154-155
Fuller, John, 149

Gallup, G. and F. Newport, 95
Gardner, Robert and Karl G. Heider, 194
Geertz, Armin, 82
Geertz, Clifford, 55, 201, 213, 214
Gombrich, Richard, 175
Goodenough, Ward. H, 103
Gould, Stephen Jay, 189, 190
Gould, Stephen Jay and Richard C. Lewontin, 28, 189
Goulet, Jean-Guy A, 122, 123, 127, 129
Greenspan, Alan, 39
Guajira Peninsula, 122, 124
Guajiro Indians, see Wayú
Guthrie, Stewart Elliott, 137, 169, 209
Guzmán de Rojas, Iván, 77

Hahn, Robert A, 103, 156
Hallowell, A. Irving, 5, 12-14, 27, 53, 82, 83-91, 207
Hallpike, C.R, 72, 79-80
Handel's Messiah, 100-101
Harris, Marvin, 13, 52
Hartley, Lesley, 51
Harvey, David, 181
Hill, Betty and Barney, 149
Hirschfeld, Lawrence A. and Susan Gelman, 205
Hodgen, Margaret, 55

Holden, Katharine J. and Christopher C. French, 155
Hollis, Martin and Steven Lukes, 72
Homo, Archaic Members of Genus, 208
Homoiousios, 35
Homoousios, 34, 35
Hopkins, Budd, 149, 153
Horgan, T. and J. Tienson, 106
Horton, Robin, 3, 61, 62
Horton, Robin and Ruth Finnegan, 72
Hudson, W. D., 25, 176, 177
Hufford, David J., 151-152
Huichol, 66
Human Nature, 201, 202
Hume, David, 96
Hultkrantz, Åke, 13
Hypostasis (-seis), 35

Ifaluk, 68, 69
Imitation, 75-76 note 1
Incarnation, 100
Integrated Theory, 200
Iroquois, 144
Irrationality, see Rationality

Jackendoff, Ray, 121, 164
Jacobs, David M., 149, 152
Jameson, Frederic, 149
Jensen, Jeppe Sinding, 82
Jepirra, Wayú Land of the Dead, 128, 129
Jesus Christ, 33-34, 38, 66
− Doctrine of Dual Nature of, 164-165, 177
− Sacrifice of, 166
Jones, Steve, 188
Jones, Todd, 106
Juya, 125, 126
Jung, Carl G., 150
Justin the Martyr, 65

Kenny, Anthony, 162
Kenny, Michael G., 78
Klass, Philip J., 154-155
Kluckhohn, Clyde, 183

Kluckhohn, Florence and Fred L, Strodbeck, 170
Kolp, Alan Lee, 35, 65
Kroeber, Alfred A. and Clyde Kluckhohn, 51
Kwoth, 43-44

Lakoff, George, 167-168, 178, 186, 216 n.21, 220
Language, Lack of Full Transparency in, 196, 211-212, 223
Leach, Edmund. R., 42, 99
"Leapfrog the Psychological," 188, 195
Leenhardt, Maurice, 62, 76
Lévi-Straussian Structuralists, 59
Levy, Marion, 138
Lévy-Bruhl, Lucien. 5, 10-12, 58-76, 81
Lienhardt, Godfrey, 13, 116, 118-120, 166
Linguistic Models, 16
Literal and Metaphorical, 81
Lloyd, G. E. R., 72, 80-81
Locke, John, 36, 101
Lorenzen, Carol, 149
Lorenzen, Carol and Jim, 149
Lowie, Robert H., 54, 202
Lubac, Henri de, 13
Lukasiewicz, Jan, 72, 77-78
Lumsden, C. J. and E. O. Wilson, 193
Lutz, Catherine A., 63, 68-69
Lyotard, Jean-François, 149

Mack, John, 149
Maleiwa, 123-125, 126, 129
Malinowski, Bronislaw, 12, 46-47, 55, 60, 98
Mandler, George, 182
Maori, 66
Martin, Luther, 159, 169
Marxism, 169
Masuzawa, Tomoko, 191
Matheson, Terry, 149, 150
Matos Romero, Manuel, 122
Mazeway Resynthesis, 211
McNally, Richard J. et al, 155

Mead, George Herbert, 87-88
Mead, Margaret, 84
Medin, Douglas L, 212, 220
Mentalities/Modes of Thought, 10-11, 58, 66, 72, 80-81
– Prelogical Mentality, 61, 63
– Primitive Mentality, 11, 58, 66, 67, 69, 74
Metarepresentational Capacities and Propensities, 206
Miller, Jon D., 95
Mind, Absence of Concept of among the Dinka, 119
Mind-Brain as General Purpose Processor vs. Assemblage of Domain Specific Modules, 202, 204, 205-206
Mithen, Steven, 28, 145, 208-210, 211
Modernity/Modernism, 3-4, 11, 99, 181
Modular Theory of Mind/Modules, 204
– (evolved, specialized mechanisms), 205-206
Monophysites, 164-165, 177
Monothetic, 121, 174, 220
Moore, Wilbert E. and Melvin Tumin, 139-140
Morgan, Lewis Henry, 7
Mother of Maleiwa (Boronka), 123
Murdock, George Peter, 183
MUFON (Mutual UFO Network), 21
Mystical: Orientation, Mentality, Beliefs, Ideas, 11, 61, 62, 69, 70, 117

Nash, Dennison, 84
Natural, Concept of in Durkheim and Hallowell, 12
Natural Numbers, 162
Natural Resemblances, 3, 41, 144, 183-184, 185-186
Natural Selection, 189
– Ad Hoc and Opportunistic, 203
Neanderthal, 209

Needham, Rodney, 41, 74-75, 95, 97, 186
Negative Theology, 39
Neoplatonist, 64
Newman, John. H., 36-38, 101
Nichomachian Ethics, 76
Nominalists and Realists, 163
Norman, Donald A., 182
Nuer, 78
Numerical Phenetics, 219-220

Object, Definition of, 12
Odd Number, 178
Ojibwa (Saulteaux), 12-13, 84, 86, 89-90
Old Hag, 151-152
Online/Offline Thinking, 18
Origen, 100
Other-Than-Human Persons, in Hallowell, 13, 14, 89

Paleolithic, 145, 146,
Paleologic, 76-77
Parmentier, Richard J., 74, 212
Parsons, Talcott, 138
Pars Pro Toto Rituals, 188, 192-193, 194
Participation, 61- 66, 75, 75-76 n. 1
Pavlov, Ivan, 210-211
Paz Ipuana, Ramón, 129
Peebles, Curtis, 150
Perrin, Michel, 124-125, 127, 129
Person
- Category of, 17-18, 19, 38-39, 41-42, 137, 170, 220
- in Ojibwa Thought, 89-90
Pflock, Karl, 154
Phillips, C. Robert III, 191
Philosophy of Resemblances vs. Philosophy of Universals, 27, 181, 185-186, 187, 223
Phonemic, 114
Phylogenetic Comparativists, see Cross-Species Comparativists
Piaget, Jean, 72, 79-80
Pike, Kenneth, 16
Pineda Giraldo, Roberto, 129, 130
Pinker, Steven, 188, 189, 190

Pístis ('Belief'), 100
Placher, William C., 33, 34,
Plato, Platonic, 64, 65, 76, 98,
Pleistocene, 27, 28, 145
Pluralistic View of Evolution, 189
Polymorphism, 142, 146
Polysemy, 212
Polythetic Classification/Polythesis, 175, 219-220, 220 n.22
Pontifex ('bridge-builder'), 4-5, 31, 45-46
Postmodernism/Postmodernist, 4, 57, 58-59, 99, 149, 181
Pouillon, Jean, 97
Popper, Karl R., 73, 205, 212
Positivists, 98
Pragmatic Coherence of Zande Beliefs, 118
Prelogical, see Mentalities/Modes of Thought
Preus, J. Samuel, 51, 52, 54
Price, Henry H., 27, 101, 102, 103, 104, 160, 181, 185
Primary Believers: see Belief
Prodigal Son, 60-61
Protestant (or Christian) Bias, 121, 213
Protocultural, 89
Prototypes (Prototypical Exemplars)/ Prototype Effects/Prototype Theory, 26, 121, 136, 137, 162, 165-169, 177-178, 179, 182, 186, 215-216, 216 n.21, 221, 222
Psychic Unity of Humankind, 54, 60,
Pulowi, 125
Pythagoras, Pythagoreans, 76
Pyysiäinen, Ilkka, 14, 16, 136, 206, 221

Quantum Principle of Complementarity, 78
Quipu, 32, 32 n.2

Radcliffe-Brown, A. R., 55
Randle, Kevin D., Russ Estes, and William P. Cone, 149, 150
Randles, Jenny, 149

Rationality/Irrationality, 58-59, 67,68, 69, 70, 71, 72, 73, 99
Reichenbach, Hans, 77-78
Religion
- Age of, 209
- As Appropriated Western Folk Category, 120, 173, 176, 215
- As Claimed Evolutionary Adaptation vs. Religion as Claimed Evolutionary Byproduct (Spandrel), 27-28, 189, 190, 207, 209
- As Claimed Causal Factor, 159, 169-170
- As Construct, 204
- As Parasitic, 207
- Doctrinal/Imagistic Modes of Religious Organization, 18, 116, 118, 120, 121, 127, 128, 130, 216-218
- Emergence of Modern Western Conception of, 215
- In the Pleistocene, 28, 208-210
- Judaism and Christianity as the Most Prototypical Exemplars of, 215-216
- Judaism and Christianity as Peculiar Developments of, 216
- Questions about, 204
- Religion-Constituting Elements, 222
- Scholarly Model of, 223
- Secular, Semi-, Quasi-, 24, 180, 221, 222
- Some Definitional Issues, 212-215
- Sui Generis, 198, 223
- Universal Distribution of, 10; see also Typicality Features
Religious Dimension and Transcending Religion, 172-173, 180, 222
Resemblance Theory vs. Theory of Universals, see Philosophy of Resemblances
Reverse Engineering, 143, 190
Revitalization Movements, 210
Rivière, Peter, 76
Rogo, D. Scott, 149
Rorschach Test, 83-84
Rosch, Eleanor, 166, 168, 216, 218

Roswell Incident, 154
Rousseau, Jean-Jacques, 140
Runciman, W. G., 107
Ryle, Gilbert, 103, 104

Sacred, in Byrne, 161
Sacrifice, 165-166, 170
Saler, Benson, 13, 33, 41, 45, 46, 57, 115, 120, 121, 127, 128, 129, 130, 147, 167, 168, 172, 182, 186, 207, 213, 216, 220
Saler, Benson and Charles A. Ziegler, 10
Saler, Benson, Charles. A. Ziegler, and Charles. B. Moore, 149, 150, 154
Schatzki, Theodore R., 73
Scheffler, Israel, 98
Schemas, 182
Science of Religion/Cognitive Science of Religion, 9, 10, 16, 28-29, 30, 90, 196, 197, 198, 199, 200, 203, 204, 205-206, 207, 208, 211, 217, 218, 222
Searle, John R., 107
Secondary Believers, see Belief
Secularism, 56
Secularization Hypothesis, 198
Self-Awareness, 82, 85, 89
Selye, Hans, 211
Sharing of Cognitive Orientations and Goals, Critique of, 138-141
Shulich, Thomas, 194
Shweder, Richard A., 72, 80
Signal To Noise Ratios
- in Evolution, 141-142
- in TV Commercials, 141
Skeptical Epistemology in Science, 135, 137
Skinner, B.F., 103
Skorupski, John, 108-109
Sleep Paralysis, 151, 152
Slone, D. Jason, 17
Slupecki, Jerzy, 77
Smart, Ninian, 160
Smith, Brian K., 33, 169
Smith, Jonathan Z., 214

Smith, Wilfred Cantwell, 23, 120, 197, 213
Sneath, Peter H.A. and Robert A. Sokal, 220
Sociobiology, 190, 207
Sokal, Robert A. and Peter H.A. Sneath, 220
Southwold, Martin, 25, 175-176, 221
Spandrel, 28, 189, 190, 207, 209, see also Religion as Claimed Evolutionary Byproduct
Sperber, Dan, 16, 19
Spiro, Melford E., 22-23, 25, 55, 69, 70, 99, 173-174, 175-176, 215, 221
"Standard Social Science Model," 196, 200, 201-203
Stausberg, Michael, vii
Steward, Julian, 8
Stich, Stephen. P., 15, 104, 114, 116
Stocking, George W., Jr., 52, 54
Streiber, Whitley, 149
Substituting or Jettisoning Categories or Disciplines, 170-171, 213
Superhuman, 23, 25, 173, 175, 221
Supernatural, 12-14, 18, 23, 62, 63, 111, 173, 208, 217, 220-222; see also Natural
Survivals, 9, 53, 55, 56
Sutton, Francis, 138

Tertullian, 35, 100
Theologism, 113
Theravada Buddhism, 25, 164, 174, 177, 221, 222
– Types of in Burma according to Spiro: Apotropaic, Esoteric, Kammatic, and Nibbanic, 174
TIME Magazine (June 23, 1997), 95
Tooby, John and Leda Cosmides, 200, 201-204
Tooby, John, Leda Cosmides, and Jerome H. Barkow, 188
Tooth-Fairy, 139
Translation, 42-45, 47
Trinity, 31, 32, 33, 34, 35, 36, 37, 38, 39, 48, 100

Trobriand Islanders, 98, 99
Trypho, 65
Tylor, Edward B., 3, 5, 6-10, 11, 12, 23, 27, 51-57, 207
Typical/Typicality Features or Elements, 24-25, 121, 164, 168, 169, 222, 223

Unbounded Category (Graded, Scalar, or Fuzzy), 164, 168-169, 172-173, 178, 179, 180
Unidentified Flying Object (UFO), 95-96, 102, 147, 154, 155
Universals, Cultural or Human, 181, 183, 184, 185-186
– Problem of Universals in Philosophy, 184-185
– Universalia ante rem, 185
– Universalia in rebus, 185

Values, 159, 160, 170, 213
Vega, Garcilaso de la, 31, 32, 42, 43
Vicente de Valverde, Fray, 31, 32, 42
Virgin Birth, Doctrine of, 99
Virtual Realities, 206

Wajsberg, Mordchaj, 77
Wallace, Anthony F.C., 77, 138-140, 144, 210-211
Wallace, Anthony. F. C., and John Atkins, 114
Walton, Travis, 149
Wanülü, 123, 127, 129
Wayú (Guajiro)/Wayú Religion, 15, 16, 18, 116, 121, 122-131
Western Monotheisms, 178-179
White, Leslie, 8
Whitehead, Alfred N., 74-75
Whitehouse, Harvey, 116, 120, 121, 127, 128, 130
Wiebe, Donald, 197, 198, 199, 200
Wikan, Unni, 63, 67-68
Wilbert, Johannes, 129
Wilson, Bryan, 72
Wilson, David Sloan, 27
Wissler, Clark, 183

Wittgenstein, Ludwig, 26, 103, 160, 162-163, 168, 176, 179, 218, 219-220
Woodfield, Andrew, 37
Woozley, A.D., 160, 185
World Religions, 216-217

Yoluja, 123, 124, 128, 129
Young, Allan, 80

Zadeh, Lofti, 77
Ziegler, Charles A., 135, 143, 147-148, 153, 155
Zuñi, 66